本书为凯里学院2020年度引进（自主培养）博士专项课题"西南地区少数民族家庭语言生态与语言规划研究"（编号：BS202005）成果。

侗族地区高校多语课堂超语语类教学研究

单菲菲 著

湖南师范大学出版社

·长沙·

图书在版编目(CIP)数据

侗族地区高校多语课堂超语语类教学研究:英文/单菲菲著. —长沙:湖南师范大学出版社，2023.3

ISBN 978-7-5648-4659-6

Ⅰ.①侗… Ⅱ.①单… Ⅲ.①侗族—民族地区—高等学校—英语—教学研究 Ⅳ.①H319.3

中国版本图书馆 CIP 数据核字(2022)第 157470 号

侗族地区高校多语课堂超语语类教学研究
Translanguaging Genre-based Pedagogy in Tertiary Multilingual Classrooms of the Dong Area

单菲菲　著

◇出　版　人:吴真文
◇组稿编辑:李　阳
◇责任编辑:李　阳
◇责任校对:李　航
◇出版发行:湖南师范大学出版社
　　　　　　地址/长沙市岳麓区　邮编/410081
　　　　　　电话/0731-88873071　0731-88873070
　　　　　　网址/https://press.hunnu.edu.cn
◇经销:新华书店
◇印刷:长沙市宏发印刷有限公司
◇开本:787 mm×1092 mm　1/16
◇印张:15.75
◇字数:450 千字
◇版次:2023 年 3 月第 1 版
◇印次:2023 年 3 月第 1 次印刷
◇书号:ISBN 978-7-5648-4659-6
◇定价:68.00 元

凡购本书,如有缺页、倒页、脱页,由本社发行部调换。
投稿热线:0731-88872256　微信:ly13975805626　QQ:1349748847

Abstract

As multilingualism has gained increasing currency in the globalized world in recent years, multilingual education has become a norm around the world. This is also true in China, "a nation of multi-ethnicities". Since English has been added to the school curriculum, the turn of the century ushered in the era of multilingual education and multilingualism in China. The past two decades have witnessed the proliferation of research on this seemingly new phenomenon. However, the majority of research has been conducted by a monolingual approach with the main focus on English. There is still a shortage of research on specifically feasible curriculum or pedagogy to truly realize the educational goal of multilingual education for ethnic minority areas, especially for the Dong area. Therefore, this research purports to design and implement an innovative curriculum for college English teaching in the context of multilingual education in the Dong area, aiming to establish a multilingual teaching/learning pedagogy that can truly realize the educational goal of multilingualism in the Dong area and other ethnic minority regions in China.

The methodology underpinning the pedagogy is drawn from translanguaging and genre-based pedagogy. Specifically, the project incorporates translanguaging as teaching strategies into every step of the Reading to Learn (R2L) cycle, which is theoretically rooted in Systemic Functional Linguistics (SFL) and genre-based pedagogy. The thesis is thus an evaluation of the implementation and impact of the design based innovative intervention program, to examine how translanguaging genre-based pedagogy (TL-GBP) is established and how the students' multilingual repertoire is utilized as a resource in the TL-GBP based English teaching, as well as the impact of TL-GBP based teaching on the expansion of the students' multilingual competence, the improvement of their metalinguistic awareness and the development of their multilingual identity.

The program was implemented in two ethnic classes of Kaili University, the local ethnic college in Guizhou Dong area, and lessons were taught in two iterations in each of the two classes. The students' progress across the lessons was systematically recorded. The data were thus collected, analyzed and evaluated, including the students' written texts at different implementation stages and qualitative data derived from interviews of the students' learning process, evaluation of the curriculum, and self-reflections of the teacher and participants. In addition, an ethnographic approach was also employed to investigate how minority students used translanguaging practices to facilitate English learning.

The research provides evidence for the value of employing the students' language resources in English teaching and learning. The major findings are as follows:

(1) The TL-GBP was constructed by incorporating translanguaging into genre-based pedagogy. Translanguaging approach was contextualised as teaching strategies that employ the students' linguistic and cultural resources to assist them in learning a new way of languaging. The R2L model was taken as a pedagogy to provide specific curriculum design for making a planned use of translanguaging strategies when gradually introducing English in steps.

(2) The pedagogy involved a deliberate use of the students' linguistic and cultural resources as translanguaging strategies in a planned and deliberate way, while introducing English in a systemic way in the R2L cycle, scaffolding students towards gradual control of knowledge about English and English language resources. Moreover, students were given agency to flexibly use their language practices to develop high-staking English writings as well as construct their own meanings and identity.

(3) Evidence showed the impact of the pedagogic practices on the students' L3 writing development and the achievement of the multilingual teaching goals. Over the iterations, students were able to write complete and longer texts with a good control of narrative genre and register with particular regard to field, literary elements, grammar (e. g. identifying clauses and verbal groups), and presentation (e. g. paragraphing, spelling, and graphic features). Throughout the program, students have also developed their multilingual competence, promoted their metalinguistic awareness, and sustained their multilingual identity.

Preface

In this remarkable book, the author conducted a first rate of study of the design and implementation of translanguaging genre-based pedagogy (TL-GBP) in the tertiary multilingual classrooms of Guizhou Dong area in China. The pedagogy, designed under the frameworks of translanguaging and the Sydney School's genre-based pedagogy theories, is both innovative and interventionist. It is an innovative curriculum of incorporating translanguaging approach into genre-based pedagogy by taking the multilingual characteristics of the Dong area in the English classroom. It proposes the intervention by activating the students' language resources and learning experiences in systemic teaching steps to gradually introduce a new way of languaging, scaffolding students towards growing independence and confidence in their use of English. Part of what the book has discovered in the research is that minority students' advantages as multilingual learners (e.g. multilingual resources, multilingual competence, multilingual learning experience, metalinguistic awareness) could be actively utilized to learn the target language in a more efficient way, and in this process, other benefits could be also observed, such as the expansion of the students' linguistic repertoire, the promotion of their metalinguistic awareness, and the developments of their multilingual identity.

Readers of this detailed study would be those who are engaging in the teaching and learning multilingual languages or in the multilingual environment, and the relative educational administrators, policy makers and other stakeholders.

Liu Chengyu, Professor
International College
Southwest University, China

Acknowledgements

This book cannot be successful without the support of my doctoral supervisor, Dr. Chengyu Liu. His thoughtful guidance and continuous encouragement throughout the research processes brought cohesion to this research. I would also like to thank Dr. Jianhua Hu, Dr. Chendan Liu, Dr. Yongfeng Zhao, Dr. Keding Zhang, Dr. Zaijiang Wei, for their careful reading of my script and thoughtful comments on my research.

I am most thankful to my mentors, Dr. Xu Wen, Dr. Shihong Du, Dr. Fangtao Kuang, Dr. Qiyang Mo, Dr. Zhi'an Chen and Dr. Li Li, Dr. Jun Cheng and Dr. Yuhong Jiang for their thought-provoking lectures and support during my study years in the College of International Studies of Southwest University. I would extend my gratitude to my friends and colleagues Huabing Li, Yunfeng Shi, Zhan Kuang, Dajun Xiang, Xiaojie Zong, Shujing Li, Changyou Zhao, Hui Shi, Tianjiao Li, Lu Gong and other fellow members for the scholarship and encouragement.

I would also like to thank Dr. James Martin and his students, who introduced me to genre-based pedagogy, and offered valuable suggestions and data for my work. I wish to thank the core members of China Society of Multilingualism and Multilingual Education, especially Dr. Bob Adamson, Dr. Anwei Feng, Dr. Yichuan Yuan, Dr. Zhen'ai Zhang, Dr. Li Zeng and Dr. Quanguo Liu, for their expert advice and exceptional support. I am grateful for every person I meet in my life, who raises me up and lets me shine.

My special thanks go to all the participants for their willingness to participate in the experiments and share their experiences and insights: instructors and students in the experimental classes, the students interviewees, faculty and administrator interviewees, and Kaili University community members who supplied me with related documents.

Finally, my deepest gratitude goes to my husband, Huiqiang Xie, my son Bokai

Xie, my beloved parents, Canyou Shan and Chuanju Ouyang, and my younger sisters Dongdong Shan, Xixi Shan and their families for their continuous inspiration and for helping me realize my goals. Their love and understanding have always given me the impetus to move forward.

Feifei Shan

2022

Kaili, Guizhou, China

List of Abbreviations

In this study, the symbols and abbreviations used to present the analysis of the class exchange follow the convention designed in Martin (1992), Martin and Rose (2007, 2008), and Rose (2014) with several additional extensions.

Symbol	Convention
dK1	delayed primary knower
K1	primary knower
K2	secondary knower
K2f	secondary knower follow up
dA1	delayed primary actor
A1	primary actor
A2	secondary actor
K1'	primary knower giving praise
K2*	secondary knower scribing
ch	challenge
tr	tracking
rtr	response to tracking
voc	vocalise
spk	speaker
=	complexing
(	dependency line
(	dependency arrow
[]	non-verbal response
()	re-instantiation

Italic font	equivalent of English from Chinese or Dong
Bold font	use of Chinese
<u>Underlined font</u>	use of Dong
//	end of a paragraph

Contents

CHAPTER ONE   INTRODUCTION TO THIS STUDY ······· 1
  1.1 Background ······· 1
    1.1.1 Contextual background ······· 1
    1.1.2 Overview of Dong ethnic minority group ······· 2
    1.1.3 General situation of multilingual education in China ······· 5
  1.2 Research Rationale ······· 9
    1.2.1 Need for effective multilingual education ······· 9
    1.2.2 Need for equally positioning languages in multilingual education ······· 10
    1.2.3 Need for reasonable language use in multilingual classrooms ······· 11
    1.2.4 Applicability of genre-based pedagogy and translanguaging approaches ······· 12
    1.2.5 Personal position ······· 13
  1.3 Research Significance and Innovations ······· 15
    1.3.1 Research significance ······· 15
    1.3.2 Research innovations ······· 17
  1.4 Research Questions ······· 17
  1.5 The Organization of the Book ······· 18

CHAPTER TWO   LITERATURE REVIEW ······· 20
  2.1 Research on Multilingual Education ······· 20
    2.1.1 Major areas of research ······· 20
    2.1.2 Domestic research on multilingual education ······· 25
    2.1.3 Problems and limitations ······· 28
  2.2 Research on Translanguaging ······· 29
    2.2.1 Major areas of research ······· 29
    2.2.2 Domestic research on translanguaging ······· 35

  2.2.3 Problems and limitations ················· 35
 2.3 Research on Genre-based Pedagogy ··················· 37
  2.3.1 Major areas of research ···················· 37
  2.3.2 Domestic research on genre-based pedagogy ······· 47
  2.3.3 Problems and limitations ····················· 47
 2.4 Summary ·· 48

CHAPTER THREE THEORETICAL PRELIMINARIES ········· 50
 3.1 Translanguaging ·· 50
  3.1.1 Tranlanguaging in education ················· 51
  3.1.2 Translanguaging and minority languages ········ 52
 3.2 Genre-based Pedagogy ································ 52
  3.2.1 The knowledge genres ······················· 53
  3.2.2 The curriculum genres ······················ 55
 3.3 Translanguaging Genre-based Pedagogy ·············· 56
  3.3.1 Translanguaging as pedagogic strategies ········ 56
  3.3.2 TL-R2L teaching/learning cycle ··············· 57
  3.3.3 Building metalanguage in stories ············· 60
  3.3.4 Building KAL: Discourse and grammar ········· 62
 3.4 Summary ·· 64

CHAPTER FOUR RESEARCH DESIGN ······················· 66
 4.1 Research Stages ·· 66
 4.2 Participants ·· 68
 4.3 Research Methods ····································· 69
 4.4 Data Collection ·· 72
 4.5 Design of the Curriculum Genres ····················· 73
 4.6 Summary ·· 82

CHAPTER FIVE PEDAGOGIC PRACTICES ·················· 83
 5.1 Iteration 1 ·· 84
  5.1.1 Preparing for reading ······················ 84
  5.1.2 Detailed reading ··························· 92
  5.1.3 Sentence making ··························· 101
  5.1.4 Joint construction ·························· 106

  5.1.5 Towards Iteration 2 ·· 119
 5.2 Iteration 2 ·· 120
  5.2.1 Detailed reading ·· 121
  5.2.2 Joint construction ··· 128
 5.3 Summary ··· 134

CHAPTER SIX STUDENTS' WRITING DEVELOPMENT IN ENGLISH ············ 136

 6.1 Writing Assessment Criteria ··· 136
  6.1.1 R2L assessment criteria ·· 136
  6.1.2 Considerations in assessing L3 writing texts ························· 138
 6.2 Assessing Pre-intervention Text ·· 140
  6.2.1 Genre and register ·· 140
  6.2.2 Discourse and grammar ··· 146
  6.2.3 Graphic features: spelling and punctuation ····························· 152
  6.2.4 The students' linguistic competence in the pre-texts ················· 153
 6.3 Assessing Individual Construction ··· 154
  6.3.1 The learning task in individual construction ····························· 154
  6.3.2 Writing production in individual construction ·························· 155
  6.3.3 The role of individual construction ··························· 164
 6.4 Assessing Post-intervention Text ·· 165
  6.4.1 Independent writing task ··· 166
  6.4.2 Narrative for ethnic stories ·· 166
 6.5 Summary ··· 181

CHAPTER SEVEN OTHER IMPACT OF THE INTERVENTION PROGRAM ······ 182

 7.1 Students' Use of Translanguaging Strategies ······································ 182
  7.1.1 Translation ··· 183
  7.1.2 Code-switching ·· 185
  7.1.3 Code-switching and translation ·· 189
  7.1.4 Application of prior knowledge ·· 191
 7.2 Additional Translanguaging Strategies for Class 2 ······························ 192
  7.2.1 Learning multilingual idioms ·· 192
  7.2.2 Composing English idioms in Dong songs ·· 193
  7.2.3 Reflections on the translanguaging strategies ·································· 195
 7.3 Tracing the Development of Students' Multilingual Competence ··········· 196

7.3.1 L3 talk development ………………………………………… 196
7.3.2 L1 literacy development ……………………………………… 198
7.4 Development of Students' Metalinguistic Awareness …………… 201
7.4.1 Translanguaging for support ………………………………… 201
7.4.2 Translanguaging for enhancement …………………………… 202
7.5 Translanguaging for Multilingual Identity ………………………… 203
7.6 Summary …………………………………………………………… 206

CHAPTER EIGHT   CONCLUSIONS …………………………………… 207
8.1 Summary of the Findings ………………………………………… 207
8.1.1 TL-GBP ……………………………………………………… 207
8.1.2 The pedagogic practices of the intervention program ……… 208
8.1.3 The impact of the pedagogy ………………………………… 209
8.2 Strengths and Implications of the Research ……………………… 210
8.2.1 Strengths ……………………………………………………… 210
8.2.2 Pedagogic implications ……………………………………… 212
8.3 Limitations and Prospects for Future Research ………………… 213

References …………………………………………………………… 216

Appendix Ⅰ Questionnaire ………………………………………… 228
Appendix Ⅱ Interview questions …………………………………… 230
Appendix Ⅲ Teaching materials …………………………………… 232
Appendix Ⅳ Scores of pre- and post-texts ………………………… 235
Appendix Ⅴ Samples of pre- and post-texts assessment ………… 236

CHAPTER ONE
INTRODUCTION TO THIS STUDY

1.1 Background

1.1.1 Contextual background

As multilingualism has gained increasing currency in the present globalized world, multilingual education has become a norm in many multilingual regions. The spread of English as a world language has added a third or an additional language to the linguistic repertoire of speakers and to the school curriculum in the multilingual regions. Schools in different parts of the world have the second or foreign languages in the curriculum. English, as the international language, is one of the most popular language opted for second or foreign language, and national and minority languages are also included in school curriculum. This is also true in China, a nation of multi-ethnicities, where multilingual education has been legitimized by a series of top-down laws and policies.

One of the distinctive features of multilingual education in China is that the ultimate goal of "Sanyu Jiaoyu" (trilingual education) is to foster ethnic minority learners as talents of "Sanyu Jiantong" [mastery of three languages, including the minority home language (L1), Chinese (L2) and English (L3), or simply trilingualism] (Feng & Adamson, 2015, p. 2). For minority students, three languages are equally important tools of communication and carriers of culture, although their educational functions are different as they play respective roles in personal and socio-economic development. Specifically, the significant role of L1 is to maintain the students' linguistic and cultural heritage, thus their identity, and for their cognitive development (Baker, 2011); L2 is crucial for their social mobility and economic development; and L3 is helpful for engaging in international affairs.

However, nowadays as China has been increasingly involved in the international affairs, it has undertaken an unprecedented challenge of balancing globalization and the preservation of a rich and diverse cultural heritage of the country's 55 ethnic minority groups. At the tertiary level, ethnic minority students must develop in a way that allows them to function in a new and ever-changing context that demands high ability in Chinese and, increasingly in English, and meanwhile to accomplish their ethnic obligations. On the one hand, linguistic, socioeconomic and cultural obstacles must be overcome to achieve academic success for these students. On the other hand, their ethnic minority language and culture, as important parts of the national treasure, should be maintained and transmitted. Therefore, it is of great importance to build bridges between foreign language teaching at school and multilingualism outside school.

This research, therefore, purports to investigate tertiary English teaching in the context of multilingual education in the Dong area of Guizhou province in China, aiming to provide a new pedagogic model that engages the resources of minority intelligence to develop minority students for the benefits of the individual, the minority community, and the nation as a whole.

1.1.2 Overview of Dong ethnic minority group

1. Demography and history

Dong, called "Geml", or "Geml Laox" in Dong language, is an ancient ethnic minority group in southern China, mainly in the border areas of Guizhou, Hunan and Guangxi provinces. The population of Dong group is around 2.88 million, ranking 10th of the total 55 ethnic minority groups in China (National Census, 2010). Nearly half of the Dong people are distributed in Guizhou, primarily in Qiandongnan Miao and Dong Autonomous Prefecture. Dong accounts for the third largest number of population in Guizhou, next only to Miao and Buyi.

The earliest ancestors of the Dong people that can be traced back are "Bai Yue" people (Feng, 1999, p. 10). Yue was a big ethnic group, which had a wide range of branches, distributed in a large area of south Yangtze river from the Warring States to Qin-Han Dynasties, known in history as "Bai Yue" (hundreds of Yue). The ancestors of Dong were one branch of Luo Yue, chiefly distributed in Lingnan area, developed into communities of Zhuang-Dong languages like Zhuang, Dong, Buyi, Mulao, Maonan, Li, etc. during the period of Ming-Qing dynasties. In fact, in the process of its development, Dong minority group interrelated with Han, Miao and other ethnic groups, and they supported and influenced each other, presenting a close relationship of

"Duoyuan Yiti" (i.e. ethnic diversity within national unity) (Yang, 2015).

2. Language and culture

Dong community has its own spoken language, but no traditional written scripts (which were created by Chinese government in the 1950s, based on Chejiang Zhanglu dialect of Rongjiang county in Guizhou province). Dong language belongs to Dong-Shui language branch of Zhuang-Dong language group, Sino-Tibetan language family. It has two dialectal varieties: southern and northern Dong dialects. Each dialect includes four local dialects respectively. Relatively speaking, the northern Dong dialect has been more greatly influenced by Chinese, thus it has a wide range of Chinese words and grammatical patterns, and its pronunciation has become simpler. The southern Dong dialect, however, has still kept the relatively ancient phonetic features.

Dong language has 32 "Shengmu" (i.e. initial consonants), 56 "Yunmu" (i.e. simple or compound vowels) and 9 tones. "Shengmu" is closely related to tones. For example, one type of tone can only appear with unaspirated plosive "Shengmu". In terms of grammar, except for numerals and quantifiers, most modifiers are put after the head-word. Both lexis and sentence structure include simple sentence and compound sentence, which suggests that Dong language has a complex phonetic system and comprehensive language system.

Dong ethnic minority group is rich in cultural resources, most of which are rooted in nature. Nature shapes their ways of life. Their economic industries mainly include agriculture, forestry, animal husbandry, fishery, etc. Their housing is also closely related to nature. They are good at utilizing woods to create exquisite architecture, such as Diaojiao Lou (a special out-seam house), Wind and Rain Bridge and Drum Tower. Their faiths are also associated with nature. They respect heaven and fear earth, and worship Gods in the forest, water and land. There are abundant forms of festivals and recreational activities, such as Dong Winter Festival (like Chinese Spring Festival), Yue Ye (group visit), Singing Festivals, etc. In addition, Dong people are also keen on singing, and they sing at all festivals. The festivals and gatherings provide a crucial platform for inter-communication among various ethnic groups, presenting a natural atmosphere of national unity.

3. Ethnic classics

Dong people are enthusiastic about literature. Dong community has been praised as "the ocean of poetry", "the world of songs", "the cradle of stories" and "the heaven of Dong drama". They like to reason things out by songs, inspire mind by interesting stories with wisdom, and mold character and instruct life by joyful Dong dramas. Therefore, Dong literary classics are their spiritual wealth, which have inspired generations of the Dong people and played an important role in the inheritance of civilization. Dong classics have been orally transmitted as a kind of oral language art due to the lacking of original written scripts, including mainly Dong song, Dong story, Dong drama, Dong Fu, etc.

Dong song, called "Gal" by Dong people, primarily includes 4 types: Grand song, Tiny song, Ritual song, and Pipa song. Among them, the most famous is Grand song, which has been listed into UNESCO intangible heritage in 2009. Dong song is an essential part of the Dong people's life. There are many famous sayings about it in Dong minority, like "rice (food) keeps our body alive, while songs keep our spirits alive", "Han people inherited their books for they have written scripts, Dong people do not have written scripts and thus inherited our songs". Dong song narrates historical legends, sacrifice ceremonies, productive labor, marriage and love, advising and reasoning, and appreciating scenery, among other things. It is not only the direct reflection of Dong culture, but also an important medium of communication and means of cultural inheritance for Dong people.

Dong story includes fairy tale, legend story, love story and life story, and story of historic figure, wise people, ghosts and gods, etc. Dong story belongs to narrative or recount folk literature, characterized by rich content, ethnic features and artistic techniques. Stories are the children's life textbooks, as the children are growing up with the accompaniment of stories. By narrating stories, Dong people can obtain information and knowledge, educate children, and thus promote cultural quality and moral cultivation. The vivid and interesting Dong stories can be seen as valuable literary heritage.

Dong drama is the development of Dong ethnic folk literature at a higher level. In a Dong drama, actors sing long narrative poems while walking slowly, accompanied by stage whisper and dance alternatively. Dong Drama can be labeled as a performing literature style or singing folk literature. "Zhu Lang Niang Mei" is a representative of Dong Drama.

Dong Fu is an ancient literature style, presented as descriptive prose interspersed with verse. It is normally divided into four types: Creation Fu, Sacrifice Fu, Lyric Fu and Reasoning Fu. Fu requires the language gaudiness and gorgeous style. Fu and Song are often interchangeably used in the Dong people's life. Fu is a kind of reciting folk literature. With free and liberate structure, it can fully express people's thoughts and feelings, thus it is popular in the Dong community.

Dong ethnic classics reflect all aspects of Dong culture. They can be viewed as important media to know the social structure, relationship of marriage and love, cultural inheritance and spiritual life, so they carry and transmit key ethnic cultural information and spirits like life style, social relationship, moral customs, wisdom etc. Dong classics, especially Dong song and Dong story, also play a significant role in shaping Dong ethnic characters of kindness, solidarity and harmony, and promoting national unity and harmony. Their huge cultural value, as an essential part of Chinese national culture, has been confirmed by scholars at home and abroad. In recent years, some works have been transcribed into the newly created Dong written scripts and translated into Chinese, but hardly any has been translated or publicized into English. Therefore, it is necessary to sustain and inherit the valuable cultural and literacy heritage for the social, cultural and economic development of Dong ethnic minority group and the nation.

1.1.3 General situation of multilingual education in China

There are 55 officially-recognized minority groups in China, with a combined population around 122 million (8.5% of total population) (2010 National Census). Residing in over 60% land, ethnic minority groups are hugely diverse in terms of history, culture and language, demography, geography, economy, policy, and so on. The rich context results in the diversity and complexity of multilingual education in terms of language status, language provision, teaching model and effectiveness, etc. The following sub-sections will present the general situation of multilingual practices and education shaped by these contextual factors on the whole and in the Dong area in particular.

1. Multilingual practices in minority communities

China is a linguistically diverse nation as a result of its multi-ethnicities. All ethnic minority groups, except for Hui and Man, have their own home languages, and some have more than one. It was estimated that a total of more than 80 languages from 5 language families (Sino-Tibetan, Altaic, Austronesian, South Asian and Indo-European) were spoken by indigenous minority groups. Twenty-four ethnic minorities, mostly with a big population, have traditional written scripts, and some have more than one, amounting to a total of more than 33 types of written scripts (Gu & Luo, 2003).

Generally, the linguistic practices in minority communities are divided into the following four categories (Wu, 1999; Zeng, 2010):

(1) Most members speak minority home language, and only a small number of people speak Chinese. They inhibit densely in the autonomous regions, such as Zang in Tibet, Mongolia in Inner Mongolian herding areas, Miao in Leishan and Dong in Rongjiang of Guizhou, etc. In these areas, except for some cadres and educated young people, minority members do not speak or understand Chinese as a result of their remote location, inconvenient transportation and underdeveloped economy.

(2) Minority members normally use their mother language to communicate, but the majority of them also speak Chinese. They mainly live in central towns or cities with Han people. They have a large population and concentrated residences and have also been influenced by Han culture, such as Zhuang in Guangxi, Buyi in Anlong of Guizhou.

(3) Most minority members shift their communicative tool to Chinese, and only a few old people speak minority language. They mainly live dispersedly near towns and cities with convenient transportation, such as Man in Liaoning, and Gelao in Qinglong of Guizhou.

(4) Some minority groups are multilingual, who speak their native language, Chinese and some other minority languages. They are usually minority groups with a small number of population and live in villages with other large minority groups. This case can be seen in Guizhou, such as Yao people in Liping, who can speak Chinese, Dong and Miao. In addition, any relatively large ethnic minority group may speak several mutually unintelligible "dialects", such as Tibetans.

The variety of multilingual practices result in the diversity and complexity of multilingual education in minority areas. The practice of multilingual education in each minority community has its particular future in terms of language use and language status in education.

2. Multilingual education in China

The concept of multilingual education can be a complex and contested construct in China's minority areas. In a broader sense, it includes teaching and learning three languages (ethnic minority language as L1, Chinese as L2 and English as L3) as parts of the curriculum within or out of formal school education. In a narrow sense, it refers to the use of three languages as the media of instruction to teach different content areas. The objective of multilingual education in China, as Adamson and Feng (2009) observed, is to "foster trilingualism in ethnic minority areas with three goals: to enhance literacy, to assure internal stability and to allow knowledge transfer in order to strengthen the nation".

Although it would be impossible to give a full description of multilingual education in all ethnic minority areas due to their huge differences, it has been found that minority students' performance in most areas was relatively poor because of their disadvantaged background. According to the statistics, one third poverty-stricken counties were found in western China. Schools in these regions, therefore, lacked basic resources (Feng & Adamson, 2015). Without sufficient teaching facilities and qualified teachers, minority students usually performed poorer than their Han majority counterparts (Jiang, et al., 2006). Many minority students could not achieve the age-appropriate proficiency either in their native language or Chinese (Tsung, 2009). Their English learning, contrary to the supportive hypothesis from some European models (Cenoz, 2003), had various cognitive, cultural and psychological problems (Adamson & Feng, 2014). It is worth noting that some minority groups in northern China boasted a better performance in trilingual education. In cases such as Koreans, students could develop trilingual competence and have strong identification with three languages. Therefore, they could be empowered by developing trilingual competence and their economy, confidently claiming their identity rather than being assimilated into mainstream society (Feng & Adamson, 2015).

In recent years, multilingual education has been implemented in the vast majority of minority areas in China, but its development is unbalanced. The use and status of three languages in education and thus their educational outcomes in various minority areas are hugely different. Furthermore, the effectiveness of multilingual education has not been so satisfying in general. English teaching in minority regions has been conducted according to the national curriculum standard. The teaching materials, pedagogy and other educational tools rarely take minority students' linguistic, cognitive and psychological factors into consideration, thus proved to benefit the minority students little. Therefore, it is essential to build suitable pedagogy and curriculum for their English teaching and developing students' balanced trilingualism.

3. Multilingual education in the Dong area

Multilingual education in Guizhou Dong area started relatively late and developed slowly. Generally, the medium of instruction in education is predominantly Chinese in both oral and script forms, and English is a compulsory course, while Dong language is limited in the curriculum provision.

At the tertiary level, minority students are expected to master not only generic skills, but multilingual proficiency in the national language—Chinese and English as well. However, the linguistic, cultural, and socio-economic gaps between the Han majority and ethnic minority groups result in the great disadvantage of the later due to the requirement of multilingual proficiency and highly demanding curriculum. For example, Dong students may face more challenges and difficulties in learning college English than their Han counterparts as a result of their poor elementary English education.

The exposure to English for them is relatively late because of the lack of funding and resources. Moreover, there are no sufficient provisions of qualified English teachers in elementary schools. As a result, students would develop inferior English communication habits, poor pronunciation and literacy competence, and thus lack the confidence of learning English at the beginning (Finifrock & Schilken, 2015; Liu & Shan, 2016). As they move to college, where though teachers with most English language knowledge and communicative capabilities are concentrated, it is difficult to correct their habitual errors developed by previous years. The teachers commented that most students were not prepared for high level English study (Finifrock & Schilken, 2015).

The situation would be worse when their first language is not well developed and the second language is used as a medium of instruction. The students have to study English in classrooms where Chinese is the dominant medium of instruction. It can be often the case that teachers explain difficult knowledge points in Chinese, and students struggle with the notes with explanations or translations in Chinese written scripts. Students who fail to acquire an effective knowledge of Chinese would lose the motivation for learning. Otherwise, students who have high motivation and are admitted to colleges would be absent from home for a long time. The lack of initiation of their own culture may result in some kind of estrangement and in the long term language loss (Finifrock & Schilken, 2015). In both cases, the result would be the reduction of the use of the students' mother tongue, and few students could develop into balanced multilingualism, irrespective of their Chinese ability or consequential educational success.

Given this situation and other factors, it is not surprising that English teaching in the Dong area is unsatisfactory. As the national goal is to bridge the gap of English proficiency between Dong minority students and Han majority students, it is urgent to seek ways to improve English proficiency of minority students in order not to limit otherwise qualified students from succeeding in the school system and society.

1.2 Research Rationale

1.2.1 Need for effective multilingual education

Globalization has given multilingualism not only visibility but also an added value associated with the ability to speak several languages (Edwards, 2004). Multilingualism can give better opportunities, and it is also linked to identity belonging to one or more speech communities. The global dimension is also clearly seen in Chinese education. In the new era, increasing tourism in many minority regions, joint ventures and "open-door" activities, have all helped fuel enthusiasm for gaining English language competence not only in big cities like Shanghai (Zou & Zhang, 2011), but also in remote minority areas (Blachford & Jones, 2011). The promotion of other policies and proposals like "overseas promotion of Chinese literature" also increase the requirements of multilingual talents, who master not only Chinese, English, minority home language, but other languages as well. However, as mentioned above, the results of present multilingual education practices are not so satisfactory, and thus there is an emergent need of effective approach to multilingual education.

Additionally, effective multilingual education is also needed for the maintenance and transmission of ethnic minority language and culture, as well as the publicity of Chinese culture. In the critical moment of developing cultural competitiveness, a series of political strategies, such as "Chinese culture going out" and "one belt one road", have been implemented to improve national soft power. The overseas publicity of Chinese culture can be an effective way of realizing the increasing internationalization of Chinese culture and cultural power. In addition, it is an important compensation to the bias of the recognition of Chinese national history and culture, i.e. "Han majority is the center and foundation", promoting the equity, respect, understanding and unity of ethnic groups. For these reasons, the translation and overseas publicity of ethnic minority classics can be taken as some national cultural strategies.

However, for quite a long historical period, the translation of ethnic classics has been a weak project of Chinese cultural communication due to the lack of minority excellent translators. Statistics show that there are about 35 thousand classical books in China, while only 0.2% of which have been translated into foreign languages (Huang, 2007), less were ethnic minority classics. The new need requires minority students to master multilingual proficiency not only in their minority language, but also in English. Therefore, effective multilingual education is needed to cultivate minority talents of mastering multilingual competence. Moreover, selecting ethnic classics as the materials of English teaching can ultimately utilize the minority students' L1 cultural and linguistic resources to not only develop their multilingual competence, but also transmit ethnic minority language and culture and publicize the ethnic classics.

1.2.2 Need for equally positioning languages in multilingual education

Multilingual education in China is an ongoing national affair. As mentioned above, recent years have seen increasing attention to the implementation of multilingual education, while the status and roles of languages in education have subtle differences.

Chinese, as the official language, is the predominant language of education. It wins the highest social status as it is perceived to be associated with social and economic capital. It is used as the medium of instruction for most subjects. For example, the students learn science, history and music in Chinese, which are specialized discourse or vertical discourse, in Bernstein's terms (1999), characterized by abstract and uncommon sense, different from students' everyday language. Knowledge discourse in Chinese is itself a challenge as the language has its own abstract and complex ideas to construct, which is especially difficult for minority students as they have to transfer the unfamiliar Chinese to their native language to understand the specialized discourse. This situation is very often detrimental to the personal development of minority students and well-being of minority language.

English as a compulsory subject occupies an important position in education. It is promoted at all educational levels throughout the country. In college education, the viewpoint on English has changed from being once "the international language of communication" to the more active role of being the language of participating in the international exchange (Ministry of Education, 2020). English education is now intended to achieve literacy competence, emphasizing particularly success in high-staking reading and writing. English is believed as an important linguistic capital to access to international affairs, while the access to English resources between urban and rural contexts is hugely different, resulting in the educational failure in many rural minority schools.

Status of minority language in education varies from regions to regions. Generally, except for a few large minority language communities, minority languages are not paid much attention. They are taught only in the pre-school or first several years of primary school, or even worse, are not taught or used in schools, as they, unlike Chinese and English, need not to be tested for further education. Because of the lack of associated economic and political capital of their minority languages, many minority students and their parents are losing their interest in learning their mother tongues. Most schools in the Dong area only pay lip service to the teaching of minority languages while taking priority to the further promotion of Chinese and English teaching.

The limited space provision of minority languages in school curriculum is the main factor that hinders the achievement of additive trilingualism. Moreover, the present practices arguably hinder the revival and development of minority languages. Therefore, there is a need for resetting the positions of languages in multilingual education to provide equal benefits for three languages.

1.2.3 Need for reasonable language use in multilingual classrooms

As discussed above, language use in classrooms, as "the medium of instruction" (MOI), of minority areas is a complex issue. Different languages are used in daily communication, involving code mixing and translanguaging as multilingual speakers make connections and navigate between languages. These flexible multilingual practices also occur in classrooms at various degrees among different ethnic minority groups. In Guizhou Dong area, minority language and multilingual practice have often been neglected in favor of a more economically viable, yet arguably less effective form of "Chinese monolingual" instruction for most subjects in the curriculum, including English (Finifrock & Schilken, 2015).

In fact, the potential role of students' L1 has been increasingly recognized (e.g. Levine, 2011). UNESCO emphasizes "using the learners' mother tongue is crucial to effective learning" (UNESCO, 2008, p. 5). The use of L1 in multilingual class is also widely believed to play an important role in the construction of ethnic minority students' identity and culture (Creese & Blackedge, 2010). In addition, the value of mother tongue-based instruction in English language teaching has been increasingly recognized and authenticated in Africa and Asia (Taylor, 2014).

However, the idea of using target language only in classrooms is still prevalent. There is a strong view of separating target language from students' L1 to avoid interference from it. Code-switching between students' L1 and the target language is often considered as a sign of linguistic and cognitive deficiency. In contrast to this traditional view, some scholars argue for more flexible classroom language practices by differentiating between the grammar-translation method and the strategic, principled use of local resources to scaffold learning. Multilingualism has been taken as a potential resource rather than a barrier to language learning, particularly when the target language is used as the medium of instruction and the learning talk is complex (Levine, 2011).

These issues are relevant to the situation of multilingual classrooms in minority areas of China, especially in the Dong classrooms where the value of students' L1 has often been overlooked. In fact, benefits of using minority language in English teaching have been reported in various types of minority communities recently, such as Korean in Jilin (Zhang, et al., 2015); Dong in Guizhou (Finifrock & Schilken, 2015) and Zhuang in Yunnan (Johnson, et al., 2016).

It is true that students' L1 or entire linguistic repertoire can be used as a resource in learning, but we still need to better understand questions as follows: How to use students' language repertoire to promote English learning? How does it exactly maintain minority students' identity? More specifically, how can the students' linguistic repertoire be taken in tertiary English teaching of the Dong area, where the students' L1 is completely neglected, to maximize their educational benefits? If the students' entire linguistic repertoire is a potential resource and can bring benefits, then what appears necessary is to establish a principled basis of using languages as teaching resources.

1.2.4 Applicability of genre-based pedagogy and translanguaging approaches

The realization of the use of L1 in multilingual education is just the first step. Then, pedagogy with planned use of L1 needs to be designed to suit best for the specific literacy need of minority students whose home language is other than educationally and politically dominant one.

The Sydney School genre-based pedagogy, developed in Australia over the past three decades, is exactly what is needed for multilingual teachers and students. It seeks to address linguistically based social and economic inequality, by providing students with explicit knowledge about social functions and linguistic properties of the modes of communication associated with academic success and social mobility, which is the same basic concern motivating most proponents of bilingual education (White, et al., 2015). Hence, genre-based pedagogy has been proved to be an effective approach to language teaching and learning for indigenous minority students. At least, these issues are relevant to the situation of multilingual education in Chinese minority areas. Moreover, the notion of "curriculum genre" (Christie, 1993) in genre-based pedagogy can be drawn on in planning the systematic use of L1, L2 and L3 in the learning process since there are different stages and phrases in a curriculum genre (Lin, 2015).

Translanguaging was firstly used as a pedagogic method that alternated the use of Welsh and English for additive Welsh-English bilingualism in Wales in the 1980s, according to Lewis, et al. (2012). It has been later extended as an approach of teaching and learning languages based on the learners' whole linguistic repertoire. There is an ever-increasing volume of literature that provided more evidence of successful classroom practices worldwide (García & Li, 2014). Translanguaging as a pedagogic approach that encourages the use of students' whole linguistic repertoire and everyday multilingual practices has been proved to be effective not only in reinforcing students' all languages but also in developing multilingual identity (García, 2009; Blackledge & Creese, 2010).

As noted above, Dong minority students face a daunting linguistic challenge on account of their socioeconomic disadvantage and the insufficient language provisions. In the new era, minority students are expected to develop multilingual literacy associated with academic success and social mobility, and the sustenance and publicity of their minority culture as well. This is certainly high staking literacy which can be beneficial for the cultural and socioeconomic development of the Dong area. Genre-based pedagogy is the methodology proved to be effective in teaching high staking literacy for these disadvantaged students. Translanguaging approach can cater to the demand of trilingual education in the Dong area. Therefore, all students' languages (L1, L2 and L3) can be used to reinforce each other and ultimately to produce additive trilingualism by appropriately incorporating these two approaches.

1.2.5 Personal position

The final point to note is the researcher's personal position. As a Dong member who grew up in a remote town of Qiandongnan Miao and Dong autonomous prefecture of Guizhou province, the researcher herself is a multilingual learner who knows well about Dong, Han and Miao cultures, as well as speaks Chinese and a little Dong language. More importantly, she has experienced pains and gains as an ethnic multilingual learner.

She began to learn English in junior high school. During that time, her English performance was very poor for reasons of a few lessons in a week, the teachers' traditional methods with more emphasis on grammar, her improper learning methods and lack of interest, among other things. In the following five years, the researcher had hardly access to English as she did not have English course as a student in secondary normal school for three years and later as a teacher in a primary school. She did not have the real English learning experience until she had her further education in Guizhou Education College, majoring in English as an undergraduate student. During the four years, she received formal training and found out some effective learning methods. Therefore, she made great progress in English proficiency, while unfortunately she was gradually losing her ethnic cultural awareness and identity.

In 2011, after finishing her master's degree, the researcher became an English teacher of Kaili University in Guizhou Dong area. In this ethnic college, most students are from local ethnic minority communities, mainly including Miao and Dong. Most of them performed badly in the English class and lacked motivations and interest, somewhat like the researcher's experience in the elementary school. During her four-year teaching periods, the researcher explored various interesting and helpful teaching methods by taking students' background knowledge and concern into considerations, which were warmly welcomed by the students. Moreover, the researcher found it successfully promote the students' motivation and learning to talk about their languages and cultures. In addition, in contact with the students and some of their ethnic cultural courses, the researcher realized the charm and value of ethnic culture. Meanwhile, when observing the tendency of ethnic minority culture to be assimilated and minority languages to be less and less spoken, she recognized that she had to do something for her ethnic minority group, and her ethnic identity was established again.

In 2015, the researcher started to study for her PhD degree, and she learned certain theoretical knowledge concerning minority language education, third language acquisition, multilingual education, and so on. She not only made sure about some of her teaching practices, but also had a deeper understanding about the related mechanism and principles, and gained new enlightenments about multilingual education in the Dong area. Therefore, she decided to initiate a project, combining what she has learned and experienced, for Dong minority students and Dong language and culture.

Above all, as a Dong learner, teacher and researcher, she is the ideal person to design and implement the multilingual intervention program in the Dong area. She is familiar with the situation to investigate the status que of English teaching in the Dong area, to understand the learning experience of Dong minority students, and to explore the suitable teaching and learning methods for them. Moreover, as a teacher in a college of the Dong area, it is convenient for her to conduct the program.

1.3 Research Significance and Innovations

1.3.1 Research significance

1. Theoretical significance

The research aims to provide a principled approach to the design and implementation of English teaching program with the focus on multilingualism, by incorporating translanguaging into genre-based pedagogy. In China, however, most multilingual education practices may only emphasize teaching and learning English as a third language on the basis of minority language and Chinese bilingual education. As indicated above, these practices, without looking at students' multilingual features and valuing their multilingual identity, were not real inclusive education, which usually resulted in less effective English teaching outcomes and at times the loss of students' ethnic language and identity. Therefore, the research seeks to establish evidence-based theoretical foundation of multilingual education in China, with the emphasis on the promotion of multilingual competence, by including students' linguistic repertoire in English teaching. This exploration provides a new perspective to the theoretical construction in terms of pedagogy and models of multilingual education in China and around the world.

This intervention program conducted in the context of the Dong area in China, aims to construct a localized pedagogic model in the context of multilingual education through adapting international pedagogic theories. On the one hand, the research presents an excellent example of employing powerful foreign theories to solve local problems and thus to promote the construction of localized theories. On the other hand, the design and implementation of the translanguaging genre-based pedagogy (TL-GBP) approach could provide evidenced-based ideas for the new trend of translanguaging as pedagogic use and effectiveness of translanguaging and genre-based pedagogy in multilingual education, contributing to the authentication, modification and extension of these theories.

2. Practical significance

This research is designed as an action project, initiated to establish theoretically strong pedagogic practice for English teaching in the context of multilingual education of the Dong area in China. The pedagogy developed is interventionist in that it advocates active intervention in the teaching, scaffolding the students towards growing independence and confidence in their use of English.

It is argued that this research could potentially inform improved multilingual education in the Dong area, with the foci not only on target language, but also on trilingualism. The pedagogy developed in this project not only emphasizes the provision of explicit knowledge about English to students, but also underlines students' own language and culture and multilingual competence. Therefore, this research attempts to promote education in the Dong area for the sake of students' academic success and personal development, local and national socio-economical promotion, and sustenance of ethnic language and culture. It is also hoped that the pedagogy could be feasible or adapted to the relevant context of other minority areas in China and around the world, and that this research could make contributions to the empirical research of multilingual education.

In addition, by translating Dong ethnic classics into English through well-planned lesson activities, the valuable cultural heritage of Dong ethnic minority could be inherited, contributing to the richness of overseas publicity of national classics and the national strategy of Chinese culture going out. Moreover, the employ of minority language and culture in English teaching enriches the research of ethnology and educational linguistics.

This project is also argued as an inclusive pedagogic practice that involves all students' linguistic repertoires and multilingual practices. This practice could provide more educational opportunities for students from disadvantaged background. Therefore, it is claimed to make contributions to educational equity and thus social justice. The theoretically strong pedagogy provides enlightenment to the development of other multilingual pedagogic models in relevant contexts.

3. Methodological significance

Action research of designing and conducting pedagogy for multilingual education in Chinese minority areas, whether in the field of FLE or multilingual education, is rare. One strength of the project is that it is positioned in the real educational context, with the focus on designing and implementing a program for realistic educational goals.

The project would have great impact on theoretical and methodological explorations of empirical study in the field of multilingual education in China and around the world. It was designed and implemented in the Dong area by combining methodology from different fields like third language acquisition, multilingual education, ethnology and educational linguistics. It is hoped that the methodology can be applied to relevant research in second language acquisition or third language acquisition in China and around the world.

1.3.2 Research innovations

The multilingual program is innovative in that it extended genre-based pedagogy by incorporating translanguaging approach, providing a principled approach to the design and implementation of English teaching in the context of multilingual education. Genre-based pedagogy has been implemented and authenticated in various contexts, including multilingual contexts, however, the major focus was one language only (mainly the national language, or target language). The TL-GBP pedagogy developed in this research takes the students' ethnic language and culture into account with the aim of multilingualism. It breaks new ground for Chinese minority areas, making a contribution to the development and refinement of the application of genre-based pedagogy and the pedagogic use of translanguaging theory.

This multilingual intervention program is a pilot exploration of using the students' entire linguistic repertoire to learn L3, and ultimately to foster real additive trilingualism. It is different from many common practices and research of trilingual education in China that usually put the major emphasis on L3 and overlook the important role of L1. As the pedagogy recorded here, teaching and learning language about language (the metalanguage) and language about a field (in this case literary language) in both the target language (L3) and students' mother languages (L1 and L2) could enhance the students' metalinguistic awareness about how all languages work. The research thus can be also viewed as interventionist in nature for it attempts to change the traditional multilingual education practices in many minority areas with the purpose of achieving the specific curriculum objective of ethnic tertiary education in minority areas, i.e. multilingualism.

Practically, it is intended that the results of the research could be taken as references in developing larger scale studies with a larger number of schools and students in multilingual education of other ethnic minority regions in China and in other relevant contexts around the world. In this sense, the research reported here might be seen as a pilot study towards more ambitious studies in the future.

1.4 Research Questions

The goal of this study is to establish a model of multilingual education for the Dong area under the frameworks of translanguaging and genre-based pedagogy from systemic functional linguistics (SFL) theories.

Specifically, the research designs and implements a multilingual intervention program by building a dialogue between genre-based pedagogy and translanguaging in multilingual education. The goal is to construct an effective approach to college English teaching and learning in the multilingual classrooms of the Dong area, and to achieve what is demanded in multilingual education of the minority areas, namely, multilingualism. Taking translanguaging and SFL as the general theoretical frameworks, particularly with reference to notions of text and context, genre and register theory and genre-based pedagogy, the research emphasizes explicit pedagogy and the use of the students' linguistic and cultural resources, aiming to scaffold them to use English independently, and ultimately to develop multilingual literacy.

Based on the above factors, this research addresses the following three questions:

(1) How is translanguaging genre-based pedagogy (TL-GBP) established under the frameworks of translanguaging and genre-based pedagogy theories for English teaching in the context of multilingual education in the Dong area, and ultimately for multilingual education with the objective of multilingualism?

(2) How is the students' whole linguistic repertoire used as a resource in the teaching of English, based on the TL-GBP?

(3) To what extent is the intervention program effective in enhancing students' learning of English, improving their multilingual competence, promoting their metalinguistic awareness, and developing their multilingual identity?

1.5　The Organization of the Book

This book is organized into eight chapters.

Chapter One is the introductory one. It first situates the research in its social context by providing the overview of Dong ethnic group and the present situation of multilingual education in China, in Guizhou particularly. It then outlines the research rational, significance, innovations and questions.

Chapter Two presents the literature review. After summarizing and comparing the previous research, it sorts out the research findings and shortcomings to serve for this research. It then examines research on translanguaging and genre-based pedagogy respectively to find out relevant research progress and limitations, based on which the approach of this research is proposed.

Chapter Three outlines the theoretical preliminaries for this research. It first outlines theories of translanguaging and genre-based pedagogy respectively, then frames the theoretical preliminaries that incorporate translanguaging into genre-based pedagogy to design the multilingual program.

Chapter Four reveals the research design. It illustrates the research procedures, the selection of sample, research methods, data collection, and how the specific curriculum genres are designed, in order to plan carefully for the implementation of the intervention program.

Chapter Five analyzes the pedagogic practices of the intervention program. It provides the examination and evaluation of the intervention program, involving two iterations of teaching and learning activities. In these iterations, translanguaging strategies are the use of multilingual texts as pedagogic resources at the macro curriculum level, and the use of all languages in structured ways as media of instruction at micro classroom interaction level, with the objectives of enabling students to develop literacy competence in English, and to reinforce their multilingual competence. In addition, the use of metalanguage to do with language knowledge and literature language to do with the field as well as cultural awareness are dealt with in all three languages.

Chapter Six examines the impact of the program on students' English writing. The students' written texts before, during and after the intervention program are assessed according to the terms of SFL. The results indicate the students' writing development, involving all language levels.

Chapter Seven investigates other impact on the development of their metalinguistic awareness and identity construction. Firstly, the students' use of translanguaging strategies during their learning process is investigated mainly by interviews. The results reveal how they use these translanguaging strategies to self-regulate and assist their learning, and how their metalinguistic awareness and multilingual identity are developed in the process.

Chapter Eight concludes this study. It summarizes the findings of the research, concluding the impact of the program implemented on the students' performance. Then strengths and implications of the research are then pointed out. The implications of the research are considered for language learning and teaching in the context of multilingual education in Chinese minority areas and in other relevant contexts of the world generally. At last, limitations of the research and suggestions for future research are provided.

CHAPTER TWO
LITERATURE REVIEW

2.1 Research on Multilingual Education

2.1.1 Major areas of research

1. Overview of multilingual education

As forces of globalization have been increasingly felt in any corner of the world, multilingualism has become more common and widely spread in education. Schools in different parts of the world have second or foreign languages in the curriculum. English, as the international language, is one of the most popular language opted for second or foreign language, and national and minority languages are also included in school curriculum. In addition, children in the same class who speak different languages at home can be commonly found because of the mobility of the population, and their languages can be part of the school curriculum or not (Hélot, 2012). Therefore, multilingual education has been broadly interpreted as the use of two or more languages in education, aiming at multilingualism or multi-literacy. Within this context, a holistic approach questions that "native-like" proficiency should be the ultimate goal when learning a language and looks at the students' whole linguistic repertoire. Multilingualism can give better opportunities, particularly in the job market, but it is also linked to identity and belonging to one or more speech communities (Cenoz & Gorter, 2015, p. 2). Moreover, multilingual education has now been seen as new solutions to bridging the gap between the local and the global in minority areas (Gorter, et al., 2014, p. 4).

The multilingual reality in education has brought together a proliferation of studies on multilingual education in European and North American context. Studies are also increasingly found in educational settings in Africa, Latin America and Asia in recent years (Feng & Adamson, 2015; Hélot & de Mejía, 2008; Skutnabb-Kangas & Heugh, 2012).

2. Third language acquisition

As an important part of multilingual education, third language acquisition (TLA) has been widely observed in recent decades. The term TLA in some cases is adopted as synonymous for "multilingualism", but it, in a strict sense, denotes the acquisition of a third language, highlighting its differences from learning a second language (Cenoz, 2009) and the complexity of its process (Safont-Jordà, 2017).

One obvious difference between second language acquisition (SLA) and TLA is that third language learners have more advantages. The reason is that they have already at least two languages in their linguistic repertoire, and thus can use them when learning a third language. These advantages have been explained in different ways, but three factors are most relevant.

The first one is metalinguistic awareness. Third language learners can develop greater metalinguistic knowledge and metalinguistic awareness compared with monolinguals (Cenoz, et al., 2017). They have a better awareness of the forms, meanings and rules of languages. Through constant interaction between two or more languages, they can reflect about language in a more abstract way and be more aware of the way languages work.

The second factor is associated with their language learning experience. In the process of learning two or more languages, third language learners can develop a range of learning strategies, which can facilitate them to learn a third language.

The third factor is the broader available linguistic repertoire as compared with SLA. As Cenoz and Todeva (2009, p. 278) pointed out, "multilinguals get many 'free rides' when learning additional languages as their prior linguistic knowledge helps on all levels of language—grammar, pragmatics, lexicon, pronunciation, and orthography".

The complexity of TLA is mostly reflected in cross-linguistic influence. Existing research on cross-linguistic influence has provided us with the information that third language learners are influenced by both their L1 and L2 at all language levels. In terms of grammar, Klein (1995) explored the acquisition of syntactic patterns and structure of a third language. Flynn, et al. (2004) proposed the cumulative enhancement model to deal with the grammar development in three languages. This model examined how previous grammar knowledge may facilitate L3 grammar acquisition while avoiding redundant syntactic structure transfer. The research showed that the learning of L3 grammar like other language systems is more complex than L2 learning. Studies on vocabulary (de Angelis & Dewaele, 2011) also indicated the complex process of the constant interaction and interdependence among third language learners' lexical systems, which may not be restricted to simple semantic or lexical transfer processes. Research on pragmatic competence of multilingual learners presented not only their advantages over monolinguals but also a different path of development (Safont-Jordà, 2005). In addition, a wide range of contextual factors like socio-economic and socio-educational status, motivation and language exposure also contribute to the complexity of TLA.

In brief, TLA shows great differences and complexity compared with SLA although it also shares strong similarities with SLA as they are both processes of acquiring a non-native language. Research of TLA has brought together SLA and multilingualism because it associated the outcomes of multilingualism with other cognitive and social outcomes. For example, in most cases the positive effects of multilingualism on TLA were reported. Meanwhile, the influence of social factors on TLA has also been found. The contribution of the research on TLA in multilingual context is important because it goes beyond the hard boundaries between languages and takes the learners' whole linguistic repertoire into account.

3. Multilingual approach to language teaching

The study of multilingual education cannot separate language acquisition, "becoming multilingual", from language use, "being multilingual", as learning language necessarily involves using the languages (Cenoz & Gorter, 2015). In contrast to traditional SLA research, the new trends in the study of multilingual education suggest that the learners' L1 and other languages can be used as resources when learning the target language. The multilingual ideas from sociolinguistics have crossed over the context of multilingual education, which implies that languages are no longer considered as separate entities, as their boundaries are becoming softer.

From a psycholinguistic perspective, Herdina and Jessner (2002) proposed "the Dynamic Model of Multilingualism" (DMM), which adapted the Dynamic Systems Theory to interpret bilingualism or multilingualism. With the aim of acquiring several languages, the DMM presents a new perspective in the analysis of multilingual data, which is different from traditional SLA monolingual paradigms. Components of the DMM are learners' multilingual knowledge and cross-linguistic awareness, produced in the constant interaction of their languages. As we can see, the DMM considers multilingual learners' full linguistic repertoire as one factor that contributes to their learning advantages and enhanced skills.

From the holistic perspective, Cenoz and Gorter (2014) proposed "Focus on Multilingualism" approach to teaching and conducting research in multilingual education. The approach relates the ways that multilingual learners use their communicative resources in real-life communication to the ways that languages are learned and taught in classrooms. It seeks to build bridges between language teaching at school and multilingualism in spontaneous conversation, involving all their linguistic resources and ways of multilingual practices. Specifically, it views that the communicative competence and metalinguistic awareness developed in previous learning experience can be activated when learning an additional language. The approach proposes to integrate different languages in the curricula, in order to enable students to use their multilingual resources cross-linguistically to learn the target language in a more effective way.

This approach, also with different names such as "pluriliteracy practices", "multilingual literacies" (Blackledge & Creese, 2010), or "translingual practices" (Canagarajah, 2013), looks at fluid code meshing and translanguaging as optimal strategies towards multiple-literacies. Language practices are considered as a dynamic process of structuration, thus reading and writing involve multilingual learners' agency in their control and management of their multilingual language systems. By adopting the temporal-spatial framework, Min-Zhan and Horner (2013) pointed out, writing in translingual practices should not be viewed as the deviation from the standard norm but as the norm of language use. In addition, Blackledge and Creese (2010) argued that literacy teaching cannot be separated from the teaching of culture so that folk narratives in students' heritage languages should be involved.

The translingual approach enables us to meet the students' need to iterate conventions and exercise agency, i.e. to use English (the third language) as a link between the cultures and people represented by other languages, which is often the case in multilingual practices.

4. New trends: towards a holistic approach

Multilingual practices in the foreign language classroom such as code-mixing and code-switching have long been observed and studied in the field of sociolinguistics. Resent research has further developed conceptions of "translanguaging" (García, 2009), "codemeshing" (Canagarajah, 2011), "heteroglossia" (Bailey, 2012), "polylingualism" (Jørgensen, 2008) and "Metrolingualism" (Otsuji & Pennycook, 2010), etc. Central to these developments is the recognition of the multilingual nature of classroom interactions and communicative repertoires of both students and teachers, and the affirmation of multilingualism as a potential resource rather than necessarily a barrier to language and content learning in the context of multilingual education (Lin, 2013). These notions have challenged the basic traditional ideas of native-speakerism, and that language use and learning are static and monolithic phenomena with solid boundaries (Pennycook, 2010).

In recent years, there has been a "multilingual turn" in language education, indicating a move toward more flexible language practices in classrooms (White, et al., 2015). There has also been a "social turn" (Canagarajah, 2007), indicating the shifting of focus from language per se to an increasing interest in learner, the communicative interaction and the context in which the interaction takes place, by considering SLA as a complex and dynamic system in which all variables are interrelated and influence each other (Cenoz & Gorter, 2011). With regard to multilingualism, according to Herdina and Jessner (2002), the development of multilingual competence can be understood as a nonlinear, interdependent and complex process. These multilingual and social turns have brought a closer interaction between foreign language education and multilingualism and challenged the long-established monolingual ideology in educational settings.

The use of L1 in the classroom is also viewed as an indicator of the development of multilingual identity by some scholars (e.g. García, 2009; Blackledge & Creese, 2010). Blackledge and Creese (2010) proposed "flexible bilingualism" as an approach that places the speaker at the center of the interaction and considered languages as social resources without clear boundaries. Research on translanguaging demonstrates that multiple discursive practices are often hybrid without clear boundaries. Some research indicated that the hybridity of multilingual interaction can be better deciphered by focusing on language features, multimodal resources and identity construction rather than by referring to languages (García, 2009).

A paradigm shift in SLA may also be observed on several fronts, with UNESCO developing a set of kits that commit to mother-tongue-based multilingual education (MTB-MLE) (UNESCO, 2016). Contrary to the traditional view of language separation in teaching, there is a new trend that L1 or other languages can be used as resources in teaching target language. This means the use of L1 or other languages is allowed when necessary while the target language can also be the medium of instruction. The use of L1 or other languages is considered as a cognitive tool when the learning tasks are complex, particularly in the model of content-based instruction (Swain & Lapkin, 2013).

In sum, the study of multilingual education has been shifting from the monolingual view that languages are stored in separate containers, to a holistic view that focuses on connections between languages and learners' full linguistic repertoire.

2.1.2 Domestic research on multilingual education

Multilingual education in China in the new era has been developed from minority language-Chinese bilingual education. Since 2002, English has been included in school curriculum, which has resulted in schools in ethnic minority areas being required to implement trilingual education (Ministry of Education, 2001).

1. Research on third language acquisition

Since the first introduction (Liu & Xie, 2006) of one ground-breaking western theoretical volume in TLA—*Cross Linguistic Influence in Third Language Acquisition: Psycholinguistic Perspectives* (edited by Cenoz, et al., 2001), scholars began to pay attention to the particular features and process of TLA of minority students and explore theoretically and practically feasible methods to instruct China's trilingual teaching.

One issue that has received most attention is cross-linguistic influence in TLA of different minority students. Studies have confirmed the results of western TLA research that bilingual learners are influenced by L1 and L2 when learning L3, and also found that L2 has a greater influence than L1 in minority education because L2 is usually chosen as medium of instruction in English teaching in China (e.g. Cai & Yang, 2010; Chen, 2012; Tan, 2012).

Some studies sought to identify patterns of cross-linguistic influence at all language levels and factors that can predict the influence. With regard to the influence at the lexical level, research mainly focused on lexical transfer and semantic access, and found that key factors that influence L3 semantic access include L2 and/or L3 proficiency and language distance (Cui & Zhang, 2009; Rebiguli, et al., 2012). At the phonological level, research reported that both L1 and L2 would influence L3 phonology learning while L1 would have greater influence, and the main factors include language distance, proficiency and the order of language learning (Cao & Xu, 2014; Ou & Liu, 2009). In addition, research also found negative transfer in the development of syntactic and pragmatic knowledge, caused mainly by their previous language knowledge and cultural differences (Chen & Huala, 2017; Liu & Zhang, 2012). Other factors found out to predict cross-linguistic influence include psycho-typology and recency (Liu & Xie, 2008), sociolinguistic context and students' language level (Liu, 2010), teaching materials and emotional factors (Zhang, 2011), etc.

Another topic that attracts the increasing interesting is metalinguistic awareness. Research showed that third language learners have higher level of metalinguistic awareness than second language learners, and that the development of metalinguistic awareness are mainly influenced by the proficiency of L1 and L2, linguistic distance and age (Zeng, 2010). In addition, research found that metalinguistic awareness is negatively related to learning burnout in TLA, so it can predict well the intensity of learning burnout (Yang, 2016).

Code-switching in trilingual teaching has also been examined. By examining types and functions of code-switching of trilingual teachers and the related influencing factors, research aimed at providing practical implications for improving the appropriate use of trilingual teachers' classroom code-switching and ultimately for promoting trilingual education (e. g. Liu, 2007; Wubaiyinna & Wen, 2015).

Research on language identity and attitude of minority students from the perspectives of psycholinguistics, sociolinguistics and anthropological linguistics has been a new trend in the study of TLA in China. Research found that ethnic minority teachers and students generally hold positive, objective and rational attitudes towards three languages and trilingual education (Yuan, et al., 2013), while students in north China have higher identification, as they have been empowered by their multilingual competence which is closely related to the development of their economy, language vitality and identity claim (Zhang & Yu, 2012). In addition, the characteristics of trilinguals' identity were carefully explored by tracing their life trajectories, and implications were provided with trilingual education and relevant policies as well as the construction of a harmonious society (e. g. Asihan, 2015; Wang, 2016).

2. Multilingual education in Chinese minority areas

The research on multilingual education started from the discussion of conceptions of trilingual education, which has been qualitatively distinguished from bilingual education (Gai & Gao, 2003). Problems in the present trilingual teaching like shortage of qualified trilingual teachers and teaching materials, inappropriate medium of instruction and teaching methods have been detected (e. g. Hu, 2007; Jiang, et al.,

2006; Liu & Shan, 2016; Shi & Xing, 2011). Moreover, challenges brought by educational policy in the new era, such as how to develop the "strong model" of trilingual education, have also been discussed (Feng & Adamson, 2015). Therefore, explorations of theoretical framework to instruct trilingual teaching and relevant empirical experiments to find feasible methods specifically for minority students have then received increasing attention.

To address the specific features and problems, trilingual teaching modes and approaches were proposed in order to promote the efficiency of trilingual education in China's ethnic minority areas. Liu and Li (2011) suggested establishing a set of trilingual education system in minority areas, including teaching objectives, curriculum system and material development and teacher training, according to particular language ecological, social and cultural basis. Xiong (2007) proposed the specific approach to trilingual education for the Dong area, i. e. to use Dong and Chinese to decode and encode in the process of learning English. Zhaogeshen, et al. (2008) suggested trilingual education system should be based on the use of Mongolian as medium of instruction.

Empirical studies have been increasing to construct and testify the teaching modes and approaches in recent years. Zhang (1998) formulated a double positive transfer teaching and learning model—to teach and learn a third language (English) based upon the students' Korean-Chinese bilingualism, the ideas then have been successfully put into practices in Korean communities. Finifrock and Schilken (2015) carried out a mother-tongue based trilingual experimental program in Guizhou Dong minority area and its result was astonishingly positive. The program conducted by Johnson, et al. (2016) in Yunnan also confirmed the important role of students' first language in effective learning.

Research also suggested training professional teachers for trilingual education. Inner Mongolia normal university began to recruit students majoring in "Mongolian as MOI in English education" since 1993, and trained a large number of excellent English teachers of "mastering both Mongolian and English" for middle school in Mongolian community (Wubaiyinna, 2010). Sichuan Normal University organized "Tao Xingzhi trilingual experimental class" to cultivate teachers for the Tibetan from 2012, addressing teachers' ability of using Tibetan to teach English (Wang & Kong, 2013). Teaching materials were also suggested to be developed in three languages following the principle of TLA to take or develop trilingual learners' cognitive advantages (Gulixia, 2011).

2.1.3 Problems and limitations

The research on multilingual education made great theoretical and practical contributions to third or additional language teaching and other fields of applied linguistics both at home and abroad, there still exist some problems and limitations to achieve the research and educational goals mentioned above.

Firstly, a thorough multilingual approach should be adopted in whether theoretical or practical studies. As discussed above, a holistic approach that takes all multilingual learners' languages and speech communities into account has been theoretically and empirically proved as a more efficient way in the study of multilingual education. However, as Cenoz (2013) pointed out, many studies, influenced by traditional SLA approach, still paradoxically adopted a monolingual focus. In China, for example, the majority of studies had a monolingual focus on English, overlooking ethnic minority students' language and other cultural elements. Therefore, a complete holistic approach should be adopted to make connections between languages, between language acquisition and language use, and between the teaching of the target language and developing multilingual competence.

Secondly, research from more disciplines and collaborations among sub-disciplines is needed. As elaborated above, studies from more disciplines like psycholinguistics, educational linguistics and anthropological linguistics would help us examine further and have a deeper understanding of the process of TLA. For example, research in China has comprehensively discussed TLA from linguistic perspectives (such as cross-linguistic influence), however, multilingual processing may be best examined by including social factors. Furthermore, given the interdisciplinary nature of multilingualism, more link between disciplines is also needed. Issues like language identity from sociolinguistics and narratives of learning experience from anthropological linguistics can provide a thorough and deep understanding of multilinguals' learning process and its related influencing factors, which may complete the results obtained from a more psycholinguistic perspective by pointing to the interaction between their emotions and other individual variables.

Thirdly, more research, especially empirical research, is needed to enable us to account for multilingual education across the globe. The situations of multilingual education in different minority regions vary, while some proposals were only identified generally based on some TLA theoretical analysis or in a specific setting. The cases discussed most in China were Mongolia, Tibetan, Miao, Uyghur and Korean, while cases of the rest dozens of ethnic minority groups are still unexplored. The research results in these areas or based on some foreign theories did not necessarily have great significance in guiding trilingual education in other minority regions. Therefore, more research, especially empirical research, should be conducted for a wide range of minority communities by taking their particular linguistic, cultural, social and psychological factors into account, so as to provide instruction of trilingual education in a particular minority region.

Bearing these research findings in mind, and taking into consideration the realistic context, this research is designed as an empirical study from the interdisciplinary perspective to implement an English teaching program in the context of multilingual education by taking minority students' language and culture as positively affective and educational elements. By adopting a "multilingual" approach, this research aims not only at English teaching and learning, but also at the development of multilingual competence and identity. The first step is to design the curriculum by looking at relevant pedagogy and strategies.

2.2 Research on Translanguaging

As described above, the holistic approach as a new paradigm in the study of multilingual education highlights the interrelationship between language acquisition and language use. It argues that the research and teaching in multilingual education should include multilingual learners' whole linguistic repertoire and multilingual identity, which goes against the well-established tradition of language separation. Influenced by the new trends, the notion of translanguaging has been proposed and developed. This section first looks at the conceptions and development of translanguaging, then reviews relevant research on it, especially on its pedagogic use.

2.2.1 Major areas of research

1. Overview of translanguaging

Translanguaging is an emerging concept. According to Lewis, et al. (2012), the term was first coined in Welsh "trawsieithu" by Williams and Whittall in the 1980s and was translated into English first as "translinguifying" and later as "translanguaging". It originally referred to the pedagogic practice of deliberately alternating the use of Welsh and English for input and output in the same lesson. The idea is to receive information by the medium of one language and to work with that information in the medium of the other language to reinforce understanding and to maximize learning. Since then, the term has been rapidly and widely extended.

Following Williams, Baker (2011, p. 288) viewed translanguaging as "the process of making meaning, shaping experiences, gaining understanding and knowledge through the use of two languages". Lewis, et al. (2012) further pointed out that the goal of translanguaging cognitive processing is to retain and develop bilingualism, rather than just for emergent bilinguals at the beginning stages. Canagarajah (2011, p. 401) defined translanguaging as "the ability of multilingual speakers to shuttle between languages, treating the diverse languages that form their repertoire as an integrated system". They argued that translanguaging can not only promote understanding of meaning but also develop balanced bilingualism by using the stronger language to reinforce the weak one (Lewis, at al., 2012).

García (2009, p. 45) agreed most with Canagarajah's idea, and viewed translanguaging as "multiple discursive practices" in which bilinguals engage in order to "make sense of their bilingual worlds". Translanguaging, she pointed out, is an approach that does not focus on languages, but on the observable and real communicative practices of bilinguals. The translanguaging practices in bilingual communities can be properly interpreted and practiced in schools as a strategy for promoting students' cognitive, language and literacy abilities. She (2011) further explained translanguaging is more than code-switching and translation in education because it goes beyond these simple practices, which takes two languages as separate systems that simply shift from each other, and takes into account the myriad multimodal ways of bilingual students' practices.

García and Sylvan (2011) have further developed translanguaging as an effective way of learning by the research in the International Network of Public High Schools in the United States. In terms of "plurilingualism from the students", they (2011, p. 397) referred it as the fact that students use "diverse language practices for purposes of learning, and teachers use inclusive language practices for purposes of teaching".

Hornberger and Link (2012) have explicitly connected translanguaging to Hornberger's (1989) "Continua of Biliteracy" in education. They (2012, p. 268) noted the importance of translanguaging in education and proposed a theoretical framework in which translanguaging can be conceptualized and contextualized, enabling the potential "to explicitly valorize all points along the continua of biliterate context, media, content, and development".

Blackledge and Creese (2010; also Creese & Blackledge, 2010) provided us with a definition of translanguaging as a flexible bilingual pedagogy for learning and teaching in the bilingual classroom. This flexible bilingualism, they argued, has been used by teachers as an instructional strategy for promoting cross-language transfer, to convey ideas easily, and most importantly to develop multilingual identity. As Creese and Blackledge (2010, p. 112) pointed out, flexible bilingualism, as students' translanguaging, can be used to "make links for classroom participants between the social, cultural, community, and linguistic domains of their lives", so that bilingual learners are placed at the heart of the interaction and languages are used as social resources without clear boundaries.

Cenoz and Gorter (2011) extended translanguaging approach, which was originally been applied to two languages in the Welsh context and for García in the US, to develop the approach "Focus on Multilingualism" which looks at multilingual learners' whole linguistic repertoire and their multilingual and multicultural identities in the context of multilingual education in Europe.

The notion of translanguaging has become prevalent but its use is not unitary. As discussed above, the term of translanguaging is dynamic, which has been developing and discussing in various aspects of sociolinguistic areas and from cross-disciplinary interaction of linguistics, sociolinguistics, educational linguistics and neurolinguistics. Therefore, translanguaging is an umbrella term. It can refer to a pedagogic strategy to promote effective teaching and learning based on students' whole linguistic repertoire in bilingual classroom. It has also been extended to the spontaneous multilingual speech and the way the real communication can be used as an instructional strategy. In addition, it has been developed recently to account for brain activity modulations when learners' all languages are activated and the results can also be used to understand, evaluate and promote the effectiveness of translanguaging strategies in education. In any case, translanguaging transgresses the strict separation of languages.

2. Translanguaging as a pedagogic approah

Translanguaging has now been largely extended and investigated in educational context. Lewis, et al. (2013) further examined the use of English and Welsh in 29 primary and secondary schools in Wales. They identified translanguaging as its original meaning when input and output were systematically varied in one language or other languages based on the observations of 100 bilingual lessons. The results showed that the language switching of input and output was more common in arts and humanities subjects than mathematics, science and the more practical subjects.

Apart from research in Wales, research on CBI/CLIL in recent years also found that the use of L1 can facilitate content understanding. Evidence showed that previous language knowledge serves as a foundation or scaffolding for acquiring new knowledge particularly when two languages have cognate connection, and L1 as a cognitive tool when the task is relatively complex, particularly in the content-based instruction (e.g. Lin, 2015; Swain & Lapkin, 2013). Moreover, connecting students' L1 everyday language with L2 scientific language can promote students' involvement in translanguaging and thus their co-construction of the thematic patterns (Lin & Lo, 2017). These studies indicate that the use of students' L1 in teaching can be a helpful pedagogic strategy, but more research is still needed to examine its effects (Cenoz & Gorter, 2017).

Other potential roles of translanguaging as a pedagogy have also been observed worldwide. For example, Mazak and Herbas-Donoso (2015) reported translanguaging can develop students' science discourses in both Spanish and English and thus has the potential to expand students' academic competence and lead to a more justice scientific community where access can be given to multilingual students. Another example showed that flexible bilingualism and pedagogy like translanguaging can promote students' creativity and criticality by examining how Chinese children in a Mandarin-English bilingual program skillfully navigated between different languages in their literacy practices (Zhang & Guo, 2017).

The new progress is the development of translanguaging pedagogic interventions, which have largely authenticated the potential role of translanguaging as a pedagogy. Lyster, et al. (2009) carried out an intervention program that French and English teachers systematically used two languages in the reading of chapters of the same books in the 2nd year of primary education in Canada. Later, they (Lyster, et al., 2013) conducted a more specific intervention with the goal of developing morphological awareness in French and English and also in Canadian immersion. The results showed that students performed better in morphological awareness. Arteagoitia and Howard (2015) conducted a program on the development of literacy skills through using students' L1 knowledge as a resource, based on the pedagogic intervention of using cognates in Spanish and English to 230 Spanish L1 students in the USA. The results indicated that the knowledge of Spanish had a positive effect in English academic vocabulary and reading comprehension.

Translanguaging intervention programs have also increased in South Africa in the last decade. Probyn (2015) explored how science teachers utilized students' linguistic resources to improve their opportunity of learning science in rural and township schools in South Africa. The results revealed that the teacher's successful practice was his systematic and purposeful use of the students' L1, and this strategy was what has been termed "pedagogic translanguaging". Makalela (2015) reported an intervention with 60 students of teacher training and found that these students performed better than other students in both the vocabulary development and oral reading competence. Furthermore, the students' reflective response to the intervention indicated that translanguaging gave them reasoning power and had a positive effect by reinforcing multilingual identity.

Another intervention work in progress was the translanguaging project in the Basque Country (Cenoz & Gorter, 2017). The instructional aim was to develop the awareness at vocabulary, morphological and discourse levels and metalinguistic awareness in three languages: Basque, Spanish, and English.

3. Translanguaging in writing

The pedagogic space that translanguaging research opens up goes beyond the way of using two or more languages in language and content classes. It considers multilingual learners' whole linguistic repertoire as a resource to raise the awareness of how languages work with the ultimate goal of developing multi-literacy competence.

Early before the term translanguaging was introduced, there was amounts of evidence that bilingual language practices would have complex influences on literacy development. Both Hornberger's (1989) "continua of biliteracy" and García, et al. (2007)'s "pluriliteracies" addressed the interrelationship of languages and different social and cultural contents as learners communicate around written form.

Studies on translanguaging as a pedagogy in writing have received a great deal of attention in the last decade, although scholars may report the process differently. Fu (2003) is one of the earliest scholars who supported the use of the students' mother tongue in the teaching of writing in the other language. She (2003) proposed a bilingual process approach to developing Chinese students' writing competence in English and argued that the ways of this approach that include thinking and expressing ideas in students' primary language assist students in writing well in a second language.

Gort (2006) demonstrated how students used their two languages interactively to facilitate bilingual literacy skills and presented how two languages were activated in the writing process to perform the writing-related tasks. Kibler (2010) described how interactional spaces where students can use both languages supported expertise enactment in different elements of the writing task. Kabuto (2011) studied on the writing development in Japanese and English of her daughter Emma. The results showed that Emma's early writing presented vertical writing in Japanese and horizontal writing in English, and she used what Kabuto referred to as "script-switching" to make close connection between writing and identity. Velasco and García (2014) explored how and why young bilingual writers used translanguaging in developing the academic writing. The results indicated that translanguaging was not only a pedagogic strategy for assisting in the instruction, but also the way bilingual learners can self-regulate and advance their learning. They also added that translanguaging had the most potential to develop learners' voices in writing, even the monolingual voice that the school expected.

Cenoz and Gorter (2011) investigated the compositions written by the same students on different topics in Basque, Spanish and English respectively. They found that students tended to use the same strategies when they wrote in different languages. Soltero-González, et al. (2012) also analyzed the written texts produced by bilingual students. They suggested that a holistic bilingual lens should be taken to analyze the multilingual strategies that bilingual students used in the written texts. They concluded that when adopting a holistic view, bilingual students can be considered as special learners who used their multilingual resources at vocabulary, grammar and discourse levels.

Another important contribution has been Canagarajah's works on translanguaging practices as pedagogies in writing. Michael-Luna and Canagarajah (2007) analyzed a number of translanguaging practices referred to as code-meshing that teachers implemented to develop students' literacy in bilingual classroom. Canagarajah's (2013) research on translingual practice explained the strategies multilingual learners adopted in the process of writing. All these practices were based on the whole linguistic repertoire and involved diverse semiotic resources.

In sum, the studies on translanguaging in writing showed that multilingual students use different problem-solving strategies and ways of expressing meanings that do not present in monolingual writings. Multilingual writers use the resources of their linguistic repertoire in drafting in one language or another, thus some competencies and skills are developed across languages in this process. What we can see from this body of research is that translanguaging can be taken as a useful and legitimate part of writing process of multilinguals. Translanguaging implies deliberate action to solve writing problems by using multilingual resources at word, sentence and whole-text levels. Many elements that have already been acquired in one language can be used and reinforced in other languages. As for translanguaging, strategies used by multilingual learners are the same with all learners, i.e. to use what they have known to solve what they do not know.

2.2.2 Domestic research on translanguaging

As a developing concept, translanguaging has been widely developed and investigated from the perspectives of a wider arrange of areas, such as SLA, TLA, social linguistics and linguistic anthropology, in western countries. Research on translanguaging in China, however, is still in its infancy.

Until recently, the concept of translanguaging in western countries was firstly introduced by Yuan and Zhou (2015). They presented the origin and conceptions of translanguaging, its related views of language and language acquisition, and research scope and progress at abroad over the past decades, and discussed some implications of translanguaging theory for college English teaching in China. Several studies that use translanguaging theory to explain some sociolinguistic phenomena were found. Li (2016) introduced some new theoretical concepts—translanguaging and Post-Multilingualism—to Chinese readers and used these concepts to analyze the emergence of New Chinese English in relation to the rapid development of the Chinese society and globalization. Li (2016) used the notion of translanguaging to examine the playful nature of multilingual practices of online English-language TV and film fans in China by digital ethnographic research. She argued the fans' translanguaging practices can create a space that allowed them to construct multiple identities, which may open up possibilities for the reconsideration, reworking, or enrichment of certain values of the official culture.

From the above, we can see research on translanguaging in China is just at its beginning stage. A great deal of theoretical and empirical explorations of using translanguaging theory in Chinese context are emergently needed.

2.2.3 Problems and limitations

The rapid development of translanguaging research reveals that the holistic approach that goes against traditional ideology of language separation and looks at connections between languages has been increasingly recognized and adopted in various educational contexts. Advantages of using translanguaging as a pedagogic strategy has been widely reported, but the research and the use of translanguaging also have some limitations and difficulties.

One apparent difficulty is to define the scope of translanguaging. Translanguaging nowadays has been widely used to explain different phenomena. As Cenoz and Gorter (2015) pointed out, translanguaging in a broad sense includes a range of terms that go across languages like "code-switching", "code-meshing" and "translation". It, in a narrow sense, refers to a specific pedagogic strategy such as cross-linguistic strategy applied in Wales (Lewis, et al., 2013) or alternated use of languages for exploratory talk in South African educational contexts (Probyn, 2015) and elsewhere. The term translanguaging used to refer to different realities shows its attractiveness, but also posits some problems related to the diversity of languages and educational contexts and the interdisciplinary nature of research on multilingual education. As Heugh (2015) argued that translanguaging ensures the educational legitimacy of using other languages in educational settings of South Africa but faces some problems when used as a blanket term compared with code-switching:

> In my view, code-switching conveys a sense that this could be two or multidirectional, whereas "trans" as in translanguaging suggests in the South African context, at least, of moving from one place to another, moving from one language to another, and possibly from an African language to English. (p. 283)

Therefore, it is necessary to solve the terminological problems and fine-tune the use of the term translanguaging. When translanguaging is used as a pedagogic tool to broaden learners' multilingual expertise, it is crucial to demonstrate its efficacy. Translanguaging is more realistic than language isolation because multilinguals process and communicate by using languages at their disposal. As outlined above, some interventional data showed positive results related to pedagogic translanguaging, but it is clear that some findings are not yet conclusive, such as its advantages in an additional language teaching or better understanding of subject content in CLIL/CBI programs. In the same vein, there is every reason to encourage further research that might demonstrate the efficacy of translanguaging at different educational levels or for different types of students.

An additional difficulty related to the use of translanguaging as a pedagogic strategy is its reaction against the well-established monolingual tradition in language teaching. The idea of linguistic divides is still well spread, and some studies that claimed multilingual perspectives in fact paradoxically adopted a monolingual focus. For example, in most cases in the USA and the UK, translanguaging has been used in the educational context of valuing the learner's prior knowledge and linguistic repertoire, but the educational focus or goal was still monolingual, namely, the trajectory was mostly one-directional and towards English. Therefore, if the term allows educational stakeholders to take the educational opportunities, there should be a need to make strategic use of the label for now. What's most important concerns the cognitive engagements that work with two or more languages simultaneously rather than separately, but the label that refers to this is to some extent less significant.

Another important challenge related to this label concerns some contexts where a minority language is spoken (Gorter, et al., 2014). As Gorter (2015) points out that there is always some social pressure to put more emphasis on dominant language than minority language. In these contexts, it is necessary to keep interactional spaces that permit the use and development of the minority language (also see Lewis, et al., 2012).

2.3 Research on Genre-based Pedagogy

2.3.1 Major areas of research

1. Overview of genre-based pedagogy

The Sydney School genre-based pedagogy is a long-running Australian-based program inspired by a language in education workshop in the Department of Linguistics at the University of Sydney in 1979. Initially, the project was designed to develop methods to enable students to succeed with the writing demands of the curriculum in primary schools.

Genre-based pedagogy is a holistic pedagogy, not just a method, or strategy, which provides a set of teaching/learning procedures guided by principles drawing from theories and action research projects. Proposed as visible and explicit pedagogy, genre-based pedagogy has been seeking to address the literacy needs of students who, either on account of speaking a language other than English or on account of socio-economic disadvantages, had few experiences of modes of communication associated with academic success and social mobility. It involves research of mechanisms that schools distribute knowledge and opportunities equally to different groups. In this sense, genre-based pedagogy resonates with the professed education policies of most nations and of UNESCO (2010) for "full and equal opportunities for education for all... to advance the ideal of equality of educational opportunity" (Rose & Martin, 2012, p. 5).

The approach has been applied at any educational levels (e.g. Emilia & Christie, 2013; in secondary school; Humphrey & Macnaught, 2011; in university sector), reaching beyond L1 teaching to L2/multilingual education (e.g. Brisk, 2014). It has not only had great influence on literacy curricula beyond Sydney across Australia, but also has been expanded as an international movement, with centers in China, Hong Kong and Singapore, Indonesia, the UK, Scandinavia, South Africa, and South and

North America.

2. Principles: language, genre and pedagogy

The Sydney School, based SFL theory, views that language is central to all the processes of teaching and learning. It is informed by a theory of language which guides its pedagogic action research. As a language-based theory of learning, language plays a significant role in teaching and learning. In the same vein, language is modeled differently from other language teaching traditions. SFL provides a functional mode of language which describes the use of language in social context (Martin, 1992; Martin & Rose, 2007; 2008).

A. Language in context

Genre-based pedagogy is informed by the evolving model of language in context provided by SFL, i.e. how language is used in social life. The functional language model involves a rich conception of language as a meaning making system. Language, treated as a social semiotic, plays an instrumental role in construing social contexts which we live in, so it is considered as the core of teaching and learning and other social activities.

A text is regarded as the unit of meaning with the specific social purpose. Teaching and learning in the functional language model are the teaching and learning of "text", and sometimes referred as "text-based language teaching and learning". (de Silva Joyce & Feez, 2012). A text includes three strata: (1) graphology/phonology: dealing with patterns of letters/sounds, (2) lexico-grammar patterns of meaning in clauses, and (3) discourse semantic: patterns of meaning across the whole text. A text is constructed to realize three general social functions: (1) interpersonal function enacting interaction relationships, (2) ideational function construing experience, and (3) textual function by which interpersonal and ideational functions are managed in unfolding communicative texts. The relationship between text and context is realization, with phonology realizing lexico-grammar, lexico-grammar realizing semantics, and semantics realizing context.

Martin further stratified context into two layers, i.e. register and genre (Martin & Rose, 2008). Register is a cover term of three dimensions of social context, which is realized by the three meta-functions of language: tenor by interpersonal function, field by ideational functions and mode by textual function. Genre is beyond register, as the global social purpose (see Figure 2-1, from Rose & Martin, 2012, p. 99). The particular social purpose shapes the type of text, which means that every text aims at realizing a particular purpose by addressing a particular audience (scientists, children, general public, etc.), focusing on particular institutions (science, news, law, etc.) and managing different modalities of communication (spoken or written, monologue or dialogue, visual or verbal, etc.)

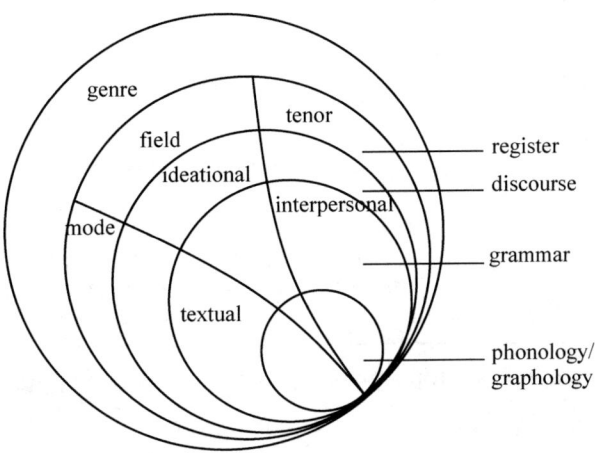

Figure 2-1 Language model in the Sydney School (Rose & Martin, 2012, p. 99)

Martin and Rose (2008) then grouped genres of a culture according to their social goals and distinguish them by their local organization. Accordingly, text types were identified in Sydney School action research to provide models of students' reading and writing in different levels of schooling, which are referred to as "knowledge genres". Three major genre families have been identified in terms of three broad social purposes: stories for engaging readers, factual texts for informing them and essays for evaluating texts of points of view (Table 2-1, from Rose & Martin, 2012), based on linguistic criteria. The relationships of the genres are distinguished based on recurrent global patterns of meaning (Martin & Rose, 2008; Rose & Martin, 2012).

Table 2-1 Genres and their stages (Rose & Martin, 2012, p. 50)

Genre families	Genre	Purpose	Stages
Stories	recount	recounting events	Orientation Record of events
	narrative	resolving a complication in a story	Orientation Complication Resolution
Factual texts	description	describing specific things	Orientation Description
	report	classifying & describing general things	Classification Description
	explanation	explaining a sequence	Phenomenon Explanation
	procedure	how to do experiments & observations	Purpose Method Results

Table 2-1 (Continued)

Genre families	Genre	Purpose	Stages
Arguments	exposition	arguing for a point of view	Thesis Arguments Reiteration
	discussion	discussing two or more points of view	Issue Sides Resolution

Genre-based pedagogy is a top-down approach. Genre, positioned at the top among the co-tangential circles in Figure 2-1, is a starting point of learning. This means that studying language begins with understanding genre—"the staged, goal-oriented, social processes" (Rose & Martin, 2012, p. 54)—through which a text unfolds. The identification of various types of text or knowledge genres has added to our understanding of teaching literacy. It thus provides tools for designing teaching and learning methods that involve more than grammar, consisting of knowledge about language (KAL). The model of teaching practice that involves different stages and activities is referred as the curriculum genre, which is directed by the principle of "guidance through interaction".

B. Guidance through interaction

The contextualization of teaching and learning in genre-based pedagogy draws on Halliday's and Painter's ground-breaking work on spoken language development (Halliday, 1975; Painter, 1984). Halliday and Painter provide the fundamental principle that successful language learning, i. e. "guidance through interaction in the context of shared experience". By observing the parent and child interaction, they described how parent's guiding interaction provides a mode or prepare child to extend knowledge and language. The idea resonates with Bruner's notion of "scaffolding", (a term introduced in Wood, et al., 1976), which refers to adult guidance supporting children to develop their competence towards independent control. The scaffolding metaphor captures the transitional role that teacher provides through unfolding dialogue in teacher and students interactions in classroom, in which teacher prepares students for task and offers elaboration after task (Rose & Martin, 2012, pp. 54-55).

The notion of "guidance through interaction in the context of shared experience" has been translated into several models of literacy teaching practices, which have developed with different representations of teaching procedures in different periods of the action research projects. Every developed model of teaching procedures has the central theme "handing over the control of genre to students". Typically, these teaching models involve firstly establishing common ground with students (context of shared experience), followed with making meaning together with students (guidance through interaction), before asking students to do work on their own (the learning task) (Rose & Martin, 2012, p. 60). These principles are contextualized into different teaching procedures, including stages and activities evolved in the development of genre-based pedagogy.

3. Models of genre-based pedagogy

A. Language and Social Power

Genre-based literacy program was initiated as the *Writing Project* and the *Language* and *Social Power* (LSP) project in the 1980s. In the initial phase, the main focus was on writing in infants and primary school to build a classification of the kinds of writing that students need to learn. The first model of teaching procedures with seven stages was designed by Rothery (in Rose & Martin, 2012, p. 55) (see Table 2-2).

Table 2-2 Rothery's language-based approach model (Rose & Martin, 2012, p. 58)

1	Introducing a Genre	Modelling a genre implicitly through reading to and by class; e.g. read *Little Red Riding Hood*
2	Focusing on a Genre	Modelling a genre explicitly by naming its stages; e.g. identifying the stages of Orientation, Complication and Resolution in the tale of *Little Red Riding Hood*
3	Jointly Negotiating a Genre	Teacher and class compose the genre under focus; the teacher guides the composition of the text through questions and comments that provide scaffolding for the stages of the genre; e.g. in a narrative the following questions may point towards a Resolution stage—how will X escape from the witch? Does she do it alone or does someone help her?
4	Researching	—Factual writing usually involves research —Selecting material for reading —Note making and summarizing —Assembling information before writing
5	Drafting	A first attempt at writing the genre under focus
6	Conferencing	Teacher/pupil consultation—direct reference to the meanings of the writer's text; e.g. questions that help the writer to resolve the Complication stage of a narrative. Young writers find Complication easy but resolving characters' problems is often hard.
7	Publishing	Writing a final draft that may be "published" for the class library, thus providing another input of genre models and a great deal of enjoyable reading

Rothery's approach of teaching procedures was recontextualized with regard to various teaching/learning cycles (TLC). The early "Language and Social Power" project model was portrayed in Figure 2-2 (Rose & Martin, 2012, p. 58).

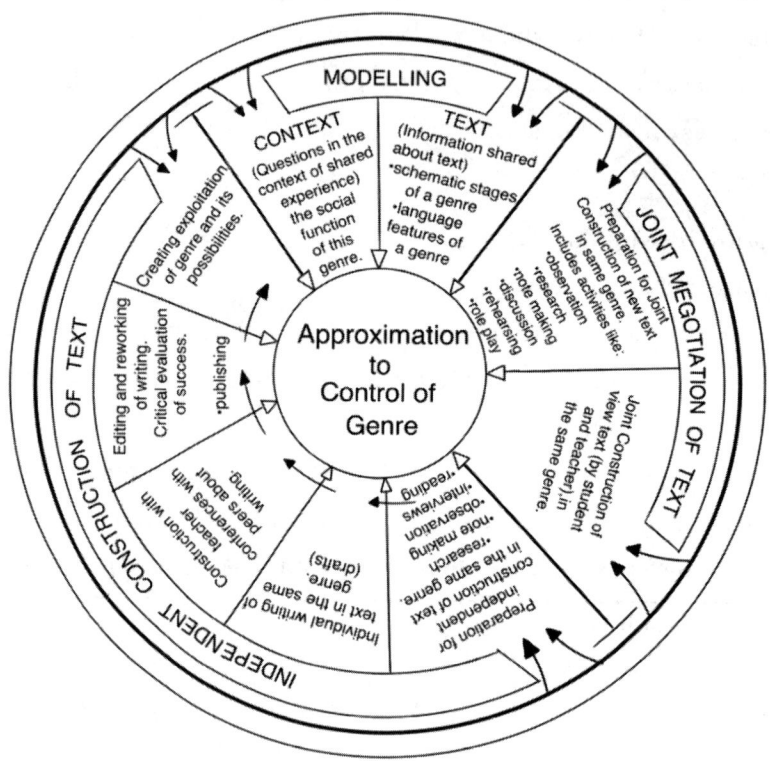

Figure 2-2　Early Language and Social Power project teaching/learning cycle
(Rose & Martin, 2012, p. 58)

As we can see in Figure 2-2, the model consists of three major stages: modelling, joint negotiation of text and independent construction of text. Each stage involves various activities, all directing to handing over control of genre to students approximately. Modelling deals with setting the genre in its cultural context and examining its structure and language feature. Joint negotiation of text includes preparing for work on a new text of the same genre and jointly constructing a text by the teacher developing a text on the board adopting suggestions from the students. Independent construction includes a range of sub-stages: work on another topic, text writing, text submitting, consulting with teacher, editing and "publishing". The aim of the final stage is to prepare for a new text which students will write on their own. It encourages creative exploitation of the genre once it has been acquired. The arrows pointing to the center indicate the flexibility of entering the teaching stages, which allows teachers to start from any points and re-cycle specific stages with different groups of students.

As the project was expanded into secondary school, the pedagogy began to emphasize literacy in specific subject domains, namely, "learning through language". The teaching procedures were planned to assemble relevant content as part of learning to write a genre, namely, language and literacy learning embedded in the subject curriculum (Rose, 2015a; b; c). The representation of this development is the best-known teaching/learning cycle by Rothery (1994, in Rose & Martin, 2012) in the Write it Right project.

B. Write it Right

The Write it Right project (WiR) focuses on language in specific disciplines. Rose and Martin (2012) pointed out that each subject domain has its own distinctive genres. The key to access the knowledge of a subject area is to bring language in each subject area to consciousness. Science, for instance, is characterized by extensive classification of uncommon sense meaning involving a large number of technical terms (Martin, 1993; 2013). The knowledge of history may be less technical, but more specialized (Martin, 1993;2013). In addition, science genres mainly concern the best understandings of the physical and biological world, while history genres focus on values (Rose & Martin, 2012). Therefore, learning science to a certain extent depends on understanding technical terms and the knowledge the terms constitute, while the most important aspect of learning history is to access historically important events and interpret them.

The teaching/learning model in WiR is presented in Figure 2-3 (Rothery, 1994, from Rose & Martin, 2012, p. 59). As we can see, the "building field" bricks and mortar motif show that it is an embedded literacy program, addressing the relevant content as part of learning to write a genre. In addition, the importance of building up the social context is highlighted across all stages so that the purpose for writing remains clear.

There are three major stages in TLC, i. e. deconstruction, joint construction and independent construction. The cycle begins with the deconstruction step, involving field-building. The teacher introduces a model of text type to students in focus, explaining its social function, genre name and schematic structure. The organization and key linguistic composition of the text are discussed. Joint construction is the second step, which involves building up a related field—the teacher guides students to write a new text of the genre by following the general patterns of the model. In this step, the teacher invites students' suggestions and wordings and then shapes the ideas and revises the wordings. The last step is independent construction, which involves building another related field. Students are expected to write a new text on their own. The basic principle for the teacher is never asking students to write anything independently until they are ready for independent writing task. If students are not ready, further cycles of deconstruction and joint construction are needed.

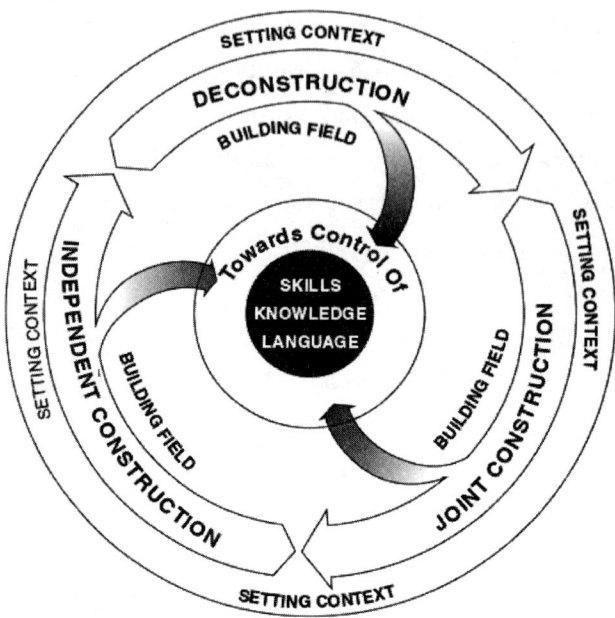

Figure 2-3 Teaching/learning cycle for teaching genre writing (Rose & Martin, 2012, p. 59)

The ultimate goal of TLC is, as the inner circle indicates, explicitly oriented to both control of and a critical orientation to the genre (Rose & Martin, 2012). Genre-based pedagogy sets this goal with two-fold purposes. One is to make the genres required for success in education and society available as widely as possible in response to the issue of social justice. Another is towards a critical perspective on genre that depends on both mastery of the genres being critiqued and mastery of the genres being used to critique (Rose & Martin, 2012).

C. Reading to Learn

The third generation of genre pedagogy is known as Reading to Learn (R2L) project, developed by Rose and his colleges to address the need of indigenous students in remote communities in inner Australia (Rose, 2011; 2015a; b; c; Rose & Martin, 2012). For students, the most difficult task in TLC is to read the model texts that are being deconstructed and joint-constructed, and the relevant materials for field-building. R2L is to address this challenge by extending principles in the previous phases of genre-based pedagogy to integrate the teaching of reading and writing at all education levels. Now it is part of mainstream education across Australia (BOSTES, 2014) and applied in other parts of the world (e.g. Acevedo, 2010; Kartika-Ningsih, 2016; Liu, 2010).

R2L provides three levels of guidance presented as a set of tools for integrating reading and teaching within curriculum (see Figure 2-4, Rose & Martin, 2012, p. 127). The teaching and learning steps in R2L deal with one high-staking reading text to be deconstructed with detailed comprehension and recognition of language choices, reconstructing a related text based on the language resources, as well as constructing a new text to achieve their own purposes in one cycle of teaching and learning.

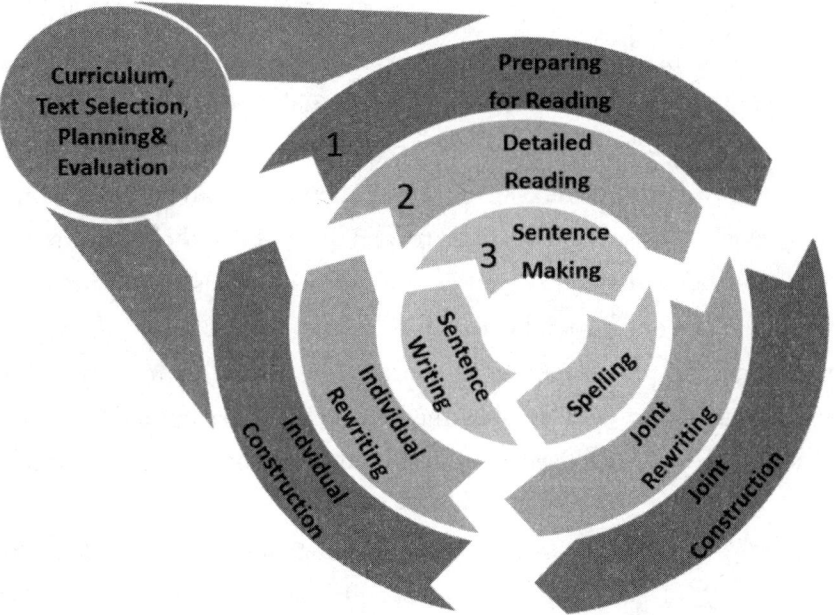

Figure 2-4　The Reading to Learn program (Rose & Martin, 2012, p. 127)

The R2L cycle has been developed to assist teachers and educators in designing carefully their teaching plan and strategies. The curriculum goals, including curriculum, text selection, planning and evaluation, are the starting point of the R2L program, which shape the genre and field to be dealt with in the outer circle (circle 1).

Circle 1 is similar to the writing-oriented TLC outlined above, but has its special deconstruction step as preparing for reading focus. In preparing for reading, the teacher reads the reading text aloud and summarizes it orally. In joint construction, the teacher and students work together to write a related text of the same genre by using the same structural patterns and language resources of the reading text. After a careful preparation, students are expected to write a new text following the stages and phases of the genre that have been modeled for them in individual construction. At this level, the teaching and reading activities mainly focus on deconstructing and reconstructing the higher strata of language hierarchy, i. e. the structure of the whole text. In a class where higher levels of support are needed, circle 2 activities are undertaken.

Circle 2 involves detailed supports for students to recognize language of curriculum text and to use language they have learned from reading in their writing. The language foci at this level are discourse semantics and grammar. In detailed reading, the teacher prepares students to identify and highlight word groups in each sentence, and then elaborates on the meaning of the identified wordings. Then in joint rewriting, students take notes from the detailed reading stage and jointly rewrite a new text by using the same language patterns. Joint rewriting involves a short passage other than a whole text compared with joint construction. It firstly involves note taking—students take turns to scribe the identified language patterns from detailed reading on the blackboard, supported by other students as reciters to read and spell for them. Then the teacher guides students to write a new text using text structure and information from the notes. Students are asked to close their reading text, then rethink their understanding of the topic and discuss the words and sentences to rewrite passages according to the notes on the blackboard. Students also take turns as reciters and scribes after negotiation to write the passages on the blackboard. During the activities in joint rewriting, the teacher supports students with guiding the sentence discussion and checking what the scribe is scribing. If students need even higher level of support, then circle 3 comes to play.

Circle 3 provides intensive strategies of teaching fundamental skills in reading and writing by the step of sentence making, spelling and sentence writing. In sentence making, one or more complex sentences are selected from the detailed reading passages for students to manipulate. Sentences are firstly printed on a large piece of paper, and students cut up them into phrases then into words under the teacher's guidance. Students then mix up the words and rearrange them into the original sentence or work out a new pattern. During this process, challenging words are selected from the sentence to practice spelling. In this step, flash card exercises can be used to practice letter patterns, letter-sound correspondences and letter formation. Finally, the grammar and spelling learned from these activities can be practiced in sentence writing. Strategies in circle 3 that focus on strata of lexico-grammar, phonology and graphology are useful for students who start to learn reading and writing, and who are struggling with literacy, as well as who are learning English as an additional language in ESL/EFL contexts.

R2L model is in effect a curriculum macro-genre, combining reading pedagogy with writing pedagogy, thus terms in the cycles are referred to as steps instead of stages. Each step has a teaching/learning curriculum genre, comprising its distinctive staging, to deal with different language strata. Each stage has different functions and activities, all orienting towards the same goal, i. e. democratizing learning in school through handing over knowledge and control of language to students. This is shown by the optional steps, providing space for teachers to start and adjust at any point according to the needs of the students and level of schooling.

2.3.2 Domestic research on genre-based pedagogy

The Sydney School genre-based pedagogy has been developed and applied in Australia and many other parts of the world, and introduced in the past few years to Chinese readers (Ma, 2010; Zhang, 2013). However, research on genre-based pedagogy, especially empirical research on the teaching of tertiary English writing, is rare.

Some research discussed genre-based literacy pedagogy only at the theoretical level. Zhang (2012) analyzed the genre of academic abstract based on genre-based literacy pedagogy and applied the genre analysis to abstract writing training. Yang (2015) argued that language teaching should cultivate students' genre awareness and the ability to use correct genres by analyzing the theories of register and genre. Zhou (2017) promoted a new literacy teaching approach by combining David Rose's R2L with Chinese scholar Chuming Wang's Writing to Learn. It is worth to mention that Ma (2017) has lead her teams to put genre-based pedagogy into practices for several years, based on which she suggested teachers in Chinese universities intervene students' writing in a top-down way, and argued that this pedagogy provides direction of English teachers' professional development.

2.3.3 Problems and limitations

Genre-based pedagogy has been developed as a series of teaching and learning approaches, by intensive collaboration between linguists of the Sydney School and teachers in real educational contexts and thus observation and reflection on the impact and results of the pedagogy for students. It interprets language teaching and learning practices in several ways. The first, the text in context model provides a deep understanding of language in its actual use linked to social context. The second, the idea of mapping curricula as systems of genres makes the differences of language use in different subject domains explicit and provides teachers with schema of the texts that they need to prepare for students. Moreover, the principle, drawing on the model of language development—guidance through interaction in the context of shared experience—provides fundamental teaching/learning mode with the notion of scaffolding in the adult and child interaction on the basis of shared experience in social context.

A point to note is multilingualism. The genre-based literacy project was initiated to address English literacy development of the students who speak a language other than standard English at home in less advantaged schools in New South Wales and inner Australia, where most students were from immigrant or indigenous background. As we can see, ESL education has been one of the main concerns in developing the pedagogy. Research implementing the genre-based pedagogy in ESL settings has now spread to other parts of the world (e.g. Brisk, 2015). However, the research on genre-based pedagogy has been strictly monolingual as it mainly focused literacy development of the foreign language—English, and emphasized English as the medium of instruction while without taking into account students' linguistic profiles. Now the consideration is to extend genre-based pedagogy to the context of multilingual education.

2.4 Summary

This chapter first reviewed the study of multilingual education abroad and at home. The present research and practices tend to adopt a holistic approach that aims at multilingualism and looks at the learners' whole linguistic repertoire. In China, however, the practices of multilingual education in most minority areas generally emphasize foreign language while ignoring ethnic minority language. In classroom teaching, consequently, the teachers usually overlooked students' cultural and linguistic characteristics. The current model was thus likely to result in the subtractive trilingualism. Therefore, this research was designed as a multilingual intervention program of teaching college English with the objective of multilingualism by taking a holistic approach. It was hoped to improve not only English teaching and learning, but also to develop minority students' multilingual proficiency and identities.

The methodology underpinning the pedagogy was drawn from translanguaging approach and genre-based pedagogy. As described above, translanguaging, as a developing concept, has been adopted as a pedagogic strategy in multilingual education practices that legitimizes flexible multilingual practices and takes all the students' semiotic and multimodal resources into account. It has been employed in various educational settings for different purposes, and theoretically and empirically authenticated to be an effective way of promoting the language learning of minority students and building their multilingual identity. Therefore, it is the best approach chosen to meet the needs of the multilingual program in the Dong area. Moreover, the application of translanguaging in the program is hoped to add up evidence-based data to the terminological and theoretical construct of translanguaging.

The research also adopted genre-based pedagogy as the particular pedagogy. As described above, genre-based pedagogy has great potential for multilingual education for at least two reasons. Firstly, the explicitness to KAL associated with the school curriculum and social functionality of classroom activities is what most bilingual and multilingual education programs need. Secondly, a range of successful experiences of implementing the pedagogy present evidence of its transferability for different educational levels and language settings. In addition, as a long-run action research project, it has developed and refined systemic teaching/learning cycles that teachers can use to plan and implement every step of teaching activities. Therefore, genre-based pedagogy can be used to plan well the use of multilingual students' cultural and linguistic resources in each step and unfolding the English knowledge at the same time.

This chapter, therefore, proposed that the intervention program could employ the students' whole linguistic repertoire as a resource in foreign language teaching according to translanguaging theory on the one hand, and provided equal access to English knowledge according to genre-based pedagogy on the other hand. The key to designing the current multilingual program was to extend genre-based pedagogy in multilingual settings by incorporating translanguaging theory into guiding through multilingual interactions in the context of shared experience.

CHAPTER THREE
THEORETICAL PRELIMINARIES

As examined above, translanguaging has been developed as an effective pedagogic strategy in multilingual education, and the Sydney School genre-based pedagogy has been acknowledged as a feasible pedagogic approach, both theoretically and practically. These facts bring the possibility that multilingualism could be considered as part of genre-based pedagogy practice in Chinese minority areas. The research was thus designed as a multilingual education program by considering translanguaging approach in genre-based pedagogy. The recontextualization of genre-based pedagogy in the multilingual context of the Dong area may provide valuable information about how translanguaging/multilingualism has been taken into account in English teaching and learning, addressing what was lacking in the current practices. The examination of the recontextualisation of genre-based pedagogy in Chinese minority areas therefore could provide the research context and basis for the development of the multilingual teaching/learning program.

Therefore, this chapter sets out the theoretical preliminary, i. e. to construct the translanguaging genre-based pedagogy (TL-GBP) methodology for this program. The chapter first reviews the notions of translanguaging in education and its links with minority languages (Section 3.1), and then examines two aspects of genre-based pedagogy in terms of the curriculum design: the knowledge genres and the curriculum genres (Section 3.2), and finally elaborates the development of TL-GBP, i. e. the idea of recontextualizing the theoretical frameworks of translanguaging and genre-based pedagogy in the multilingual context of the Dong area (Section 3.3).

3.1 Translanguaging

In this research, we attempt to adopt translanguaging as pedagogic strategies in the multilingual classrooms of Guizhou Dong area in China with the specific purpose of developing confident and additive multilingual students, and hoping to sustain and inherit Dong minority language and culture at the same time.

3.1.1 Tranlanguaging in education

As a teaching method in its original formulation, translanguaging approach has been widely developed as pedagogic tools that could activate all students' multilingual and multimodal resources in education. As García and Kano (2014, p. 261) pointed out, translanguaging as a pedagogic approach in education is "a process by which students and teachers engage in complex discursive practices that include ALL language practices of ALL students in a class in order to develop new language practices and sustain old ones, communicate and appropriate knowledge, and give voice to new socio-political realities by interrogating linguistic inequality."

Translanguaging is a holistic approach developed as a reaction against many years of separate monolingualism. It can not only promote the understanding of content but also develop the weaker language compared to the dominant language (García & Li, 2014). It has been postulated to have the potential advantages of facilitating students to develop multi-literacies (Cenoz & Gorter, 2015). Moreover, translanguaging, as García and Li (2014) contended, highlights two fundamental concepts of multilingualism: creativity and criticality. As a socio-educational process, translanguaging encourages students to establish and constantly negotiate their social identities and values as a result of critical and creative reaction to their historical and present social conditions. Kenner (2004) demonstrated various ways that multilingual students combine different modes and linguistic resources, and make connections and differences between their available writing systems to creatively construct bilingual texts. By this way, Kenner (2004) indicated, students could express their sense of living in multiple social and cultural worlds.

Translanguaging in education has been foregrounded as legitimate pedagogic practices (García & Li, 2014). Adopting a translanguaging lens means that there can be no way to educate inclusively without recognizing the diverse languages and meaning-making practices as learning resources to show what they know and to extend these. Translanguaging in classroom has the potential to offer a "safe space" (Auer, 2010) in which a teacher can: "meaningfully educate when they draw upon the full linguistic repertoire of all students, including language practices that are multiple and hybrid" (García & Kleifgen, 2010, p. 43). Moreover, translanguaging space can give students agency to negotiate their linguistic practices, and recognize each other as resources and develop new ways of languaging, so that it changes the way to learn and to teach.

3.1.2 Translanguaging and minority languages

Translanguaging provides an opportunity of minority language revitalization efforts by offering minority language space in education. Although multilingual education has been spreading throughout the world, most practices still took a monolingual approach that only focused on the target language or dominant language while ignoring minority language. Most multilingual education programs, as we have seen, do not always connect school teaching with language practices at home. Translanguaging provides not only a navigational space that goes beyond discursive boundaries, but also a space in which competing language practices, knowledge and doing, emerging from both home and school, are brought together. It has been precisely bringing together of all students' languaging and doing that generate new knowledge and learning, as well as new languaging and texts (García & Li, 2014, p. 68). Translanguaging approach to minority language revitalisation, as Otheguy, et al. (2015, p. 283) argue, "allows us to graduate from the goal of "language maintenance", with its constant risk of turning minoritisied languages into museum pieces, to that of sustainable practices by bilingual speakers (...)".

Translanguaging has been considered as a mechanism for social justice, especially when teaching students from minority communities (García & Leiva, 2014). It is not only an approach that multilingual students use their full linguistic repertoire to access content or language, but also transformative for the students, for the teachers and for the education itself. With the purpose of clearing away the hierarchy of languaging practices that view some languages more valuable than others, it conceptualizes bilingual/multilingual education as a democratic attempt, aiming at ensuring the right to learn of language-minority students, which is usually undermined by teaching practices that jeopardize this reality.

3.2 Genre-based Pedagogy

Another approach the program drew from is genre-based pedagogy, based on SFL, particularly Martin's text-in-context model (with Martin's notion of genre) (Martin, 1992; Martin & Rose, 2007; 2008). Language learning and reading involve the control of genre, i.e. "a category of texts with similar language patterns used to achieve similar social purposes" (de Silva Joyce & Feez, 2012, p. 14). Therefore, there are two aspects that text and context are referred to in this research. The first is "knowledge genres" concerned with KAL, i. e. the text types of schooling (Rose & Martin, 2012; 2014) that students need to read and write for success in education and society. Another is referred as "curriculum genres" (Christie, 2002), concerned with knowledge about pedagogy, i. e. pedagogic text types of schooling, which are used to illuminate classroom context and its language use. The curriculum genres adopted in the study are the model that Rose and his colleagues (Rose & Martin, 2012; Rose, 2014) have developed, as we shall elaborate, by drawing in part on Bernstein's (2000) model of pedagogic discourse and in part on the SFL model that Christie (2002) first proposed.

3.2.1 The knowledge genres

The text-in-context model, as expounded above, focuses on teaching and learning text by modeling it in social context. Text is realized across language strata (graphology/phonology, lexico-grammar, and discourse semantics), which is controlled by register, including the particular institution (field), the particular audience (tenor), and the modalities (mode), and genre (social purpose). The Sydney School has mapped genres (i. e. the text types that students are expected to read and write for success in school) by their social purposes as outlined above in Table 2-1. Genres are categorized into three families according to their common purposes: stories to engage readers, factual texts to inform readers, essays to evaluate readers. The functions and stages in each family that go through to achieve its social purposes are set out in Figure 3-1 (Rose & Martin, 2012, p. 128).

These text types are termed as the knowledge genres that are taught and learned across the curriculum in schooling, because they are "field constituting texts, through which institutional knowledge is acquired" (Rose, 2015b; Rose & Martin, 2014). These genres involve "patterns of written discourse in which the knowledge and evaluations unfold through a text, and patterns of grammar in which discourse is realized in written sentences" (Rose, 2015b). As already outlined in Table 2-1 and Figure 3-1, there is shared metalanguage about the names, stages and phases which can be offered to students to talk about the language of the field. As with genre-based pedagogy, what to note first should be issues of designing the intervention program and building the metalanguage or KAL. The starting point of building the metalanguage of knowledge genres is to do with pedagogic task of reading and writing them. The curriculum field, along with the focus on tenor in reader's engagement and some discourse patterns for reading and writing in three families of genres set out in Figure 3-1 are generalized in Table 3-1 (Rose, 2015 c, p. 6).

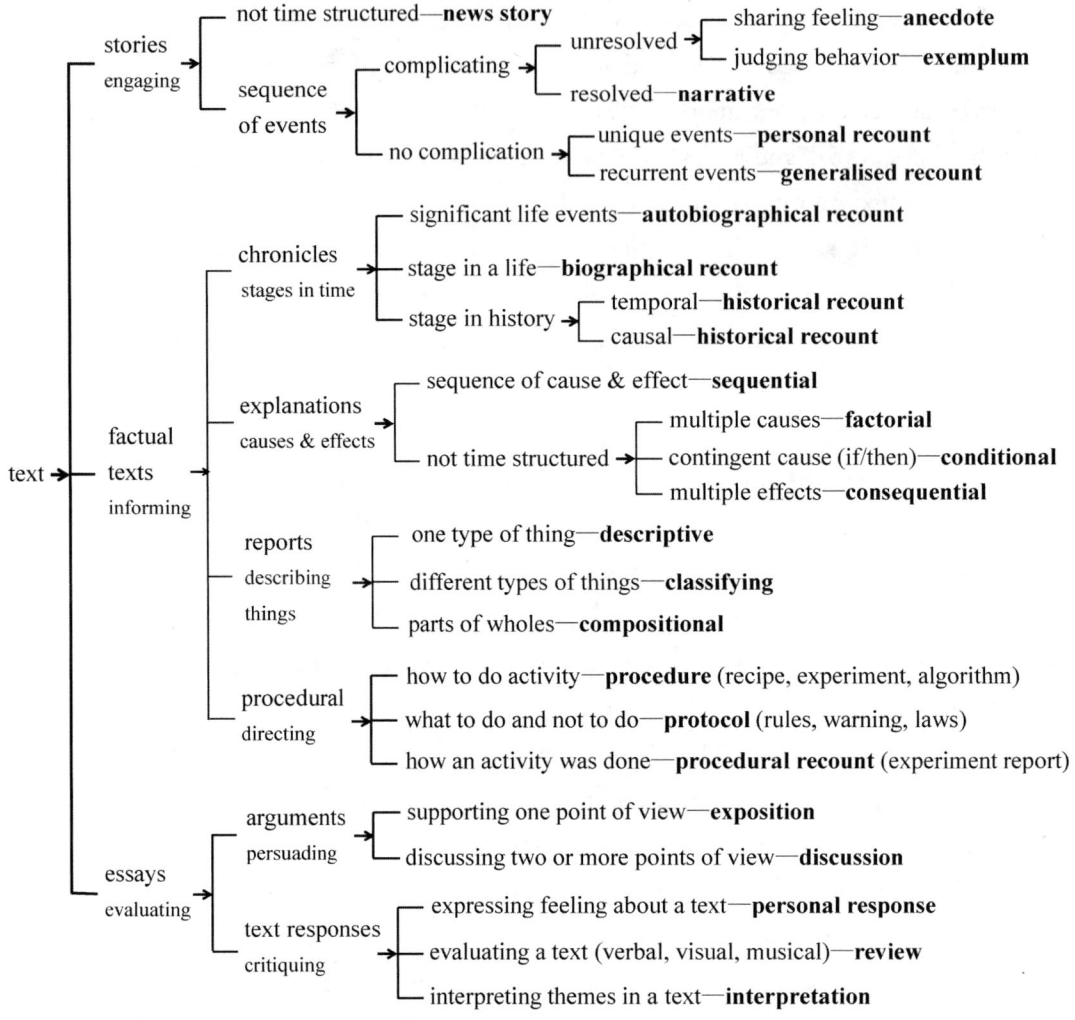

Figure 3-1　Map of genres in school（Rose & Martin，2012，p. 128）

Table 3-1　Language foci of reading and writing tasks（Rose，2015 c，p. 6）

Genre	Field	Tenor	Discourse patterns
stories	plots, settings, characters, themes	pleasure in literature, judgements of characters	literary devices for engaging readers and encoding themes
factual texts	knowledge of social and natural worlds	interest in knowledge	structuring of knowledge, using abstraction and technicality
arguments & text responses	issues, positions, analyses, critiques	negotiation of positions (critical evaluation)	structuring of arguments and evaluation

The mapping of genres provides an overview for teachers to prepare lesson plans, so that the task for students can be made explicit. The organization of genres function as a systematic principle for teachers to select and analyze text in their curriculum, starting with their functions, stages and phases. The language resources mentioned above provide essential tools for the realization of the genres. These resources made it possible to be explicit about the curriculum content in the process of teaching and learning these genres across all sectors of schooling.

3.2.2 The curriculum genres

The curriculum genres focus on the patterns of classroom discourse in which school knowledge and values are taught and acquired. These constitute two fields: one is the knowledge being exchanged; the other is the pedagogic activities through which the knowledge is negotiated between teachers and students. Types of knowledge can be both domestic, recreational and manual trade knowledge that can be acquired in daily life, namely Bernstein's "horizontal discourses", and knowledge of professional occupations with specialized discourse, namely Bernstein's "vertical discourses". Knowledge always embodies social values so that they are acquired together with knowledge.

Other dimensions of curriculum genres were further proposed by Rose (2014). Pedagogic relations and modalities along with pedagogic activities are register variables of curriculum genres. First, knowledge and value are construed through pedagogic activities that are unfolded as sequences of learning activities. Learning activities are enacted as exchanges in cycles of interaction between teachers and students. The social relations enacted between teachers and students are referred as pedagogic relations, which position students in hierarchies of success and failure and may be inclusive and exclusive, explicit and implicit. Pedagogic modalities are modes of pedagogic discourse, involving spoken, written, visual, gestural and manual modalities.

The relationship between the two fields of curriculum genres can be represented as projection, proposed by gests that knowledge and values are projected by the entire configuration of pedagogic activities, relations and modalities. That is the students' success in the classroom depends on their engagement and status in pedagogic exchanges, their control of modalities, and continual evaluations. The whole configuration of curriculum genres can be schematized in Figure 3-2 (Rose,2015a; b; c; Rose & Martin, 2012, p. 274).

The entire configuration of pedagogic activities, relations, and modalities shapes pedagogic practice. They are projected by the overall pedagogic discourse. It projects both knowledge and the learners' identities, whether success or failure, and inclusive or exclusive. The learners' identities are often established in teaching and learning as "a product of (1) continual evaluation, (2) varying degrees of engagement in lesson activities and classroom interactions, and (3) varying control over modalities of learning" (Rose & Martin, 2014, p. 278).

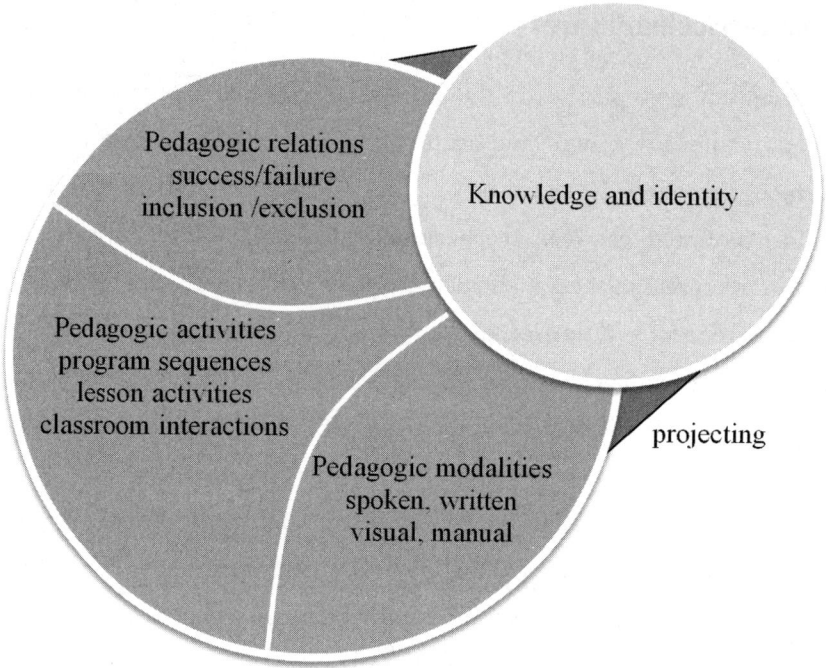

Figure 3-2 Dimensions of a curriculum genre (Rose & Martin, 2012, p. 274)

3.3 Translanguaging Genre-based Pedagogy

This section aims to establish the teaching/learning model to plan and implement the curriculum of this research by incorporating translanguaging into genre-based pedagogy. On the one hand, genre-based pedagogy is used to design the general curriculum, including macro genre of curriculum goal and micro genre of every lesson step and activity, which will be analyzed by the knowledge genres and the curriculum genres introduced above. On the other hand, translanguaging is deconstructed as pedagogic strategies incorporated into every step of genre-based pedagogy to deal with every aspect of multilingual classrooms in the Dong area.

3.3.1 Translanguaging as pedagogic strategies

From the above, translanguaging approach in education allows the use of all languages to develop new language and sustain the old ones. It can be also taken as an opportunity for minority languages to be revitalized in the multilingual education of minority areas. It is a mechanism of not only educational justice but also social justice. In this sense, it provides a tool of scaffolding minority students towards the ways of English languaging by connecting it with their whole linguistic repertoire for multilingual education in the Dong area, in which English was the focus while the minority language was overlooked in most cases, and students had little access to English resources in their daily lives and thus usually poorly performed in English classes.

This research, therefore, adopted the translanguaging approach, seeking to use the ethnic minority students' language and cultural resources in English teaching and learning, meanwhile allowing their flexibly language practices in order to develop strong English writings and ultimately additive trilingualism, and at the same time to claim for their multilingual identity (see Figure 3-3).

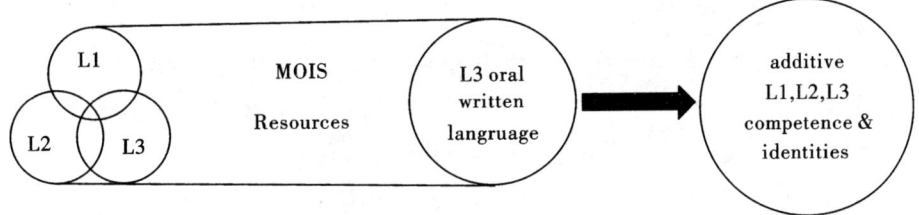

Figure 3-3 Translanguaging approach in this program

As we can see in Figure 3-3, this translanguaging approach involves the use of students' L1 (Dong), L2 (Chinese) and L3 (English) as media of instruction and teaching resources in English teaching and learning. In this process, it is argued that, not only L3 written language but also oral language can be developed, and ultimately additive trilingualism and multilingual identity can be also maintained. In addition, minority language and culture can be sustained and publicized by using them as teaching resources and re-instantiated into English.

3.3.2 TL-R2L teaching/learning cycle

As elaborated above, translanguaging approach has been conceptualized as specific teaching strategies in this research, and these translanguaging strategies were planned in every step of the curriculum. The design of the curriculum was drawn from genre-based pedagogy, specifically from R2L program. Hence, a TL-R2L teaching/learning cycle has been developed shown as in Figure 3-4.

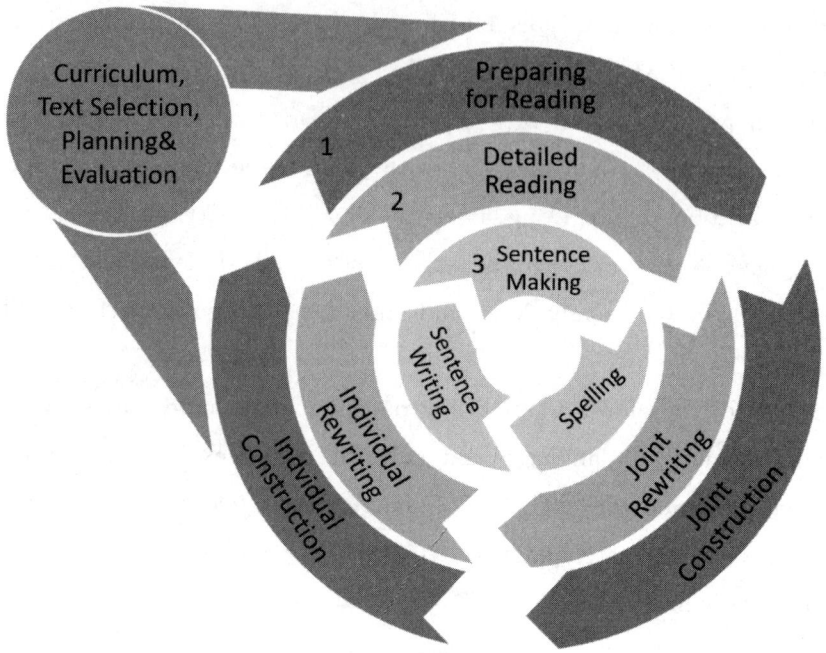

Figure 3-4　The TL-R2L teaching/learning cycle in this program

From Figure 3-4, we can see that the TL-R2L teaching/learning cycle was designed to incorporate translanguaging into the curriculum genres. The design of the curriculum genres involved the three-layered circle of R2L including different stages and steps. Two iterations of the R2L program were planned, with each involving one cycle of R2L teaching for one reading text, following the same sequential and selected steps. These steps are chosen and sequenced following the same principles of genre-based pedagogy from the notions of SFL.

The knowledge genres in this program were concerned with multilingual goal. The design of the knowledge genres, or specifically the selection of reading texts, involved the use of multilingual resources as translanguaging strategies. Specifically, the reading texts in the program were in both the target language—English (L3) and Dong students' mother language (L1) which has been translated into Chinese (L2), for Chinese is the main medium of instruction in school subjects and it can also be regarded as part of students' resources as previously acquired L2. Moreover, the fields of English text and Dong text are relevant. L1 reading text aimed at preparing the students for (1) entering into the genre and knowledge as they are what the students need to learn in L3 text, and (2) preparing to write English narratives. L3 reading text was first presented with the affordance of translanguaging strategies to facilitate students to access the new text and genre in English. Next, L1 reading text with the translation of L2 was used to help them familiarize new knowledge about English language (KAEL) and prepare for the construction of new text.

The curriculum genres involved the planning of lesson steps and classroom interactions. The lesson steps were selected from the three-layered cycle according to the curriculum goal and students' need. Translanguaging approach was used as teaching strategies of alternatively using L1, L2 and L3 in the classroom interaction of each lesson stage for different purposes. The general principle was that the classroom activity can start by using any language (L1/L2/L3). In the first iteration, L1 and/or L2 were mostly used as a scaffolding independence and confidence in their use of English, and L3 was increasingly used in Iteration 2 as students have gradually developed their English proficiency to reinforce the new knowledge. In most cases, L1 and/or L2 were chiefly used in the preparing phase to facilitate building up the new knowledge by relating it to students' existing knowledge and experience, while L3 was chiefly used in the affirming and elaborating phases to bring new ways of English languaging to students and to realize the accumulation of curriculum knowledge. In addition, code-switching or multilingual media of instruction (the use of L1/L2/L3 in one phase) was also used in order to reinforce the learning.

In contrast to the immersion approaches with the ideology of teaching the target language through the target language only (or: multilingualism through parallel monolingualisms), translanguaging approach in this program allowed the use of L1 and other languages to scaffold L3 learning with the aims of what refer to as multi-competence (Cook, 1992) and multi-literacy. Multilingual speakers could develop a complex type of competence, which is qualitatively different from the competence of monolingual speakers of a language. They cannot be judged by the standards of native speakers because they can never be monolingual native speakers. As most learners do not achieve the goal of native-speakerism, the process can result in a sense of failure and lack of self-confidence when learning languages. In the same vein, multilingual learners' whole linguistic repertoire is strategically and systemically used to access to new knowledge and ways of languaging. There is every reason to provide the maximal amount of L2/L3 input, but the input that is made maximal is useful only when that input is also made comprehensible. The potential role of L1 in helping to make the L2 input comprehensible should not be neglected and we should not throw the baby out with the bath water just for fear of using too much L1 (Lin, 2015).

Translanguaging approach that legitimates the use of L1 is also different from the traditional grammar-translation method and the emergent mother-tongue based multilingual education (MTB-MLE). The former supports the overuse of L1 to explain every point of L2/L3 language knowledge. It is true that if L1 is overused to the extent that the entire lesson is full of L1 without any L2 input then it is disastrous (Lin, 2015). The latter also favors the use of L1 as a scaffolding, while the L1 use is usually random and unsystematic. Translanguaging approach in this program is the principled and systemic use of the students' whole linguistic repertoire as a resource. The use of L1 is well planned from the curriculum design perspective in that both written L1 literature and spoken L1 are systemically used in the curriculum to enhance the curricular goals of the program. In addition, by incorporating translanguaging into genre-based pedagogy, students' all languages (L1, L2 and L3) are systemically positioned at different stages of the curriculum genre to achieve recurrent typical functions at different stages and phases.

The next subsections then discuss the elements of the knowledge genres involved in this program, i.e. metalanguage in stories as the choice of genre in focus, which includes aspects of metalanguage at stages and phases, as well as discourse and grammar in L1, L2 and L3. The curriculum genres in this program that involved the design of the specific lesson activities will be elaborated in the next chapter (Section 4.5).

3.3.3 Building metalanguage in stories

Stories were selected to be part of the intervention program. As mentioned above, the purpose of stories is to engage readers. Stories are central genres in all cultures. They are told in all social groups to interpret life chaos and rhythms, to evaluate each other's behavior, and to educate and entertain our children (Martin & Rose, 2008, p. 49).

Story genres include recount, narrative, anecdote, exemplum and observation. Narrative is the main knowledge genre in the intervention program. Like other genres of stories, narrative genre involves a disrupting event that is evaluated, with the purpose of resolving the disruption in a story, thus the equilibrium is disturbed and restored. The stage of narrative is "Orientation—Complication—Evaluation—Resolution". The essential point of narrative is to resolve the complication after the evaluation of the complicating action with some types of attitude.

It is commonly found that traditional stories in widely divergent cultures have some similarities in terms of their organizations and their fields, which indicate social functions to encode certain ideological principles. For example, *Just So Stories* invented by the famous novelist Rudyard Kipling has been recontextualized as the dominated model for interpreting Australian mythology in indigenous education in Australia. This recontextualization is referred as an insensitive "infantilization" of indigenous Australian culture, and in particular as its "Dreaming" in English.

Text 3-1 is an example of story by recontextualizing Kiplings's *Just So Stories* to focus on indigenous Australia.

Text 3-1　An example of a story

"Phenomenon to be explained"
This is the story of how the birds got their colours.

Orientation

Long, long ago—in the Dreamtime—when the land and animals were being made... all the birds were black—all one colour.

Complication

Till... one day, a little dove flew around looking for food. He flew down to the ground to catch a big juicy grub. But instead, he landed right on a sharp stick! It pierced his little foot and made him very sick. For days, he lay on the ground in pain. His foot swelled up. He was dying! All his mates gathered around to see how they could help. All except crow. He just wandered around with his hands behind his back.

Resolution

Suddenly, the parrot rushed forward—and with her sharp beak... burst the little dove's swollen foot! Colour splashed out all over the parrot. Red and green and blue ran down her chest, wings and tail. It splashed out all over the other birds. Some got red, some brown, some blue, some yellow. Some got spots. Some got stripes. All got colours. All except crow, who was standing away from the others. Crow got no colour at all! So that's how the birds got their colours. And as for the dove, he soon got better, thanked the parrot... and was able to fly away.

This indigenous story is told to children not only to entertain or engage them, but also express values—to establish the axiological understandings. The text is organized according to the stages and phases of narrative. At the beginning, it introduces the phenomenon to be explained, i. e. "how the birds got their colours". The Orientation presents the background information characters, places, times, namely, all the birds were black in the old time. The Complication then builds with problems that a little dove meets and the reaction of other birds, which raises tension. The Resolution releases tension by presenting the solution to the problems: the dove got better and the other bird got colours except for crow.

To uncover the purpose of a text and name its stages and phases bring two benefits in teaching and learning. First, teachers have metalanguage to talk about sections of the reading text, so they can unpack the reading text. For example, by analyzing the phases in stories, teachers can recognize the complexity of choices of the text and scaffold students to access a challenging text. Another related aspect is that students acquire the social purpose of the text and recognize the structure of the text that realizes the social purpose so that they are enabled to follow the text with deep understandings of literature literacy, and in this process, the values and cultural sensitivity are promoted.

Stories like Text 3-1 told to aboriginal children are recorded so as to pass on "Aboriginal culture" and "Dreaming stories" to future generations, and at the same time, to meet the need of improving literacy, which are the major concerns for Aboriginal people. In the same vein, the materials of ethnic minority classics can be carefully analyzed drawing on SFL genre theory with a view to exploring their cultural sensitivity, and recontextualized in the English classroom in minority areas, in particular drawing on R2L pedagogy with the purpose of improving literacy and passing on the Dong cultural value and classics.

3.3.4　Building KAL: Discourse and grammar

Alongside the KAL terms of stages and phases, other metalanguage that needs to be considered is related to the strata of discourse semantics, lexico-grammar, and phonology/graphology. In terms of discourse semantics, the main focus of narrative is on the "literary language" of written stories that realize the events, problems and characters' reactions and reflections. In lexico-grammar, word groups are highlighted with the general terms: people, thing, process, place, time and quality, including verbal group, nominal group, prepositional phrase, adverbial group and adjectival group. Lexical metaphor, grammatical metaphor, material processes, mental and verbal processes are also the language resources. The KAL is all relevant when considering the different realizations in various languages. As these languages (English, Chinese, Dong) have developed specialized discourses in terms of literature, there is a potential "load" in learning English for students, as students need to access the characters and values which are different or unknown for them. We can take the language from one extract of Kipling's *Just So Stories* as an example.

Text 3-2 One extract of Kipling's *Just So Stories*

NOW this is the next tale, and it tells how the Camel got his big hump. In the beginning of years, when the world was so new and all, and the Animals were just beginning to work for Man, there was a Camel, and he lived in the middle of a Howling Desert because he did not want to work; and besides, he was a Howler himself. So he ate sticks and thorns and tamarisks and milkweed and prickles, most excruciatingly idle; and when anybody spoke to him he said "Humph!" Just "Humph!" and no more.

With regard to word groups, some expressions in English have no equivalent words in Chinese or Dong. For example, the character is the Camel in English, "骆驼" in Chinese, while there is no relevant vocabulary in Dong for there is no such animal in the Dong community and when they meet new words they will use Chinese directly. Another example is "Desert", in Chinese "沙漠", and there is no equivalent translation in Dong.

With regard to grammar, the realization of place or environment in settings is prepositional phrase with the phrase "in the middle of" in front of "a Howling Desert" in English. In Chinese, the equivalent expression to realize the same environment presents opposite order. The word order in Dong is usually the same with that in English when expressing place, while Dong students tend to use the Chinese expressions when meeting the alien words. Samples of grammar structure in English, Chinese and Dong are presented as follows:

"in the middle of a Howling Desert"
"广阔的沙漠中间"
"Howling Desert in the middle of"

The differences between languages and cultures would bring the potential "learning" load for learners, so the difficulty is how to ease semiotic load in teaching and learning. Dong students keep their own language and cultures, while they are also influenced by the dominant Chinese language and culture. Besides, as they lived in the mixed communities with other ethnics such as Miao and Buyi, they have experienced and recognized a diversity of languages and cultures. These experiences can be used as resources when learning another language.

3.4 Summary

This chapter set out to answer the question, "How is translanguaging genre-based pedagogy (TL-GBP) established under the frameworks of translanguaging and genre-based pedagogy theories for English teaching in the context of multilingual education in the Dong area, and ultimately for multilingual education with the objective of multilingualism?"

The TL-GBP has been developed based on the frameworks of translanguaging and genre-based pedagogy for the multilingual pedagogy programming. It employed the Sydney School genre-based pedagogy, while took multilingualism into account. Specifically, it used the R2L program, which is itself based on genre-based pedagogy, as basis for its curriculum genres, involving developing English literacy practices in the selected stories of folk literature. It also deconstructed translanguaging as pedagogic strategies to employ students' language and cultural resources into every steps of the R2L cycle. The pedagogy established suggests the additive multilingual teaching and learning, i. e. the teaching and learning of an additional language can promote students' multi-literacies by using translanguaging and genre-based pedagogy approaches.

The TL-GBP has the following characteristics:

(1) Directional. The pedagogy was specifically designed for ethnic college students in the Dong area. It took the students' cultural and linguistic resources into consideration in order to provide a scaffold for the learning of L3 on the one hand (the academic purpose), and to sustain their ethnic language and culture and build their multilingual identity (the social and cultural purposes).

(2) Operable. Planning for teaching and learning was specific and detailed in the TL-GBP, and it covered all language strata. The three-layered TL-R2L cycle provided a principled basis for proceeding in planning curriculum design and implementing the pedagogy.

(3) Integrated. The TL-GBP set out clear goals for teaching and learning. It was designed as an integrated curriculum, including teaching objectives, teaching contents, teaching materials, teaching steps, and teaching methods. In addition, the R2L method also provided a holistic rubric for assessing the students' written language development.

(4) Adaptable. The TL-GBP was an integrated curriculum system, which can be adapted and used in other contexts. For example, the languages involved could be other languages, and the number of languages could be more than three, four or five. In

terms of languages use, it can start by L1 or L2 to maximize the teaching efficiency. In addition, other elements like the teaching materials and teaching steps can be flexibly selected to suit for a specific context.

    The next chapter will discuss the detailed information of this TL-GBP program, including the research stages, the specific curriculum design and data collection, etc.

CHAPTER FOUR
RESEARCH DESIGN

This chapter will present the specific design of the TL-GBP program, including a brief description of two research stages, the research methodology—participant information, research methods and data collection, and the detailed design of the curriculum genres of the program.

4.1 Research Stages

The project was carried out by two stages. The first one was the descriptive stage, in which a pilot survey was carried out to investigate the current teaching and learning practices of multilingual education in the multilingual classrooms of the Dong area. The second stage was the intervention stage, in which the TL-GBP program was implemented and evaluated.

1. The description stage

The description stage was to portray a broad picture of the present situation of English teaching and learning in multilingual classrooms of Guizhou Dong area, including how languages were used during teaching and learning, how the teacher organized the teaching/learning activities, whether minority students' resources and agency were recognized and how, etc. Furthermore, research at this stage also sought to identify key issues in multilingual classrooms and conditions for the implementation of program.

Both description stage and intervention stage took place in Kaili University, the only ethnic college in Guizhou Dong area of China. Ethnic classes in Grade 1 were observed. Students in the ethnic classes, most of whom are from the local ethnic communities, are specially cultivated as ethnic talents for the protection and inheritance of ethnic minority culture and the contribution of local social-economic development. Therefore, the training of these students is distinctive from the normal graduate education in terms of students, curriculum and educational goal, and so on.

The investigation of present teaching and learning practices was conducted by classroom observations, document analysis, questionnaire and interviews. Classroom observations were carried out to investigate the language use and teaching methods of the teaching and learning practices by (1) attending classroom sessions of each class for a complete unit of teaching, and (2) recording the teaching activities by the means of audio recording, videotaping and note taking. The teaching sessions took place during the lessons of English as a subject. The total time spent for classroom observations were four weeks.

Document collection included two parts. The first part was to do with policy analysis, including collecting and examining the national and regional policies, laws and legislations about minority languages and multilingual education in minority areas. The second part was to collect the relevant curriculum documents and teaching materials, including: (1) textbooks for students, (2) teaching guidebooks for teachers, (3) the syllabus and teaching materials used by the teachers, (4) the demands of students' reading and writing, and (5) curriculum documents and other related documents.

The description stage is the basic step for first interpreting the status quo of multilingual education in Guizhou Dong area, detecting its problems and difficulties, and then shaping the design of the innovative multilingual intervention program.

2. The intervention stage

After the description stage, the intervention stage was to implement and examine the TL-GBP teaching/learning program. This stage is the major focus of the discussion in the dissertation.

At the intervention stage, the design of the program was put into experiments in two classes, both are in the first grade of the five-year ethnic heritage classes for junior college education. The researcher acted as the teacher to implement the program, teaching literacy of English and literature. The data were collected during the implementation.

The total time of the intervention stage was nine weeks. The aim of this research was to recontextualize the theoretical framework of genre-based pedagogy in the multilingual classroom in the Dong area in China while incorporating translanguaging strategy throughout the whole teaching and learning stages. The research methods at the intervention stage will be further elaborated in Section 4.3 after the description of the participants in Section 4.2.

4.2　Participants

Participants involved in this research are students and their class teacher of Kaili University in Guizhou Dong area, where there are also other ethnic minority groups such as Miao, Buyi, Yao and Han majority. Kaili University pays great attention to the ethnicities in education and has cultivated a large number of qualified graduates for the local, especially many teachers for towns and villages of the Dong area. Moreover, it was selected as "training school of national intangible cultural heritage inheritors" by China's Ministry of Culture.

Two ethnic heritage classes for five-year junior college education were chosen, specifically Miao class (Class 1, 30 students) and Dong class (Class 2, 31 students), as they are typically characterized by multilingualism. The majority of class students are bilinguals or multilinguals who speak their mother languages, Chinese Mandarin, the local dialects and/or other ethnic minority languages, and they have also developed multicultural knowledge including Chinese, Dong and Miao in this multilingual context. Though the minority language involved in this program was mainly Dong, Miao class was also selected, because both Miao and Dong classes have been educated based on the same syllable with the same educational goal of cultivating them as inheritors of both Miao and Dong cultures regardless their ethnicities. These students were both enrolled after junior high school and now in the second term of grade one. They had the same curricula, mainly including ethnic songs, dances, instruments, Miao language and some fundamental educational courses. In addition, the design was also to test whether different degrees of translanguaging incorporated in genre-based pedagogy have different impact on students' literacy development and other aspects.

The English text book for students was New Trend Basic English, which was compiled for professional training college with the focus on practical and basic English. Their teacher before the program was not the local minority member and did not share the similar linguistic background with the students. In the first term, the students have been taught some kinds of basic practical writings, mainly factual texts, such as Business Cards, Thanks Note, Agenda and Telephone Message. The teacher mainly used traditional teaching methods and never applied genre-based pedagogy and students' minority language before. In this case, the students had no idea about story genres and the classroom practices of genre-based pedagogy.

The students have already had some multilingual learning experiences in the college. English was a compulsory course, Chinese was still the medium of instruction in most courses, and their minority languages were used as the medium of instruction in some courses. For examples, Dong, together with Chinese, was used in the course of Dong song; Miao was mostly used in Miao language course. They were both proficient in their mother tongue and Chinese, while not in English, for they had little chances to practice English and access to English culture and resources in their daily lives. For example, in the last terminal exam, only 4 students passed in each class. The summary of the participant information is presented in Table 4-1.

Table 4-1 Summary of the participant information

Information	Class 1 (Miao)	Class 2 (Dong)
Students	30	31
Grade / Age	Grade 1 offive-year ethnic junior college students (15-17 years old)	
Teaching	Traditional teaching methods (grammar translation)	
Curriculum	Practical and basic English, involving simple factual genres	
Language	* Chinese is the main medium of instruction throughout the schooling years & minority languages were used as a transitional tool to help students understand Chinese in the first years of primary school; * Chinese and English are used in English course, Chinese and Dong are used in the course of Dong song, Chinese and Miao are used in the course of Miao; * Students mostly speak minority languages among peers or to their ethnic minority teachers, but speak Chinese to other teachers.	

The class teacher was invited to engage in the experimental classes during the researcher's teaching program to observe the process of teaching and learning. She sometimes assisted the researcher in managing the students. She was also interviewed before and after the program. The interview at the beginning stage aimed to provide background information related to her teaching and learning, such as an overview of curriculum syllabus and units, content of knowledge, teaching methods, medium of instruction, etc.

4.3 Research Methods

This research is an evaluation of an innovative curriculum for English teaching, initiated to examine the effectiveness of the designed multilingual program combining genre-based pedagogy and translanguaging. This innovative curriculum was designed and implemented by the researcher, who also acted as the teacher, to address the problems and difficulties of English teaching in the context of multilingual education in the Dong area. It was argued that this research could potentially inform improved practices of multilingual education in the Dong area in the future.

The program was considered as a pedagogic intervention. On the one hand, its goal was to subvert typical teaching and learning practices found in many Chinese ethnic minority schools. On the other hand, the project was conducted by the researcher in real educational context, with the focus on designing and implementing a program for realistic educational goals. The project, therefore, was conducted during the regular teaching and learning of English as a subject in students' regular classes. Moreover, the intervention program was designed in iterations.

This research was also conducted following ethnographic research principles. The ethnographic approach values authentic settings of minority education and researchers as insiders in such natural settings. The current research, as mentioned above, took place in natural teaching/learning classes in ethnic minority schools. The researcher acted as the teacher rather than letting the class teacher enact the program. In so doing, there were several advantages: (1) there can be the minimum risk of reinterpreting the design of the curriculum genres by other enactors, such as the class teacher; (2) because the researcher was in the classroom with students, this approach enabled her to observe the students' learning and language practices in and out of the classroom and thus to have deeper understanding of students' learning performance and language practices, being familiar with the recorded data, while also collecting the unrecorded and incidental data as more as possible; (3) it also provided valuable insight into the everyday challenges teachers faced in multilingual classrooms. Except for the role of teacher, the researcher also played some other roles: such as the designer of the program to plan teaching procedures; the evaluator of the process of the program to react on any natural or real life challenges in classroom; and the evaluator of the whole results of the intervention.

To obtain the comprehensive data in real educational context, the research adopted a mixed method approach by means of triangulation employing both qualitative and quantitative research methods. The records of teaching situation were collected by the participants (students), the implementer (researcher and teacher) and the observer (students' original teacher), thus triangulation can be viewed as a democratic and professional approach of evaluating classroom activities. Therefore, apart from the implementation of the program, the following methods were involved.

1. Literature study

On the one hand, by comparing and analyzing the literature data, the researcher found out the limitations of current research and problems and difficulties of multilingual education in Chinese minority areas, and then sought out the suitable pedagogy for English teaching in the context of multilingual education. On the other hand, by collecting and analyzing document and literature, the researcher obtained the background information of the multilingual education in the Dong area, including the linguistic and educational policies, Dong language and culture, history and customs, demography, etc., and the status quo of college English teaching, including information of syllabus, curriculum, textbooks, teachers, students, etc., helping select the sampling region, institution and classes.

2. Questionnaire

A questionnaire was designed for the students. The questionnaire was conducted before the program to get the basic information of students, including their background, original English and minority language proficiency, and the identification of ethnic language and culture, etc.

3. Interview

Semi-structured interviews were designed and conducted for the teacher and students before and after the program. As for the teacher, the interviews were to get the information of her English teaching experiences, such as teaching methods, language use, attitude towards all languages (L1, L2 and L3), and the use of students' language and culture in class, as well as to check her comments about the teaching and learning of this program. The sample students were chosen according to the results of their pre-intervention writing texts representing all levels of low, medium and high scores. As for the students, the interviews were to investigate their English learning experiences, language use in the classrooms and in their daily lives before the program, as well as to examine their translanguaging experiences and metalanguage awareness during the program, identifications of ethnic language and culture after the program and their attitudes towards the program. In addition, interviews were conducted after the students wrote their three texts before, during and after the intervention to reflect their translanguaging experiences in their writing activities, including the strategies they used and the purposes during different periods of the intervention.

4. Observation

Observations were performed to capture the overview of English teaching and learning in the classrooms, including language use, teaching process, teaching methods and classroom interactions, as well as to record the teaching procedures, teaching activities and students' involvement in the classrooms during the program. In addition, language use among students and between teacher and students after the class were also observed to know well their language practices in daily communication.

5. Self-reflection

Self-reflection was conducted by the teacher researcher to look back at the teaching process in order to examine the problems and teaching results during the implementation process, and thus can adjust the research design at any time to achieve the optimal effect of the program.

6. Comparative study

Comparative study was carried out to compare, analyze and induce the literature materials and data. The students' texts before, during and after the intervention were compared to trace their literacy development. Furthermore, their processes of cognitive development, metalanguage awareness development and identity establishment at different learning stages were also compared.

4.4 Data Collection

In this research, data were collected from several sources: (1) program-related data, (2) data of questionnaire, interviews, observations and self-reflections, (3) informal conversations with the teacher and students before, during and after the program. The research dealt with the collection of data about the program and its implementation through the transcription of selected video and audio recordings, and collections of photographs taken during the program as well as collection of materials from the students. In recording the program, a video camera and an audio recorder were used. The video camera was put in the back of the class facing the blackboard to record the activities that the teacher researcher enacted the lesson plan and the students participated in and doing the tasks. The audio recorder was placed as close as possible to the teacher researcher during the teaching process, and sometimes was carried by the teacher researcher to capture teacher/student(s) interactions or students' group works. The interview data was also recorded by the means of audio recording or notes. The interviews were transcribed for thematic data analysis; some were translated for data presentation.

Table 4-2 presents the types of research data collected in the study, including texts written by students before, during and after the intervention program, and audio, video and photographic records capturing the classroom activities, interviews and casual conversations with teachers and students.

Table 4-2 Summary of data collected in each class

Data source	Teacher	Class 1 Students	Class 2 Students	Total
Pre-intervention written texts		23 handwritten texts	25 handwritten texts	48 handwritten texts
During-intervention written texts		28 handwritten texts	25 handwritten texts	53 handwritten texts
Post-intervention written texts		22 handwritten texts	24 handwritten texts	46 handwritten texts
Photographs of class activities		10 digital copies	8 digital copies	18 digital copies
Videos of class		±460 minutes	±480 minutes	940 minutes
Audio of class activities		±60 minutes	±65 minutes	125 minutes
Records of pre-intervention interviews	±10 minutes	±15 minutes	±20 minutes	35 minutes
Records of interviews during the intervention	±15 minutes	±55 minutes	±90 minutes	160 minutes
Records of post-intervention interviews	±25 minutes	±30 minutes	±35 minutes	90 minutes

4.5 Design of the Curriculum Genres

The intervention program took a TL-R2L teaching/learning cycle, which employed R2L methodology and adjusted it by incorporating translanguaging approach in relation to multilingual education of the Dong area in China. The program followed the principles of R2L methodology in several ways. Firstly, reading was positioned as the first and foremost step of learning in school, so choosing reading texts was the foundation for developing the teaching/learning program. Secondly, the program employed the steps in the three-layered R2L curriculum genres. Lastly, the teacher and students' classroom interactions were also some parts of the lesson plan, thus the teacher was prepared with classroom talk during the implementation of the program.

Moreover, R2L methodology was extended through incorporating translanguaging pedagogic strategies. At the macro level, multilingual reading texts were chosen drawing on the notion of translanguaging in order to facilitate students to write their folk stories with the similar topic in English. Specifically, there was an English story, and a reading text in the students' mother tongue from Dong ethnic literature on the relevant topic, coupled with a parallel translation in Chinese. In addition, the use of the students' resources for translanguaging was to assist them in developing deeper understandings, learning new text modes and gaining confidence. At the micro level, translanguaging strategies were also used in a well-planned and systemic way in the classroom interactions at every teaching and learning step and stage to facilitate the teacher to organize the teaching activities and students to do lesson tasks successfully.

1. Multilingual reading texts

Two stories were selected as reading texts for the intervention program. The first reading text (RT1) is an English story and the second one (RT2) is a Dong story. The texts were selected according to three principles of R2L (Rose & Martin, 2012). With regard to field, the texts provide the key information of the demands in the curriculum. With regard to mode, the texts are appropriate for the students' level at the schooling year. With regard to genre, the texts are good examples for writing. In addition, the texts are representatives of the community culture with the specific objective of promoting students' cultural sensitivity and values, and further sustaining their ethnic culture and language.

RT1 is a story from *Just So Stories* written by the British author Rudyard Kipling, in which each story tells how a particular animal was modified from the original image to its current image by the acts of man or some magical beings. This collection of the origin stories is viewed as a classic of children's literature, by which indigenous Australian stories have been reformulated to educate their children with the purpose of passing on aboriginal culture and improving literacy, by the R2L approach. RT1 is *How the Camel Got His Hump*. It narrates how the Camel was given a hump by a "Djinn" as punishment for the Camel's refusal to work. RT1 serves as a good example of narrative to provide genre and language knowledge to be learned and preparation for the recontextualization of Dong story in English.

RT2 is a story from a selected collection of Dong ethnic folk literature. The story is about how the Ox was controlled by the Man and began to work for the Man. RT2 was selected to appropriate students' entire linguistic and semiotic resources, which are useful for students to engage with the materials and interact cognitively and socially in ways of producing and extending their languaging and meaning making. Except for literacy development, it can be also helpful to transmit Dong ethnic classics and claim students' agency, which are intrinsically interlinked.

The English and Dong reading texts are both challenging for students, because they both bring new language practices into classrooms. The differences between the two reading texts provided students with the information that the literature or stories from different communities contain various values as well as ways of communication and thinking. Analyzing reading text is the essential part of apprenticing students into literature writer.

2. Two iterative learning cycles

The reading texts include new knowledge to be learned and language practices to be extended for students. The complexity of KAL and cultural topic bring a potential load to students. Therefore, the program, on the one hand, needs to deal with the rigorous knowledge in the reading texts to ensure that students could successfully complete the learning tasks. On the other hand, it needs to tackle the cultural value in the reading texts to give students voice and establish their identities.

To achieve these goals, the program systematically tackled the complexity of the context and text in the reading texts while taking the students' resources into account. This complexity was managed by focusing on one reading text at one time. Each reading text was used as a basis for one iteration, thus the curriculum genres were iterated in two cycles of the intervention program. Each iteration dealt with deconstructing and reconstructing the language strata in the reading text, adopting the available options of steps in R2L methodology. A sequence of activities were systematically organized to deal with the strata of language to build students' control over language in manageable steps.

Five steps from the R2L three-tier cycle were chosen: (1) preparing for reading, (2) detailed reading, (3) sentence making, (4) joint construction, and (5) individual construction. With regard to preparing for reading, field and genre were deconstructed, i.e. analyzing the topic and structure of the text. Detailed reading dealt with discourse and grammar, enabling students to be familiar with patterns of wording and meaning within and between sentences. Sentence making involved reconstructing the difficult sentences in reading texts so that the new knowledge about grammar and graphology can be practiced and mastered. Joint construction focused on every stratum, including genre, field, discourse, grammar and graphology. Individual construction focused on discourse, grammar and graphology. The knowledge dealt with in each step is presented in Table 4-3.

Table 4-3 Sequence of teaching/learning activities and language focus

Preparing for reading	Detailed reading	Sentence making	Joint construction	Individual construction
field & genre	field, discourse, grammar, phonology	discourse, grammar, graphology	genre, field, discourse, grammar, graphology	field, discourse, grammar, graphology

The two iterations were brought together to achieve the unit of teaching/learning the story genre of English and writing ethnic story in English. Each iteration was designed to scaffold listening, speaking, reading and writing in English and focused on the transmission of social values and the promotion of ethnic identity. The stages of the iterations had different functions as each constituted its own genre to achieve its purposes.

Translanguaging approach was employed at every lesson step to facilitate the realizations of these goals. At the reading stage, including the sequences of "preparing for reading, detailed reading and sentence making activities", translanguaging strategies were used to deepen understandings and help learn new ways of languaging. Specifically, multilingual resources were used to create a rich experiential context to build background knowledge so that students can grasp the main gist of the experience. In addition, students' multilingual practices in daily life were encouraged in the group work in sentence making to enable cooperative tasks and engage cognitively in the ways of new languaging.

At the next stage, joint construction, translanguaging strategies were used to raise awareness of different types of communicative expressions and promote metalinguistic awareness and thus to learn the target language in a more efficient way. Strategies like translating, bilingual notes, code-switching were used to help students learn the new ways of meaning making.

At the last stage, individual construction, translanguaging strategies were used in the whole process of writing—planning, drafting and production. Strategies like word transformation, glosses and retrieval of multilingual repertoire were used for scaffolding, effectiveness, rhetorical engagement and at times for agency claiming. The whole configuration of the curriculum genres can be seen in Table 4-4 and Table 4-5 below.

Table 4-4 The configuration of the curriculum genres—Iteration 1 (English reading text)

Translanguaging	Step	Prepare	Task	Elaborate
L1, L2 & L3 resources	Preparing for reading	Preview text in L1, L2 & L3	Read English text	Review field
Students' familiar languages	Detailed reading	Preview, read sentences	Identify wordings	Review field, language
Multilingual practices	Sentence making	Preview, deconstruct sentences	Rewrite sentences	Review field, grammar
Code-switching	Joint construction	Plan field, deconstruct model	Use English notes for a new text	Review genre, language
Multilingual repertoire	Individual construction	Review genre, language	Use English notes for a new text	Check sentences, spelling, punctuation

Table 4-5 The configuration of the curriculum genres—Iteration 2 (Dong reading text)

Translanguaging	Step	Prepare	Task	Elaborate
Multilingual resources	Preparing for reading	Preview text in Chinese & Dong	Read Dong text	Review field
Students' familiar language	Detailed reading	Preview, read sentences	Identify wordings	Review field, language
Multilingual notes	Translating	Deconstruct model	Scribe identified wordings in Dong	Re-instantiate wordings in L3
Code-switching	Joint construction	Plan field, Deconstruct model	Use English notes for a new text	Review genre, language
Multilingual repertoire	Individual construction	Review genre, language	Use English notes for a new text	Check sentences, spelling, punctuation

As indicated in Table 4-4 and Table 4-5, the iteration of English text teaching is "preparing for reading—detailed reading—sentence making—joint construction—independent construction", while the iteration of Dong text teaching does not necessarily need "sentence making" step but involving the translation of Dong notes into English, thus activities in Iteration 2 are "preparing for reading—detailed reading—translating—joint construction—independent construction".

The curriculum sequence in the TL-GBP program serves as the macro-structure of the program. The next section is to plan for the enactment of the design, applying the lesson plan to involve interactions as the micro-structure.

3. Classroom interactions: analytical tools and program design

The lesson planning was to design classroom interactions which (1) incorporate the enactment of the curriculum sequence, and (2) plan teacher talk to ensure success for all students in accomplishing a learning task. The program was designed and evaluated by analyzing how the dimensions of curriculum genres were realized, from global structures to local structures. Specifically, the analysis focused on how lesson sequences were organized in the series of lesson activities that were realized in a series of learning cycles (Rose, 2014).

The curriculum genres cover three dimensions: pedagogic activities, pedagogic relations and pedagogic modalities, from the perspective of register. Pedagogic activities deal with the field of the teaching, concerning "what the teaching is about". Pedagogic relations have to do with the tenor, involving the relations between the teacher and students. Pedagogic modalities focus on the teaching and learning modes, including language and other tools of communication involved in the lesson. The configuration of the three dimensions contributes to the pedagogic practices of the TL-GBP program, which will be elaborated in the following sections.

A. Pedagogic activities

The macro curriculum genres of R2L are realized in lessons, including a series of lesson stages which consist of a series of learning activities. The pedagogic activities are carried out by a series of learning cycles, in which knowledge is taught and acquired. The core structure of a learning cycle is "Focus—Task—Evaluate". In the Focus phase, the teacher specifies the learning task for students, which demands knowledge from them. Only the students can do the task by proposing knowledge from their experience or identifying in a text. In the Evaluate phase, the teacher gives an evaluation to students' responses, ranging from various degrees of affirmation and rejection.

The phase "Focus—Task—Evaluate" is a common practice in classroom discourses. It is expanded in R2L program by providing more information related to students' experience in Prepare phase before Task and more support to accumulate detailed technical or abstract knowledge in Elaborate phase after Evaluate.

The Evaluate phase is very important as it indicates the effectiveness of the Prepare and Focus phases. The teacher has the authority to evaluate the students' task. The evaluation can either affirm or reject the students' responses, grading the force of affirmation or rejection from strong to week. The options for Evaluate phase are diagrammed in Figure 4-1 (Rose, 2014, p. 18):

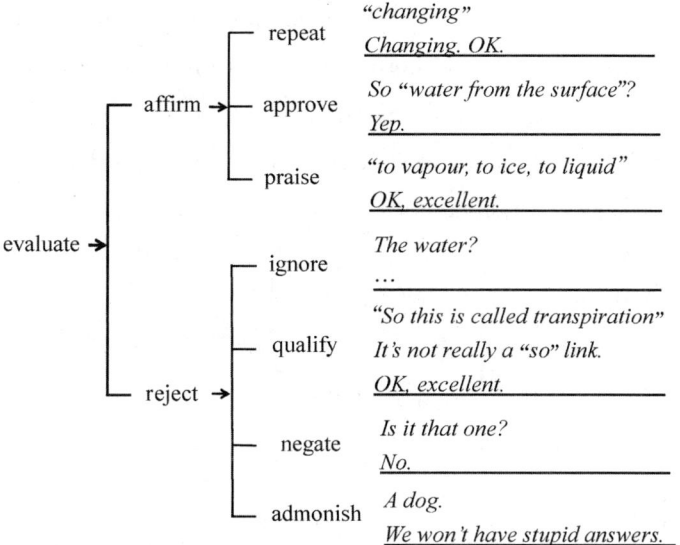

Figure 4-1　Options for Evaluate phases (Rose, 2014, p. 18)

In R2L, affirmation is equally assured around the class for careful planning of learning interaction to ensure success for all students at all points of a lesson. Therefore, all students are included in the learning community of the class and their identities as successful learners of foreign language can be ensured.

B. Pedagogic relations

The pedagogic relations are enacted in the pedagogic activities. Two types of pedagogic exchanges are generally found in class, i.e. action exchanges and knowledge exchanges. In an action exchange, the students usually perform the action, known as primary actor or A1. The action is often demanded by the teacher, known as secondary actor or A2.

A1 is a core role in action exchanges. An action exchange may just compose of an A1 action. More often, the teacher may ask or direct students to do an action, so the sequence is A1—A2. In some cases, students may ask permission for an action which referred to as delay A1, or dA1 moves, and the teacher permits the action (A2), then students perform the action (A1), so the sequence is dA1—A2—A1.

In knowledge exchange, the teacher is usually the primary knower or K1, the authority to provide knowledge for students to acquire. Students then require or receive the knowledge, known as secondary knower or K2. As the K1, the teacher has the authority to evaluate the students' knowledge. The evaluation is K1's core role in pedagogic exchange, as it shows if the acquisition is successful or not.

K1 is a core role in knowledge exchanges. A knowledge exchange may just consist of a K1 role. Typically, students may demand information or the teacher may ask a question that students do not know before K1 gives information or evaluation, so the lesson sequence is K2—K1. More often, the teacher's evaluation is delayed by asking a question (dK1) and after students' response (K2), so the sequence is dK1—K2—K1. These options for pedagogic exchange roles are outlined in Figure 4-2 (Rose, 2014, p. 8).

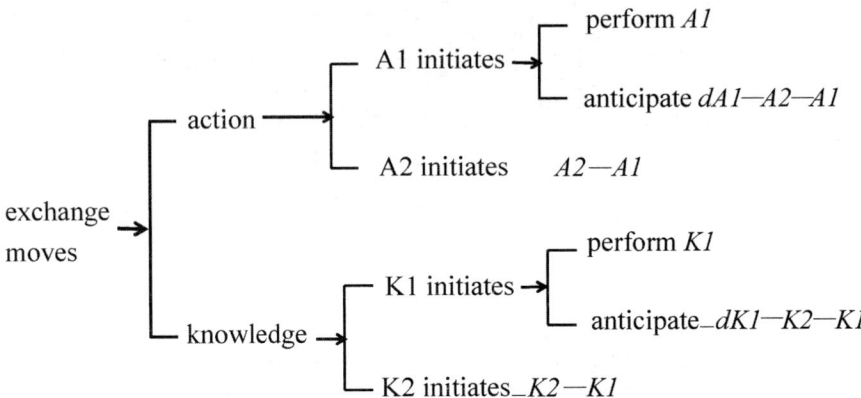

Figure 4-2 Common options for pedagogic exchange roles (Rose, 2014, p. 8)

Apart from these basic types of pedagogic exchange roles, the teacher or students may follow up an A1 move with thanks or a K1 move with comments (A1f/A2f; K1f/K2f). Moves may also be tracked to clarify understanding or be challenged, referred to as tracking (tr), response to tracking (rtr), challenge (ch) and response to challenge (rch).

Analyzing the students' participation in pedagogic exchanges is crucial because it presents the number of students who are actively included in the classroom interactions, as Rose (2014, p. 9) pointed out "inequality of participation is a critical factor in the formation of the hierarchy of inclusion and exclusion in classroom learning". The students' role can be a speaker or addressee. The participants can be the whole class, a group of students, or an individual. By taking students' participation into consideration, the students' role and how they enact their role can be made clear in the analysis.

C. Pedagogic modalities

Pedagogic modalities are employed in various ways to bring meanings or deal with meanings to the discourse, so the sources of meanings are crucial for the teacher and students in a lesson. The analysis in the intervention dealt with identifying and thus facilitating choices about sources and sourcing of meaning in classroom learning.

The source may be spoken by the teacher and students (known as discussion) or recorded. Recorded texts can be visual or verbal, and shared or individual. Meanings may be sourced into the discourse by reading aloud, pointing to or verbally referred to a recorded text. Spoken sources in the classroom discussion can be either shared knowledge learned from prior cycle or prior lesson, or individual knowledge of the teacher or students. The teacher may present his/her knowledge or elicit the students' knowledge. Students may recall their prior knowledge or infer knowledge implied in teachers' questions. The most common options for sources of meaning are set out in Figure 4-3 (Rose, 2014, p. 20).

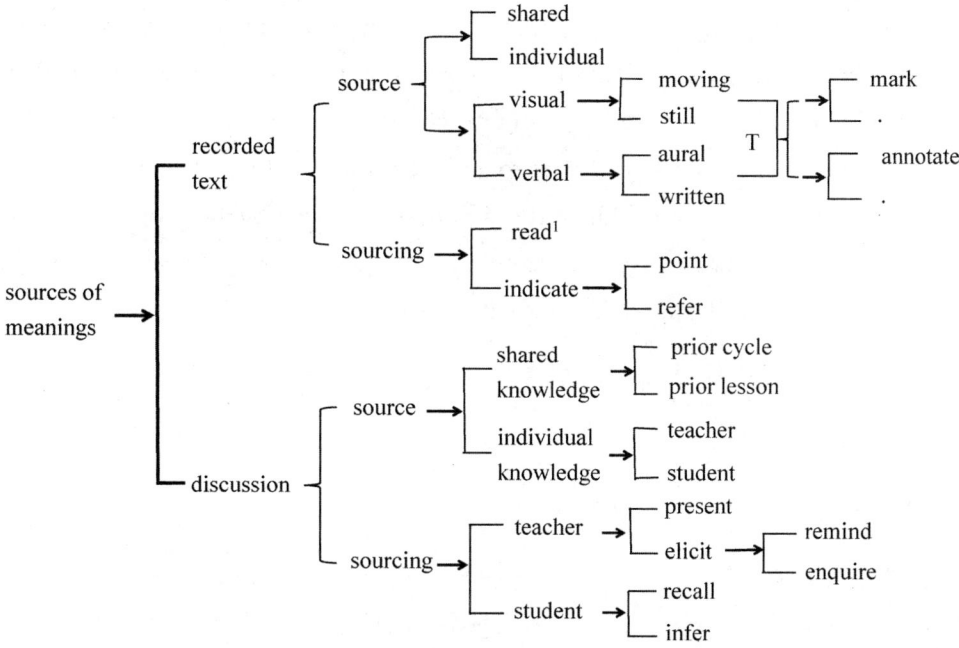

Figure 4-3 Basic options for sources of meanings (Rose, 2014, p. 20)

The curriculum genres, including pedagogic activities, pedagogic relations and pedagogic modalities, provide the analytic tools for classroom interactions during the implementation of the program. By analyzing pedagogic activities, we can know how the knowledge and values are exchanged. By analyzing pedagogic relations, we are clear that whether students are included and excluded in the teaching activities, which is vital for the teaching and learning outcomes and knowledge transmission. By analyzing pedagogic modalities, we can get the information of the teaching and learning resources involved, and how the students' semiotic resources are applied in the teaching activities. In short, by analyzing the curriculum genres, we have a clear picture about what happen in the classroom and the effectiveness of this program.

4.6 Summary

This chapter discussed the details of the research methodology. Two research stages were designed: the description stage was to present an overview of English teaching and related educational variables in the Dong area; and the intervention stage was to implement the designed curriculum.

The multilingual pedagogy programming developed here was designed as an innovative intervention program. The program was implemented in two multilingual classrooms of Guizhou Dong area in China. By using the selected Dong folk literature, it aimed at not only L3, but also multilingualism by involving all students' language resources. The pedagogic practices of the intervention program then will be analyzed in details in Chapter Five, where classroom curriculum genres, covering pedagogic activities, pedagogic relations, and pedagogic modalities, will be examined. The results or impact of the program, including the students' L3 writing development (Chapter Six) and the development of students' multilingual competence, metalinguistic awareness and identity (Chapter Seven) will be then presented.

CHAPTER FIVE
PEDAGOGIC PRACTICES

There are two major concerns in developing this intervention program. The first one is to consider the use of separate language in contemporary practices of multilingual education program. The second one is that although now genre-based pedagogy has been widely approached in the contexts of EFL teaching and multilingual education around the world, multilingualism has hardly taken into account. The pedagogy developed to address these concerns is based on translanguaging and genre-based pedagogy theories, by extending multilingualism into English teaching in the Dong area. The main goal of the intervention program is to facilitate students to access the ways of English languaging. In addition, by involving students' whole linguistic repertoire and semiotic resources in L3 teaching, it is hoped that the program can also help develop students' L1 literacy competence and multilingual identity. In brief, the program aims to provide guidance through translanguaging interaction in a context of shared experience.

The pedagogic practices of the program are analyzed in terms of pedagogic activities, pedagogic relations and pedagogic modalities described above in two sections. Section 5.1 analyzes the curriculum genres of Iteration 1, using L3 reading text. Four steps are discussed, i.e. preparing for reading, detailed reading, sentence making, and joint construction. Every step is elaborated to gain insight in how translanguaging practices are organized and KAL in L1, L2 and L3 takes place in the program. Some excerpts from the interview serve anecdotally to inform the students' views about the intervention. Section 5.2 examines the curriculum genres of Iteration 2, which involves multilingual reading texts. Two steps, detailed reading and joint construction, are elaborated to describe more frequent and flexible translanguaging practices and more use of L3. Data from the students' interviews add to the documentation of the intervention.

5.1　Iteration 1

This section analyzes the process of Iteration 1 that used the reading text in target language (L3). At the beginning stage of the intervention program, the main focus was on English essay structure and language resources, so that English reading text was firstly dealt with in Iteration 1 to provide students with the access to English genre knowledge and language resources. The main functions of Iteration 1 were to (1) model ways of phrasing in L3; (2) provide access to the field of the text; and (3) assist students in being familiar with the patterns of teacher/learning iterations of genre-based pedagogy.

The reading stage began with L3 text to provide explicit knowledge about text organization and quality of ideas that students need to know. The steps in deconstructing the language strata in L3 are "preparing for reading, detailed reading and sentence making". The step of reconstruction activity is joint construction, aiming to re-build the language strata. Each step, together with translanguaging practices, is elaborated below.

5.1.1　Preparing for reading

Preparing for reading deals with the genre and field or background knowledge, aiming to support all students with general comprehension of the text. The stages of preparing for reading are "Preview text—Read text—Review field". The Preview text stage plays an important role in preparing students to follow the text as it is read aloud, by providing the field knowledge, and the sequence in which the field unfolds through the genre. After the students have accessed to the text with general comprehension, the next is Read text, in which the teacher reads the text aloud. Then it comes to Review field, in which the class discuss the topic and some of its key elements in the reading text.

1. Preparation for English knowledge

Before the intervention, the preparation was to distribute handouts of the reading text with printed images for Iteration 1 to the students (see Appendix Ⅲ). As presented above, the English text was taken from one extract of *Kipling's Just So Stories—How the Camel Got His Hump*. The reading text was adjusted to an appropriate length as a proper teaching material for multilingual beginners to learn a complete structure of story genre (see Appendix Ⅲ). The reading text was for students to highlight, and the printed images were to present a vivid picture of the plot of the story. Students were asked to sit in groups of five or six for it was easier for the teacher to move around and check the students during the lesson activities, and for students to conduct the task cooperatively during the lesson activities.

In preparing for reading step, it was the teacher's main task to explain the genre and field of the reading text in order to build new knowledge for students. As story genre is a new way of languaging for students, the first previewing activity was to deconstruct its genre structure for them. The teacher then explicitly previewed the text by providing the background of the text and pointing out the key elements, such as the basic premise and events, by labeling the genre of the text, its stage and phases.

Translanguaging strategies like code-switching and appropriating the students' multilingual repertoire were used to reduce students' semiotic loads in preparing for reading step. Chinese, as the dominant MOI at school, was used to introduce new topic and knowledge at the Preview stage. English was to refer to KAL terms in English, such as the genre name and its stage and key elements. Dong words were to relate the text to students' background knowledge or compare it with their languages and cultures. The students had never learned English story genre and approached genre-based pedagogy before, so that the repetition of new knowledge in different languages could help them be familiar with new terms and the steps of genre-based pedagogy quickly.

The teacher's brief preparation by using translanguaging strategies could relieve the students' semiotic load and thus enable them to closely follow the words as the text was read. After reading, the class had a discussion about some key elements, led by the teacher.

Tables 5-1 to 5-3 present the typical exchanges at the Preview stage of preparing for reading, in which only the teacher is the speaker. The exchange is taken from Day 1 of the intervention in Class 1. The pedagogic activities, pedagogic relations and pedagogic modalities are respectively dealt with in separate tables. A gloss is provided here in English in italic font.

Table 5-1 presents the pedagogic activities of this initial exchange. Two columns are analyzed. The first column labels the phases in lesson cycles. The second column specifies the matter of each phase, i.e. what is the focus of the phase. A sequence of

Prepare phases were provided for students. The teacher firstly prepared the students' task by explicitly telling the students the genre of the reading text (Prepare: task), then the focus was to prepare students the genre of the text, including its generic structure.

Table 5-1　Pedagogic activities in Text 5-1

Speaker	Exchange	Gloss	Phases	Matter
T	我们将学习一篇英文故事,然后参照这篇故事学习用英文写我们的民族故事(da'u)。	*We will learn an English story, then learn how to write our story (da'u) in English.*	Prepare	task
T	So today we will learn "story genres"(故事类语类,指语篇类型). One of the typical story genres is "narrative", to recount personal experience and sequence of events. "Narrative"为记叙文,用来叙述个人经历和一系列的事件,为写故事的常用语篇类型。	*("Story genres" are text types) "Narrative" is to recount personal experience and sequence of events, a typical text type to write a story.*	Prepare	genre
T	Firstly, we will get to know the "stages" of "narrative"(首先,我们来了解一下记叙文的语篇结构). The stages include (包括以下阶段) Orientation—Complication—Evaluation—Resolution.	*(Firstly, we will get to know the "stages" of "narrative")* *(include Orientation—Complication—Evaluation—Resolution)*	Prepare Scribe	genre

In this exchange, translanguaging was employed to provide a well and inclusive preparation for students. Chinese was the main MOI, Dong was supplementary, and there was also code-switching to English. These languages were used for different purposes: L1 was for connecting new languaging to their experience of listening and telling L1 stories, L2 for acquiring new information quickly, and L3 for accessing new academic language. Moreover, code-switching and translation were also applied to highlight the key points and maintain students' attention as the preparation was a little long for the introduction of new knowledge.

Table 5-2 presents the pedagogic relations in two columns too. In the first column, the roles of the teacher and students in the pedagogic exchange are identified, and participants are identified in the second volume, whether they are speakers or addressees. The exchange was realized by the single K1 role, in which the teacher addressed the whole class. The single K1 role was characterized by a move complex, including three K1 moves. The expansion of the relations among each K1 is indicated by an equal "=", referring to elaboration. The relations are connected with each other by the dependency lines on the left (see Martin & Rose, 2007).

Table 5-2   Pedagogic relations in Text 5-1

Speaker	Exchange	Gloss	Roles	Participants
T	我们将学习一篇英文故事,然后参照这篇故事学习用英文写我们的民族故事(da'u)。	*We will learn an English story, then learn how to write our story (da'u) in English.*	K1	class
T	So today we will learn "story genres"(故事类语类,指语篇类型). One of the typical story genres is "narrative", to recount personal experience and sequence of events. "Narrative"为记叙文,用来叙述个人经历和一系列的事件,为写故事的常用语篇类型。	*("Story genres" are text types) "Narrative" is to recount personal experience and sequence of events, a typical text type to write a story.*	= K1	class
T	Firstly, we will get to know the "stages" of "narrative"(首先,我们来了解一下记叙文的语篇结构). The stages include (包括以下阶段) Orientation—Complication—Evaluation—Resolution.	*(Firstly, we will get to know the "stages" of "narrative") (include Orientation—Complication—Evaluation—Resolution)*	= K1	class

Table 5-3 also shows the pedagogic modalities in two columns. The sources of meanings in the exchange are labeled in the second column, and the sourcing of these sources is labeled in the first column. In this case, the teacher first prepared the new topic for students by referring to the reading text. In terms of the options in Figure 4-3 above, the source was shared & verbal: written, and sourcing was to indicate: refer (to the reading text). The teacher then prepared by pointing to notes on the PPT, which presented specifically the definition and stages of narrative. As this was new knowledge for students, the teacher also wrote down some key points on the blackboard and asked the students to take notes. The sources here included shared texts and individual manual notes, and the sourcing included for the teacher: point, present, annotate, and for students: copy, which showed the multimodal functions of projecting the text, so that the teacher may point to it and all students can see and understand.

Table 5-3　Pedagogic modalities in Text 5-1

Speaker	Exchange	Gloss	Sourcing	Sources
T	我们将学习一篇英文故事,然后参照这篇故事学习用英文写我们的民族故事(da'u)。	*We will learn an English story, then learn how to write our story (da'u) in English.*	refer	reading text
T	So today we will learn "story genres"(故事类语类,指语篇类型). One of the typical story genres is "narrative", to recount personal experience and sequence of events. "Narrative"为记叙文,用来叙述个人经历和一系列的事件,为写故事的常用语篇类型。	*("Story genres" are text types) "Narrative" is to recount personal experience and sequence of events, a typical text type to write a story.*	point	notes on PPT
T	Firstly, we will get to know the "stages" of "narrative"(首先,我们来了解一下记叙文的语篇结构). The stages include(包括以下阶段) Orientation—Complication—Evaluation—Resolution.	*(Firstly, we will get to know the "stages" of "narrative") (The stages include Orientation—Complication—Evaluation—Resolution)*	point	notes on PPT

As the teacher has just begun the Preview stage by introducing the conceptions of story genres and narrative, she continued the exchange by discussing English and Chinese genres, mainly in Chinese. Table 5-4 presents the next exchange at the Preview stage, using the same sequence of analyses.

In this exchange, a learning task was orally specified by the teacher requiring students to relate the newly learned knowledge to their prior knowledge. Some students proposed some implicit items. To help students to compare the items more explicitly, the teacher prepared other questions about the genre structure. The students then accomplished the task by referring to their prior language knowledge. The teacher then affirmed it by approving and repeating their responses in both English and Chinese.

Table 5-4 Pedagogic activities, relations, modalities in preparing for reading (2)

Spk	Exchange	Gloss	Phases	Matter	Roles	Pts	Sourcing	Sources
T	请同学们对比一下,英文"narrative"和中文的记叙文有什么异同吗?	Please compare it with Chinese narrative, do you find any similarities and differences?	Focus	task	dK1	class	remind recall	prior knowledge
Ss	有很多相似之处。	There are many similarities.	Propose	item	K2	Ss		prior knowledge
T	比如说,我们用中文写故事时会先写什么? 再写什么? 最后写什么呢?	For example, if we write a story in Chinese, what will we write first, what's next, and what's in the end?	Focus	genre structure	dK1	class	remind	prior knowledge
Ss	故事的开头、过程、结局。	Orientation, the process of the event, and the ending.	Propose	genre structure	K2	Ss	recall	prior knowledge
T	Yes, good. 中英文故事的结构相似,都有开头(Orientation)、过程(Complication)和结局(Resolution)。	Whether we write in English or Chinese, we will have Orientation—Complication—Resolution.	Affirm	approve	K1'	class	point	notes on PPT

The series of Focus and Propose moves in Chinese enabled all students to experience brain storming and draw from their linguistic repertoire quickly and easily. Their success was affirmed by praising them in English and repeating the knowledge of genre structure both in Chinese and English, which helped them have deeper impressions and keep the knowledge in mind unconsciously.

To appropriate the students' early required linguistic knowledge, a dK1 question was proposed to focus the students' task. The students' K2 Propose was followed by the teacher's affirmation (K1'—the prime symbol was adopted to show K1 as praise).

K1's role showed an expected move, following the students' correct K2 answer. The pedagogic purpose of K1's affirmation was to promote students' confidence. Moreover, it was in English with the specific purpose of starting to introduce the target languages in a positive way. In addition, the pedagogic purpose of repeating items in both Chinese and English was to pack up the knowledge so that students can acquire the terms and wordings in two languages.

The source of meanings was primarily the prior knowledge. The teacher first asked students to compare English narrative with Chinese. In responding, students recalled their previously learned knowledge about Chinese narrative. The function of referring to the students' prior knowledge about other languages was to relate the new knowledge to what students have already known, which enabled them to accomplish the learning task successfully. The students' response became the step for the teacher to associate it with the present lesson.

After preparing English genre and reviewing it by comparing it in two languages, the teacher moved to the exchange of deconstructing the text in terms of field. Table 5-5 presents another sequence of Prepare phase, in which the field unfolds through the genre. The teacher prepared the background knowledge of the reading text with the basic premise of the story and the main characters. She then summarized the sequence of Complications to the point where it started getting resolved. The preparation was designed with translanguaging tools such as translation and repetition of the key words in two languages (e. g. the Camel, 骆驼), facilitating all students to engage in the story with full understanding of the context.

Table 5-5　Pedagogic activities, relations, modalities in preparing for reading (3)

Spk	Exchange	Gloss	Phases	Matter	Roles	Pts	Sourcing	Sources
T	The story is about how the Camel got his hump. 这是一个关于骆驼(Camel)是怎样长出驼峰(hump)的故事。	The story is about how the Camel got his hump.	Prepare	field	K1	class	refer	reading text
T	从前,世界还是崭新的时候,人类向动物寻求帮助:马(Horse)驮东西(carrying),狗(Dog)取东西(fetching),牛(Ox)耕田(ploughing)。故事的主角骆驼(Camel)一点儿活儿都不愿意干,对所有的请求都只是傲慢地回复一句"哼"。	Once upon a time, when the world was new-and-all, Man turned to the animals for help: to the Horse for carrying, the Dog for fetching, the Ox for ploughing. The main character camel refused to do a lick of work, haughtily replying "Humph!" to all requests.			K1		point	reading text notes on PPT
T	你认为其他动物对骆驼这种行为会有什么反应?骆驼的驼峰(hump)和他挂在嘴边的这句"哼"(humph)有关系吗? OK, let's start reading the story and find out what happens.	What do you think about the reactions of other animals to the Camel's behavior? Is there any relation between the Camel's hump and his word "humph"?			K1		refer	reading text notes on PPT

As for the pedagogic relations in the exchange, the teacher presented the knowledge to the whole class as K1 role. The single K1 role was presented as a move complex. The series of elaborations ("=") both supported and motivated students to attend to the text as it was read.

As for the pedagogic modalities, the teacher first prepared by referring to the reading text, then pointed to it and the image on the paper, and finally referred to it again. Meanwhile, the teacher also pointed to the reading text on the PPT, in which stages and phases of the story were labeled, sometimes along with some gestures, to present the knowledge.

The exchanges analyzed above are typical examples in the Preview text stage of preparing for reading. They are characterized by the complexity, normally involving continual switches from genre to field focusing in the phases of learning cycles, from the teacher to students in the negotiation of exchange roles, and from the teacher's knowledge to students' knowledge in the sources and sourcing of meanings.

2. Reflections on preparing for reading

In the program, it was primarily the teacher who spoke in preparing for reading step. It seemed to be a teacher-centered model but as in all R2L activities, the focus was actually on the students' task. To this end, the sufficient preparation with translanguaging strategies reduced the students' semiotic load and provided supports in several ways.

Firstly, the teacher unpacked the reading text, using students' familiar languages and KAL terms to explicitly explain the genre and field of the text, for every student to access new knowledge and way of languaging. Since it was the teacher who introduced the new knowledge and ways of languaging to the students, the teaching was strongly classified [in Bernstein's (2000) terms]. The use of translanguaging strategies created the connection of learning a new written genre and field with the students' previous knowledge, which enabled them to be more aware of the new way of languaging without overloading them. These practices, compared with some practices that students had to response from their prior knowledge only, were ways of inclusive teaching, aiming to subvert a common practice of ranking students in a hierarchy of knowledge by distributing the necessary knowledge for all students. It was effective to prepare the students for their readings, to access the reading text with general comprehension, and to provide foundations for them to engage in the next lecture.

Secondly, the teacher guided students to follow the previewing by employing multilingual and multimodal resources. For instance, the use of students' everyday language and academic language in L1, L2 and L3 scaffolded them to develop knowledge of academic languages and genres in all their languages. Moreover, comparing the languaging ways, referring and pointing to the shared reading text, along with images and gestures, as the teacher discussed the reading text, enabled students to catch up with particular parts and make connections between the text and the metalanguage used for its structure.

Last but not least, preparing for reading step was conducted as briefly as possible, which ensured students to do their task successfully as their tasks at this stage were to follow the teacher's presentation and obtain a general framework of the text. Therefore, the brief preparation motivated students to study reading and minimized the chance for students to get distracted, confused or bored.

5.1.2 Detailed reading

After preparing for reading, detailed reading was conducted with the purpose of assisting all students in reading passages of the reading text with full understanding and recognizing the author's language choices. As for stories, passages are selected for detailed reading as "they use rich language resources for building tension in stories, include a series of descriptive devices and are engaging for the students to using the language resources in writing their own passage" (Rose & Martin, 2012, p. 134). This step focuses on the language strata of field, discourse semantics, and lexico-grammar. As the reading text was relatively long, only several passages at each stage were selected for detailed reading with the focus on unpacking and identifying: (1) key elements of the text, (2) literature language resources and devices, and (3) the organization of the key elements and the literature language.

1. Identifying wordings

In detailed reading, the teacher guides students to identify the key words in each sentence of a short passage through various learning cycles in the recursive movement of exchange phases. The students' tasks are to identify and highlight the key elements and words in recursive verbal tasks. Detailed reading usually begins with reviewing the context and phases of the selected passage. After preparing a sentence of the passage and reading the sentence aloud as students read along, the teacher prepares students to identify words by providing them a meaning cue and a position cue. After identifying, the teacher directs the class to highlight the identified word group and then elaborates it in the context of the events. The sequence of moves continues for the next sentence and wordings in the selected passage, so the generic structure is recursive, i. e. Preview, Read sentences—Identify wordings—Review field, language.

In each exchange, the sequence of moves consists of Prepare—Focus—Identify—Affirm—Elaborate. Prepare and Elaborate moves are deliberately planned by the teacher for deepening students' understanding of the language and field so that these moves may be realized as move complexes. Translanguaging are used in all moves, with more use of the students' L1 and L2 in Prepare and Focus moves. L3 is used when L3 wordings were recognized or prepared.

Table 5-6 is a typical example of a lesson cycle in detailed reading from Class 2. Before the lesson cycle, the teacher first explained the learning activities of detailed reading to the students so that they would look at the text in details and identify wordings when guided by the teacher. The lesson cycle dealt with the first passage of the text, with the focus on the Orientation stage of the narrative *How the Camel Got His Hump* (see Text 5-2 below).

Text 5-2 One extract from *How the Camel Got His Hump*

Orientation

In the beginning of years, when the world was so new and all, and the Animals were just beginning to work for Man, there was a Camel, and he lived in the middle of a Howling Desert because he did not want to work; and besides, he was a Howler himself. So he ate sticks and thorns and tamarisks and milkweed and prickles, most excruciatingly idle; and when anybody spoke to him he said "Humph!", Just "Humph!", and no more.

The teacher began this exchange by preparing students with the general background knowledge and phases of the passage (Prepare passage). She then directed students' attention to the first sentence and read it (Prepare sentence). After reading, she told students that "The start of the sentence tells us when the story happened" and asked them to find out the time phrase (Focus wording). After the students identified "in the beginning of years" (Identify wording), she affirmed the answer by both approving and repeating it (Affirm: approve, repeat).

Table 5-6 Pedagogic activities, relations, modalities in detailed reading

Spk	Exchange	Gloss	Phases	Matter	Roles	Pts	Sourcing	Sources
T	This is the Orientation(开头). It tells us the setting of the story (故事的场景). 从前,人类请动物帮忙干活,但是骆驼不干。What did the Camel do and say? Let's find out.	(Orientation)(the setting of the story) Previously, the man asked the animals to work, but the Camel did not listen.	Prepare	passage	K1	class	point	passage
T	The first sentence tells us the setting, including time, place, character and event. Look at the sentence as I read it (请同学们边听我读边看这句话). [Reading] The start of the sentence tells us when the story happened (句子的开头告诉了我们故事发生的时间).	(Look at the sentence as I read it) (The start of the sentence tells us the time)	Prepare Prepare	sentence wording	=K1 =K1	class class	point refer	passage passage
T	Can you find when the story happened (你能找到故事发生的时间吗)?	(Can you find the words that tell the time)	Focus	wording	dK1		point	passage
Ss	In the beginning of years.		Identify	wording	K2	Ss	read	passage
T	Good! In the beginning of years.		Affirm	praise, repeat	K1'	class		

Translanguaging tool used here mainly referred to multilingual practices to scaffold students to understand KAL in English and follow the pedagogic discourse in English. Since some English terms in this exchange have already been presented in preparing for reading step, the exchange was chiefly conducted in English, along with some repetitions of key terms (e.g. Orientation,开头) in Chinese for emphasis, and some Chinese translations to help all students to identify the time phrase with full background knowledge. Their success was affirmed by praising them in L3 and repeating the wording.

The pedagogic relations in this exchange are also presented in Table 5-6. The Prepare phases were carried out as a complex K1 move, with the teacher addressing to the class. Then the Focus was specified by a dK1 question. The students responded to the question as K2, which was followed by the teacher's affirmation as K1'.

The complex K1 move with translanguaging practices provided explicit meaning cues for the students repeatedly. In so doing, every student can identify the wording, and most importantly, be affirmed by the teacher. The affirmation offered the students a sense of success, enabling every student to engage equally and actively in the learning activities. English was also introduced and repeated in a positive way to develop the students' interest and motivation.

The source of the knowledge was the first passage of the text, which was pointed by the teacher to the relevant part of the passage "In the beginning of years..., he was a Howler himself." As the wording was explicitly sourced, the students can easily identify it in the text, which ensured the success of completing the challenging task of locating the English time phrase.

This pattern of the learning cycle was conducted recursively to identify key elements in the text. As the text is a kind of children literature, in which relatively easy wordings can be prepared as "wh" meaning cues such as *who, what, when, where, how far*. In so doing, the students identified specific wordings from these general meanings. These general meanings focused the students' attention on the semantic functions of word groups that make up sentences. As the students became familiar with the discourse, they were prepared to transfer this work to the next iteration. By providing explicit meaning sources, the teacher handed control of reserving semiosis to the students.

2. Dense elaboration

The students' success in identifying the wordings provided a sound basis for the teacher to elaborate the word meanings. Table 5-7 analyzes how the wordings were elaborated in aspects of grammar, meanings and pronunciation after the students' successful identifications.

Table 5-7 Pedagogic activities in elaboration (1)

Spk	Exchange	Gloss	Phases	Matter	Roles	Pts	Sourcing	Sources
T	Please repeat "In the beginning of years".		Prepare/ Focus	pronunciation	dK1	class	present/ gesture	knowledge
Ss	In the beginning of years.		Rehearse	pronunciation	K2	class	recall	knowledge
T	Excellent! In the beginning of years. "In the beginning of years" is a phrase, means long time ago. 就是汉语讲故事常用的开头"从前",侗语的 xic unv。	*It is the same with the phrase "cong qian" when we start the story in Chinese, "xic unv" in Dong.*	Affirm Elaborate	praise, repeat word meaning	K1' K1	class class	present	knowledge knowledge

As for the pedagogic activities in the elaboration, the phrase "in the beginning of years" was the most useful resource in story writing but it was new for most students, so the students needed to pronounce the phase and keep it in mind as it can be used in their own writings. The students' pronunciation in response (Rehearse) was affirmed by praising and repeating. The teacher defined the phrase and explained it in Chinese and Dong context again. Connecting the meaning and usage of the phrase with the students' previous knowledge reinforced the use of the phrase in specific contexts. A short direction from the teacher was added along with gestures in this exchange to introduce more English pedagogic discourses in the teaching activities.

As for the pedagogic relations, the teacher specified the Focus as dK1, and the students rehearsed the phrase as K2, which was affirmed by the teacher as K1'. Finally, the teacher elaborated the meaning of the phrase as K1.

As for the pedagogic modalities involved, the teacher first presented her knowledge of pronunciation, along with the gesture to direct the students to take the knowledge. The students recalled what they had learned as they pronounced it. The teacher presented her knowledge to elaborate.

Elaborations facilitated students to access the text by inferring their knowledge and experience, and to interpret the context. The next exchange presented in Tables 5-8 and 5-9 shows the elaboration of the inferred meanings.

In Table 5-8, the exchange is presented as a cycle complex. Firstly, the teacher prepared students with the sentence meanings. Then she engaged students interactively in elaborations, by asking their experiences or common sense about the place where the Camel usually lives in the first two learning cycles of the exchange. In the next learning cycle, the Focus was to identify two qualities of the desert, dealing with the grammar about nominal groups. Here the teacher explicitly named the nominal groups as qualities of the Desert and explained what these qualities refer to. The teacher then elaborated the meaning of the phrase "in the middle of" by translating it into Chinese and Dong. This learning cycle complex showed the typical learning activities in detailed reading. The functions of these activities that directed the students' attention to common structural patterns were to raise the students' recognition of the word and grammar patterns in English in their reading and of using them in their own writings later.

Table 5-8 Pedagogic activities in elaboration (2)

Spk	Exchange	Gloss	Phases	Matter
T	The next sentence tells us where the Camel lived.		Prepare	wording
T	Can you see where the Camel lived?		Focus	wording
Ss	In the middle of a Howling Desert.		Identify	wording
T	Exactly right.		Affirm	praise
T	He lived in the middle of a Howling Desert.		Prepare	sentence
T	这是什么地方呢？同学们知道骆驼住在什么地方吗？	*Where is the place? Do you know where the Camel lived?*	Focus	wording
Ss	沙漠。	*Desert.*	Propose	wording
T	Yes, 沙漠, desert.	*desert*	Affirm	praise, repeat
T	In the middle of a Howling Desert. This word group describes two qualities of the desert (这个词组描述了沙漠的两个性质). The first quality is what part of the desert.	(*This word group describes two qualities of the desert*)	Prepare	grammar
T	Can you see what part of the desert (沙漠的哪个部分)?	(*What part of the desert*)	Focus	wording
Ss	In the middle of.		Identify	wording
T	Yes, great.		Affirm	praise
T	In the middle of 的中文意思是在中间，侗文 tal caih 的 tal。	*In Chinese " zhongjian", in Dong, "tal" of the "tal caih".*	Elaborate	wording

Table 5-9 analyzes both the pedagogic relations and modalities in this exchange. The teacher prepared the students by pointing the text in a K1 move. She then reminded the students to recall their common sense in elaborations as dK1. After the students recalled the knowledge in Chinese, the teacher affirmed it in a K1' move. The next cycle began with a K1 move, by teacher presenting her English grammar knowledge. She then focused the students' task by a dK1 question, pointing to the text. The students proposed a response to the question by reading the word group from the text. The learning cycle was repeated to deal with other grammar knowledge. After explicit preparation, first of the sentence, then of the wording and grammar by using multilingual and multimodal resources, the students accomplished the tasks successfully, whether proposing or identifying a meaning. By repeating the learning patterns, the students can follow more English instructions and practices. For example, as the teacher read the English word, the students rehearsed it without being asked.

Table 5-9 Pedagogic relations and modalities in elaboration (2)

Spk	Exchange	Gloss	Roles	Sts	Sourcing	Sources
T	The next sentence tells us where the Camel lived.		K1	class	point	text
T	Can you see where the Camel lived?		dK1	class	refer	text
Ss	In the middle of a Howling Desert.		K2	Ss	read	text
T	Exactly right.		K1'	class		
T	He lived in the middle of a Howling Desert.		K1	class	refer	text
T	这是什么地方呢? 同学们知道骆驼住在什么地方吗?	Where is the place? Do you know where the Camel lived?	dK1	class	remind	knowledge
Ss	沙漠。	Desert.	K2	Ss	recall	knowledge
T	Yes, 沙漠, desert.	desert	K1'	class		
T	In the middle of a Howling Desert. This word group describes two qualities of the desert (这个词组描述了沙漠的两性质). The first quality is what part of the desert.	(This word group describes two qualities of the desert)	K1	class	present	text
T	Can you see what part of the desert (沙漠的哪个部分)?	(What part of the desert)	dK1	class	point	knowledge
Ss	In the middle of.		K2	Ss	read	knowledge
T	Yes, great.		K1'	class		text
T	In the middle of 的中文意思是在中间,侗文tal caih 的tal。	In Chinese "zhongjian", in Dong, "tal" of the "tal caih".	K1	class	present	knowledge

In detailed reading, deconstructing English reading text involved both reading the field and negotiating the meanings of some wordings. Elaborations involved extending the students' knowledge with various learning foci. Firstly, the literature language and devices in story genres were unpacked in that the students can be sensible of and process them. Secondly, the repetitions of English wordings brought consciousness of new knowledge to the students, even when the teacher did not construe it in a learning cycle. Moreover, the students can also perceive of the new knowledge as key elements with the assistance of translanguaging strategies. It seemed that the repetitions and translanguaging practices in dense elaborations have created a space for the students to access knowledge of English language. Finally, as they have been familiar with the learning pattern, the metalanguage of English grammar introduced here paved the way for the next activities—sentence making, without obstructing the students to do tasks.

After dealing with each sentence, it was read aloud, and when all sentences were completed, the whole passage was read again. The stages and phases were also labeled on a projected passage on the PPT and the students labeled them in their own copies. Finally, the students were asked to do exercises and assignments of translating the English passage into Chinese and Dong. These exercises reinforced the students' knowledge of genre and field on the one hand, and assisted them in reviewing the word meanings and thus reinforced their understandings on the other hand.

3. Reflections on detailed reading

In detailed reading, it was the students' task to identify and propose the wordings. The teacher's tasks were to carefully prepare the students to do the task and elaborate the meanings after the task. Since the goals of the lesson were to build both knowledge and successful multilingual learners' identities, it was crucial for the teacher to provide both sufficient preparation and explicit elaboration to assure that all students were continually successful in the TL-GBP program.

Firstly, preparing sentence by using translanguaging strategies was fundamental, which enabled all students to understand the sentence as it was read. Since English wordings were alien for most students, the sentence preparation that correlated the meanings with their familiar expressions liberated the students from struggling to decode unfamiliar words, and assisted them in processing the wordings, meanings and soundings easily. In addition, this preparation provided a meaningful context in the text as students identified and understood each wording in the sentence.

Additionally, translanguaging strategies also played an important role in providing students with meaning cues. Simply "wh" cues and synonyms were used in this text, and Chinese and/or Dong translations were also important scaffoldings as students had not yet been familiar with the teaching and learning patterns and KAEL. The ways of repeating the meaning cues in various languages helped reduce the semiotic load and emotional stress on students, so that any student, including the weaker readers in the class, can easily identify the wordings from the meaning cues.

After the successful identifications, translanguaging strategies in elaborations helped build and extend students' knowledge. The elaborations were fulfilled by defining words and grammar structures in both English and Chinese or asking students to propose responses from their individual knowledge and linguistic resources. In so doing, the students had deeper understandings of the new meanings and structures while sustaining their identities as they could use their agency.

In fact, the students and their English teacher made a great deal of positive comments on detailed reading activities. The students actively engaged in the activities. Most students made an agreement that they have never enjoyed English class like this before and they always felt included in the lesson for there were numerous activities or tasks they wanted to take part in. Some students' comments are shown in Text 5-3.

Text 5-3　Interviews: some students' comments on detailed reading

S1：英语课有很多有趣的活动,我们都被吸引了。

S1：There were a lot of interesting activities, and we were all involved in the class.

S2：很开心,很好玩儿。我很喜欢这些活动,因为参与这些活动,我们上课总是很活跃,上英语课不那么无聊了,不再使我想睡觉了。

S2：Fun, enjoyable! I like the activities very much, they made us active. English lesson made me happy, it's not boring, not sleepy.

S3：和以前的英语课完全不同,因为有很多活动,大家都积极参与。学习氛围比以前好了,我上课也更专注了。

S3：Different from the English class before. Because everyone took part in the activities actively, the learning atmosphere was better, and I was more attentive to the class.

S4：更轻松更好玩儿了,让我们有兴趣,因为你解释的(英语知识)让我很容易懂。

S4：More relaxed and funny! You attracted us more because your explanations of (the English knowledge) were easier to be understood.

S5：我现在敢站起来回答问题了,以前从来不敢单独回答问题。

S5：Now I had the courage to answer questions, and I had never dared to answer questions alone before.

Their English teacher commented that it was quite unusual that most students were actively involved in the activities, even the weaker learners who were often doing other things unrelated to learning such as talking and sleeping. In detailed reading, the students often raised their hands and were pointed to answer questions, which indicated that the students were confident to engage in the activities and can do the task successfully even knowledge and meanings were new for them. The teacher also observed the dynamic change in the pedagogic relations in the process of the teaching activities because more students were included than usual practices.

5.1.3 Sentence making

After detailed reading, some intensive strategies were provided to practice the fundamental skills of reading and writing before the students moved to reconstruction. Therefore, sentence making step is to provide a higher level of support for the students to prepare them for reconstruction, as the students were relatively new and weak learners, and it was the first time for them to learn in a R2L model.

1. Building knowledge about English language

Sentence making was carried out after detailed reading and before joint construction. One or more sentences from the passage in detailed reading were written or printed on papers. The teacher guided the students to identify and cut up the wordings, using the discussion as in detailed reading. The students manually dealt with the word groups, first mixing them up, and re-arranging them into a complete sentence, then re-reading the sentence aloud. In sum, the stages in sentence making include Preview sentence—Identify grammar structures—Rearrange sentences. The stages of sentence making were repeated for each sentence.

Knowledge of English grammar was handled at the stage of Identify grammar structure. This was done by a "top-down" approach as the teacher introduced it at higher levels after contextualizing the text within their field and genre, and each sentence within its phase. After the word groups were repeatedly dealt in different activities with different modalities in detailed reading, it was ideal to introduce KAEL in sentence making step. As the students were already familiar with the sentences contextualized in a whole text, they can focus on grammar patterns in the sentences without overloading. To further reduce their learning loading, translanguaging strategies were employed to introduce English metalinguistic terms by comparing KAL in Chinese and to make the intuitive KAL in the students' consciousness in both L2 and L3.

Sentence making has several pedagogic functions (David & Martin, 2012, p. 187): (1) it intensifies the discussion of meanings and wordings from detailed reading; (2) it enables the students to take control by manipulating wordings to create meaningful sentences since they are already familiar with the sentences from a passage; (3) the individual words from the sentences can be also used to practice spelling. In addition, sentence making practices are particularly effective for the students to take control of grammar and lexis in the target language based on more abstract understandings of KAEL and metalanguage. To fulfill these functions in the program, sentence making was well-adjusted and adapted by incorporating translanguaging strategies into its stages.

Table 5-10 analyses the exchange of introducing grammar structures. Like the sequence in detailed reading, after the passage and sentence were briefly prepared, the teacher focused the students on identifying the grammatical item. Since this learning cycle has already practiced many times in detailed reading and the students have been familiar with the "wh" questions, they identified the word group quickly. The meaning of the word group was carefully prepared and repeated before its grammatical type was presented. When the students proposed the answers in Chinese, the teacher repeated them in English to reinforce the understandings of metalanguage. The introduction of grammar structure in Chinese and English promoted the students' awareness of metalanguage in both languages. The grammar learning activities based on the already learned language sources ensured the introduction of grammar knowledge without overloading the students but reinforcing genre knowledge and meanings discussed before.

As for the pedagogic relations in this exchange, as the common sequence, the teacher first specified the students to identify the grammatical item, and then introduced the related grammar knowledge as K1, which was followed as A2 by asking the students to scribe the key point of the grammar knowledge. The students then performed the demand as A1.

Table 5-10　Pedagogic activities, relations and modalities in sentence making (1)

Spk	Exchange	Gloss	Phases	Matter	Roles	Sts	Sourcing	Sources
T	Can you find when the story happened?		Focus	wording	dK1	class	point	previous lesson
Ss	In the beginning of years.		Identify	wording	K2	S1	read	previous lesson
T	Well-done! "In the beginning of years"整体是一个英语短语,是"从前"的意思,表示时间,因此为时间类词组。	"In the beginning of years" as a whole is an English phrase, which means "conqian" and indicates the time, so it is "time word group".	Affirm Elaborate	grammar	K1	class	present	text
T	[Scribing "time (时间) when" on board]		Scribe					knowledge
T	Please write them down. 请同学们把这些表示语义类别的词记在笔记本上。	Please write down the words of semantic categories on your notebooks.	Focus		A2	class		
Ss	[Scribing "time (时间) when" on notebooks]		Scribe		A1	class		

The next exchange negotiated more details of KAEL—distinguishing the main types of word groups, and the names of KAEL followed the labels suggested in Rose and Martin (2013) and Rose (2015c).

The exchange in Table 5-11, taken from the same source of data, continued to deal with the next item of KAEL—the grammar structure. The teacher first introduced the grammatical item "prepositional phrase", then explained it in Chinese by presenting her English grammar knowledge and comparing it with Chinese as K1. After that, she scribed it on board as A2 and asked the students to follow the scribing.

Table 5-11 Pedagogic activities and relations in sentence making (2)

Spk	Exchange	Gloss	Phases	Matter	Roles	Sts
T	"In the beginning of years" expresses the meaning of time. It is introduced by the preposition "in", thus named as prepositional phrase, which usually expresses the meaning of places or times. "In the beginning of years" 以介词 in 开头,所以叫介词短语,介词短语通常表示时间和地点。	*"In the beginning of years" is introduced by the preposition "in", thus named as prepositional phrase, which usually expresses the meaning of places and times.*	Elaborate	grammar	K1	class
T	[Scribing "prepositional phrase" (介词)]		Scribe		A1	class
	Please write them down (请同学们把这些表示语法的词记下来).	*(Please write them down)*	Focus		A2	class
Ss	[Scribing "prepositional phrase" (介词)]		Scribe		A1	class

Exchanges like Table 5-11 were carried out in iterations to introduce all types of word groups in the text after the identifications of word meanings. Moreover, key points were written down on the board. After all grammar activities have finished, the grammar knowledge was concluded in the table and presented to the students on PPT (see Figure 5-1). At the same time, the teacher elaborated the overall grammar by using various languages, which reinforced the grammar structures of the text and laid solid foundations for the next step in writing.

After negotiating the grammar structure, the teacher guided the students to identify each word group in the sentence and then labeled them as prepositional phrase, nominal group, verbal group, adjectival group, adverbial group and conjunction according to the meanings. In this process, the teacher also instructed the students to negotiate the position of each group in the sentence. Figure 5-2 shows an example.

```
name (英汉)          wh-word (英侗)              word group
people(人物)         who (nouc)─────────→nominal group (名词)
thing (事物)         what (mangc)──────↗
process (过程)       what doing/happening─→verbal group (动词)
                     (duc mangc)
place (地点)         where (nyaoh nup)────→prepositional phrase
time (时间)          when/how long (xic nup)    (介词)
quality(of process)  how like (il nup weec)──→adverbial group (副词)
(性质，修饰动词)
 quality(of thing)   what like (il nup yangx)→ adjectival group(形容词)
(性质，修饰名词)
```

Figure 5-1 Classes of word groups presented on PPT in the lesson

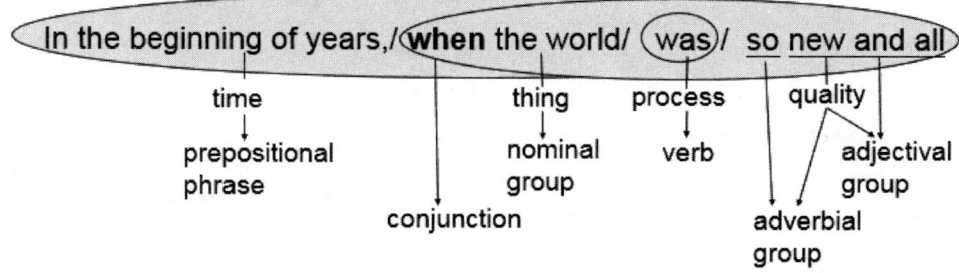

Figure 5-2 Identifying and labeling word groups

After identifying and labeling all the sentences of the first passage, the students cut up the paper into lines of sentences, then into word groups that they have marked. In the end, the students mixed the chunks of the first sentence and rearranged them into a sentence again. They finished the task by completing all sentences in the first passage.

Sentence making activities were repeated for each passage in detailed reading of the text. The practices were conducted in groups, with each 4 or 5 students. They were allowed to discuss in any language when doing the task. The teacher circulated and supported each group. Within each group, the teacher helped one with his task and the other group members followed. After they finished the task, each group showed their sentence by either reading it or writing it on the broad.

The assignment for students at this stage was to do linguistic analysis of the passage by marking the word group with a slash /, and then labeling below it. Text 5-4 shows one student's homework.

Text 5-4   One student's homework of doing linguistic analysis

Presently/the Horse/came/to him/on Monday morning/,
    Thing   *process* *thing* *time*
with a saddle/ on his back/ and a bit/ in his mouth/,

thing   place   thing   place
and said, / "Camel, O, Camel," / come out/ and trot/
process   thing   process process
like the rest of us/.
thing

In addition, other intensive strategies were used to provide students with sufficient supports to deal with long and difficult sentences. One strategy was making sentence activity. The sentences were firstly written on the blackboard or displayed on PPT, then some key words were erased as the class read them, finally leaving just a few grammatical words as a skeletal framework. Meanwhile, the students were asked to remember the sequence of the sentences and then wrote the erased words. Another example was the tense practice of verbal groups. This activity was similar to the making sentence activity. Sentences were also written on the blackboard or displayed on PPT, but this time it was the verbal words that were erased, then students needed to write the verbal words. During these activities, the teacher provided supports for the weaker students.

2. Reflections on sentence making

The main foci of language strata in sentence making were discourse and grammar. The specific purpose of the intensive strategies, set out by the teacher, was to provide a higher level of scaffold for students to learn KAL so as to reinforce fundamental skills in reading and writing. This has been realized by a number of meaningful practices, working on the same passages in the preceding sections, with the teacher's guidance, through students' cooperation, along with the learning of graphology and phonology.

During sentence making, translanguaging strategies were used to scaffold students to have a deeper understanding about KAL in both Chinese and English. When explaining grammar knowledge, Chinese was used to concentrate students and help them grasp the meanings easily and quickly. When introducing the metalanguage, the students' familiar L1 and L2 were used to affirm terms that they did not know, such as giving supplementary Chinese word "名词" for "nominal group", and to create explicit and direct connection with word meanings and grammar, such as using "who (noun)" to connect with "nominal group". By these activities, students' grammar knowledge in both L2 and L3 has been build. In addition, since the teacher's role was also to enact students' roles that were realized in Direct and Focus phases, translanguaging strategies were used in these phases to avoid the unnecessary burden on students in understanding the questions or commands, which may slow down the lesson activities.

Sentence making was a key step to scaffold students to take control of KAL. Firstly, the discourse and grammar knowledge were dealt with in the contextualized texts that the whole class have been worked on, so that students can understand and construct new knowledge in a meaningful context rather than in isolation. By this way, they can have a full understanding of the meanings and knowledge. Secondly, they repeatedly experienced each language feature by a great deal of practices so that they can build the knowledge by dealing with it for several times. Thirdly, when students handled with various modalities of reading and writing, by cutting up sentences on paper strips, reading and writing words and sentences on the blackboard and their notebooks, they also took control of them.

There were also several benefits concerning some social aspects. Firstly, translanguaging activities in groups encouraged cooperation and communication among students, and increased their confidence to do the tasks. It was often the case that when a task has just finished, some students asked for the next task immediately. Some students commented in the interviews that they liked to engage in the activities, as discussing in their own languages made them relaxed and their communication easier, just like the ways they talked to their Dong peers after class and in their hometowns. Therefore, the step helped them befriend and learn from each other. They had less fear when being asked by the teacher, because they were fully aware that they represented a group and other group members would assist them. Secondly, as the students had increasing confidence in participating the activities, the class became less disruptive and noisy. The biggest challenge in these classes before was to maintain the students' attention. Pointing every student to engage in the group work ensured that all students got opportunities to answer questions for their groups, and the teaching/learning activity was under control at the same time.

5.1.4 Joint construction

The goal of joint construction was to support all students to appropriate the language resources of experienced writers into their own writing, so that they can grasp the genres for assessment tasks. This step further reconstructed all language strata following the same language patterns deconstructed in preparing for reading and detailed reading, from the notes in the reading text but with a new field, i.e. new characters, settings, events.

The sequence of joint construction was Preview genre—Plan field—Use language sources for a new text—Review genre and language. The teacher guided students to jointly write a Dong story by applying the sentence patterns in the reading text. This was a way to model the independent writing as it built up language resources that students can use to construct their own writings.

1. Lesson activities in joint construction

Joint construction began with previewing the genre. As the reading text was used as a model for joint construction to follow its stages and sequence, the teacher first guided students to analyze the stages and phases of the reading text again. The reading text was projected on the PPT, and prepared, read and discussed in the ways like those in preparing for reading. The teacher then directed students to identify each phase in the text, and wrote a label for it beside the related passage. The students at the same time labeled on their own copies. This stage facilitated students to be more familiar with the structure and the rhetorical devices of the model, and the metalanguage used to discuss it.

Next, a new field for joint construction text was chosen, which was brainstormed by the students from their Dong folk stories. The teacher then guided them to choose new details for each phase of the text, by pointing out what the writer has done at each step, and asking the ideas or information that should be chosen for the new text. The students' ideas were evaluated and elaborated, and their Dong or Chinese expressions were translated into English to fit the requirements of developing joint construction. In other words, the teacher gave any language resources that the students proposed for the text, incorporating the students' ideas into a fine product.

As ideas produced for wording each phase, they were written on the blackboard. As many ideas as possible were listed for students to choose in their own writings, the teacher then guided students to discuss appropriate wordings and organize them into a sentence. Following the Plan field, in which the teacher scribed the students' ideas on the board, the students began to take more control in Use language sources for a new text. At this stage, students were asked to take turns scribing the new text on the board. Figure 5-3 presents typical organization in joint construction.

Most importantly, joint construction activities did not just support students to use the particular language features of the reading text, rather the repeated processes like detailed reading apprenticed them to recognize useful language resources in reading and writing. Moreover, metalanguage introduced at the previous learning stages was applied and reinforced as the new text being constructed.

Figure 5-3　Joint construction activity in Iteration 1

2. Negotiating wordings and sentences for the joint text

The starting point for joint construction was to select a character who was also viewed as an "excruciating idle", and "the golden" in the downtown but refused to work for man in the Dong people's mind. Characters like this in the Dong area included animals like the Dog, the Horse and the Ox. Finally, the Ox was chosen to substitute the Camel for joint construction.

Discussion began with planning field by unfolding the stages and phases. It started with the term Orientation, which has been introduced in the previous reading. The students organized its phases in a new text. The teacher provided supports for the students to propose details in each phase by pointing to the wordings in the passage of detailed reading and naming the types of language knowledge. In the interactions, Focus questions were more open for the students to propose ideas from their own repertoire. After the key elements of the field were built up, the teacher then guided the students to organize sentences and wordings.

Table 5-12 presents a typical interaction. It started with the precise preparation by the teacher for the students' recognition of the specific language pattern. Identifying the wordings and pointing to the terms "time phrase" prepared the students to propose appropriate ideas, which were followed by the teacher's affirmation and choice of the proposes. The students' proposes and the teacher's elaborations of the wordings were important steps towards individual construction.

Table 5-12 Pedagogic activities, modalities and relations in joint construction (1)

Spk	Exchange	Gloss	Phases	Matter	Sourcing	Sources	Roles	Sts
T	The Orientation of the reading text starts with a time phrase (阅读语篇中的开头部分以一个时间短语开头).	(The Orientation of the reading text starts with a time phase)	Prepare	wording	refer	text	K1	class
T	What is it?		Focus	wording	refer	text	dK1	class
Ss	In the beginning of years.		Identify	wording	read	text	K2	Ss
T	Right.		Affirm	praise				
T	So we can start with a time phrase (所以我们可以以时间短语开始).	(So we can start with a time phrase)	Prepare	wording	present	knowledge	K1	class
Ss	Long long ago, long time ago.		Propose	wording	recall	knowledge	K2	Ss
T	[Scribing] 很好, 就用 Long time ago 吧。我们写作也可以用阅读语篇中的这个短语。	Good! Let's try "Long time ago". We can also use the phrase in the reading text.	Elaborate	wording	present	knowledge	K1	class

Table 5-12 analyzes the significance of sourcing and sources in the pedagogic activities. The meanings were indicated, presented and elicited by the teacher, and read, recalled or inferred by the students. From the analysis of sourcing and source, we can see that careful preparations were efficient ways to help students to make appropriate responses, by referring to the reading texts and presenting the language features. Metalanguage was used to direct attention for students to propose ideas for the new text. All these were sufficient for the students to propose appropriate wordings, no needing of a dK1 Focus. By this stage of the lesson, the students were familiar with the pattern of interaction in the TL-R2L cycle, and thus can predict the role in the learning cycles. Metalanguage that was repetitively used to point to the language patterns promoted the students' familiarity of knowledge about English grammar.

In the next exchange, the teacher then appointed a student to scribe the wording discussed in the new text. In Table 5-13, the exchange started by the teacher appointing a student to scribe (S1), then initiating a command for S2, which was realized as a dK1 role, to read the new wording in the new text for the class. S2 interpreted it as K2 and proposed the wording again, then S1 followed her reading to write down the wording on the blackboard.

Table 5-13 Pedagogic activities and relations in joint construction (2)

Spk	Exchange	Gloss	Phases	Matter	Roles	Sts
T	现在请一位同学为我们把第一个短语写在黑板上,S1。	Now, I want a student to write the first phrase of our new text, S1.	Direct	activity	A2	S1
S1	[Coming up]				A1	
T	再请一位同学为我们读一下这个短语,S2。	Now, I want a student to read this phrase for us, S2.	Focus	wording	dK1	class
S2	Long time ago.		Propose	wording	K2	S2
S1	[Scribing]		Scribe	wording	K2	S1

Following the wording discussions, in which the teacher provided language resources and wrote them on the board, the students took more control to scribe the wordings and sentences by themselves. The students' roles were to scribe the propositions on the board and dictate the proposed wordings and sentences. Thus, the student who scribed plays the role as the scribe and the one who dictated is the role as the reciter. Students took turns playing these roles, which gave all the students the ownership of the new text. With regard to appointing to the scribe and reciter, the teacher may select the weak learner or those who did not pay attention to the class, ensuring that all students could get involved in the teaching activities. When the pointed students dictated and scribed on the board, the other students wrote on their notebooks.

Tables 5-12 and 5-13 are typical examples of joint construction interactions. The wordings were proposed by students and selected by the teacher, then wrote down by students for the new text. In some cases, more scaffolding was provided to assist in creating sentence.

Table 5-14 follows tables 5-12 and 5-13 to present how the teacher provided grammar supports after proposing wording in order to make complete sentence and prepare for later individual writing. Here the teacher reinforced the function of commas to mark phrases and extended the students' knowledge about the punctuation.

In Table 5-14, the class discussed the use of punctuation when creating the first sentence in the orientation of the new text. The exchange began by the teacher focusing the students' attention on the use of punctuation after the phrase, by referring to the new text. Then the teacher elaborated the use of commas that functions as the end of the starting phrase in a sentence, like "In the beginning of years" or "Long time ago". In this interaction, translanguaging strategies were employed to assist the students in understanding and accessing new terms and knowledge. Chinese was used to focus the students' attention and elaborate new knowledge about English punctuation. Terms were also translated into English to reinforce the English metalanguage and prepare for the next step.

Table 5-14 Pedagogic activities and relations in joint construction (2)

Spk	Exchange	Gloss	Phases	Matter	Sourcing	Sources	Roles	Sts
T	这个短语后面需要什么标点符号(punctuation)? Right, comma.	What punctuation do we need after the phrase?	Focus	grammar	refer	new text	dK1	class
Ss	逗号。[S1 scribes]	Comma.	Propose	grammar	present	knowledge	K2	Ss
T	逗号标记短语(phrases)结束,它还标记了小句(clauses)。	Commas mark the end of phrases. They also mark clauses.	Elaborate	grammar	present	knowledge	K1	class

Another way of scaffolding in the program was comparing the grammatical realizations of meanings in different languages. In table 5-15, the class was negotiating the next sentence in the orientation, about the place of the setting. After reviewing the language patterns in the reading text, the students proposed wordings for the new text. The teacher then elaborated English grammar by comparing the grammatical features of prepositional group in L1, L2 and L3. All these were sufficient scaffolding for the students to propose a prepositional phrase in English, which was approved and used in the new sentence by the teacher.

In Table 5-15, the teacher provided support for the students to acquire knowledge about English grammar by comparing the structure of a prepositional phrase in L1, L2 and L3. In Chinese, the preposition is normally placed at the end of the phrase, while it is in front of the phrase in English, and the case in Dong is the same. By the careful preparations that the teacher presented her grammar knowledge as K1 complex while reminding the students' own language knowledge, the students can easily infer an appropriate wording without a dK1 Focus.

Table 5-15 Pedagogic activities, modalities and relations in joint construction (4)

Spk	Exchange	Gloss	Phases	Matter	Sourcing	Sources	Roles	Sts
T	Where did the Ox live?		Focus	wording	refer	new text	dK1	class
Ss	水边,河边,溪边……	*by the river, by the stream...*	Propose	wording	recall	knowledge	K2	Ss
T	Good, "by the river", "by the stream" in English.		Affirm	approve	present	knowledge	K1	class
T	英语介词短语中的介词 "in""by""on"在短语最前面,如"by the river"中的"by",这与汉语相反,与侗语相同。在阅读语篇中,介词短语"on the edge of the desert"意为"在沙漠边",所以"在河边"可以怎么表示?	*Prepositions like "in", "by", "on" are usually put in front of the phrases in English, such as "by" in the phrase of "by the river", which contrasts to Chinese while is the same with Dong. In the reading text, the prepositional phase "on the edge of the desert" means "zai sha mo bian", so how to say "zai he bian"?*	Elaborate Focus	grammar wording	refer	reading text	=K1 dK1	class
Ss	On the edge of the river.		Propose	wording	infer	prior move	K2	class
T	Yes, excellent! 这句话,我们就用"by the river"。	*We will use "by the river" in this sentence.*	Affirm Elaborate	wording	present	knowledge	K1' K1	class

After preparing the sentence patterns in the reading text and proposing the wordings, a new sentence was created as shown in Table 5-16. This exchange dealt with grammar knowledge in terms of verbal tense. The teacher guided students to compare the verbal groups in clauses in L2 and L3. In Chinese, there is no need to change verbal tense to construe a Process in the past time, but in English the verb should be changed into the form of the past tense. The careful preparations assisted students in recognizing the changed verbal form, as negotiated in sentence making.

In Table 5-16, the teacher prepared the students to identify the verbal tense change in the sentence of the new story, by pointing out the grammatical differences between Chinese and English sentences. The teacher further elaborated the tense change in story writing to prepare the students for the next sentence writing and further independent writing. Translanguaging strategies were used to not only assist the students in full comprehension of the grammar knowledge by comparing the previously acquired knowledge with the newly learned knowledge, but also avoid negative transfer from their familiar language knowledge.

Table 5-16　Pedagogic activities and modalities in joint construction（5）

Spk	Exchange	Gloss	Phases	Matter	Sourcing	Sources
T	So what's our next sentence? He lived...?		Focus	sentence	refer	new text
Ss	He lived on the edge of the river.		Propose	sentence	infer	prior move
T	Excellent. 汉语句中动词没有时态变化，而英语中，我们说过，在表示过去行为的动词要用过去式，这句话的动词"live"的过去式是？	*There is no change of verbs in Chinese, while in English, we have learned, verbs need to be changed into past tense to show the past process. So what's the past tense of the verb "live" in this sentence?*	Affirm Elaborate	approve grammar	present	knowledge
S3	Lived.		Propose	wording	infer	prior lesson
T	Exactly! Lived! 故事类写作通常描述过去的事情，因此句中的动词通常用过去时。	*Story genres usually describe the past events; thus we need to change the verbs into past tense in the sentences.*	Affirm Elaborate	approve grammar	present	knowledge

3. The jointly constructed texts

In Iteration 1, each class jointly created a new story in English in joint construction. The jointly constructed texts were seen as the standard writing model that the students were to independently construct texts for their final task. The jointly constructed texts followed the same stages and phases of the reading text, i.e. Orientation—Complication—Resolution, in which problems raised and resolved, tensions built and released with new protagonist and field, presenting one complete and interesting story. They were less detailed than the reading text, without sentence-by-sentence rewriting following the original patterns, as the main goal was simply to practice the structuring of a whole text for the new learners, and there may be no enough time to expand every detail like the reading text. In addition, some language resources, knowledge and writing devices obtained from the reading text have also been practiced in the process of creating the new text. Besides field differences described above, other differences in Iteration 1 texts from the original texts were language resources, patterns and discourses, which were negotiated through joint construction activities.

Two texts from the two classes are presented here. Both texts narrated stories about how the Ox began to work for the Man but with slight differences in terms of the plots of the stories. Text 5-5 is from Class 1, and Text 5-6 from Class 2. The comparison of the two texts illustrates that joint construction is a significant step, directing both classes to produce complete high staking folk stories in English as far as the TL-GBP program is concerned, and it is also a crucial step towards the students' independent construction.

Text 5-5   The jointly constructed text of Class 1

Long time ago, when the world was brand new, there was an Ox, and he lived on the edge of the river, because he did not want to work. He liked to take a bath, most excruciatingly idle.

One day, the Ox did not want to work, and he went to the river to take a bath. And he stamped the Crab accidentally. The Crab cried with pain. That made the Crab very angry.

Presently, the Crab nipped the Ox's nose. The Ox cried with pain.

The Man came to the river, and he put the Crab in the river, and put the rope into the Ox's nose.

Text 5-6   The jointly constructed text of Class 2

In the beginning of years, when the world was so new, there was an Ox, and he lived on the edge of a river, because he did not want to work. So he ate grass. He liked to take a bath and he was happy every day.

Presently the Dog came to him, with a bone in his mouth, and said, "come and fetch and you can eat bone".

The Ox said "Moo" and stamped the Dog. That made the Dog very angry.

Presently, the Dog called the bird to bite the Ox's nose. And the Ox cried with pain. The Man heard the Ox's cries and came to him. He put the rope into the Ox's nose.

And from that day to this the Ox always wears a rope. And he began to work for Man.

The two stories have almost the same Orientation and Resolution, but greatly different Complications. They have also different language features in terms of wordings and sentences even with the same content at some stages. Table 5-17 compares the first passage (the Orientation) of Texts 5-5 and 5-6. Both texts began with time phrases: "Long time ago and In the beginning of years". After the first phrase, the next three sentences were almost the same, except for the words to intensify new, in text 5-5 "brand" and in text 5-6 "so". Next, Text 5-6 had one more sentence "So he ate grass". The last sentences were differently constructed but referring to the same setting: "most excruciatingly idle and he was happy every day".

Table 5-17 Comparison of sentences in Texts 5-5 and 5-6

[Text 5-5]	[Text 5-6]
Long time ago,	In the beginning of years,
when the world was brand new,	when the world was so new,
there was an Ox, and he lived on the edge of the river, because he did not want to work.	there was an Ox, and he lived on the edge of a river, because he did not want to work.
He liked to take a bath, most excruciatingly idle.	So he ate grass. He liked to take a bath and he was happy every day.

4. Handing over the control to students

Various kinds of guidance were provided by the teacher for different tasks. After careful preparations and discussions, most wordings and sentences were clear to recite and scribe. It was sufficient for the teacher to point or direct the students to recite the sentences and spell the wordings. In such case, the teacher handed over the responsibility to the class to recite for the scribe. On some occasions, when the scribes were weak learners or the sentences were long or difficult for the scribes, the teacher may direct the reciter's attention to a particular wording or repeat it for the scribe.

Table 5-18 presents an example of such a case. This exchange comprised two learning cycles. In the first cycle, the teacher directed S2 to recite for S1 in scribing the first phrase of the sentence and focused her attention on the first letter. The reciter did not immediately respond, but the scribe began to write a small "l" without noticing that the first letter should be the capital "L". In the second cycle, when the teacher focused the reciter's attention on the first letter case again (dK1), the scribe was not sure about the writing, and looked expectantly at the reciter. This time, the reciter identified the capital "L" (K2), then the scribe wrote the word (K2 ∗). The teacher immediately affirmed both the reciter and the scribe in one K1' move.

Table 5-18 Pedagogic activities and pedagogic relations in joint construction (6)

Spk	Exchange	Gloss	Phases	Matter	Roles	Sts
T	请帮助 S1 写下第一个短语"Long time ago"。	Help S1 to write the first phrase "Long time ago".	Direct	activity	A2	S2
T	请注意句子中第一个单词的首字母是否要大写？	Please check whether the first letter of the sentence is capital?	Focus	letter	dK1	S2
S2	[No response]					
S1	[Scribing "long" with a small "L"]		Scribe		K2	
T	"L"应该大写还是小写？	Is the "L" capital or small?	Focus	letter	dK1	S2
S2	大写。	Capital.	Identify	spelling	K2	
S1	[Erasing the small "l" and scribing "long" with a capital "L"]		Scribe		=K2*	S1
T	Yes, right!		Affirm	approve	K1'	S1, S2

On other occasions, the scribe wrote the wording incorrectly, and other students noticed the error and reacted to it. Table 5-19 presents such an exchange. This sample was taken from the iteration in Class 2. After the teacher directed the reciter to identify the sentence, the scribe wrote and made a mistake when scribing "world". Other students yelled at this mistake. The teacher then stepped in and directed the reciter to be responsible for the correct writing.

Table 5-19 Pedagogic activities and pedagogic relations in joint construction (7)

Spk	Exchange	Gloss	Phases	Matter	Roles	Sts
T	S5,下一句话是什么？	S5, what's the next sentence?	Focus	sentence	dK1	S5
S5	When the world was so new.		Identify/Dictate	sentence	K2	S5
S4	[Scribing world incorrectly]		Scribe			S4
Ss	[Yelling "错了,错了"]	[It's wrong, it's wrong.]	Reject	wording	=K2*	Ss
T	是谁负责这句话的？	Who is responsible for this sentence?	Direct	behavior	K2f	class
T	请负责"world"的拼写。	Be responsible for the spelling of "world".		behavior	K1	class
S5	W-O-R-L-D.		Dictate	spelling	A2	S5
S4	[Correcting]		Scribe	wording	dA1	S4
T	Excellent!		Affirm	approve	K1'	S4, S5

There were two learning cycles in this exchange. In the first cycle, the teacher asked the reciter to dictate the sentence for the scribe (dK1). After the reciter did the task (K2), the scribe began to write but spelt one word incorrectly (K2*), and some students followed up the K2 to remind S4 of the mistake (K2f). The teacher then responded by rejecting the behavior with a rhetorical question, i. e. "Who is responsible for this sentence", which explicitly meant "no one spells for the scribe, so it is not her fault". This rejection triggered a further cycle. In this cycle, the teacher first directed the class to take the responsibility to spell for the scribe (A2). After the reciter spelt the word for the scribe and the scribe corrected the word (K2), the teacher simultaneously affirmed both the reciter and the scribe as K1' role.

The exchanges like Tables 5-18 and 5-19 are typical activities in joint construction, in which students took control of negotiating the meanings in English. As the reciter identified and dictated the wording, the scribe recognized it and wrote it in a right way. In the exchanges, the teacher initiated the activity as A2 to demand for an action, while what was negotiated was the exchange of knowledge. Knowledge was embedded in the action of the exchange since the English sentence patterns and wordings like "when the world was so new" are the language resources that the students were expected to grasp for their later independent writing. Therefore, in Tables 5-18 and 5-19, the teacher's Direct to the activity was treated as A2, but the students' Identify/Dictate as K2, and their scribe as K2*. The asterisk was used to indicate the response in a written form.

5. Reflections on joint construction

In the intervention, the students were most enthusiastic about the activities in joint construction. Everyone had opportunities to come and write on the blackboard. Most importantly, everyone was able to make a contribution to their jointly written text. In both classes, all students actively engaged in the activities, to propose meanings and wordings, to take turns reciting and scribing, and to support each other. In Class 1, when the lesson ran out of time, the students still did not want to stop, and showed the disappointment when told to do the activities in the next class.

Joint construction was a crucial step to hand over control of learning tasks to the students. In this step, the frame was weakened and the students were given the agentive roles as reciters and scribes. The reciters read and spelt the sentences and wordings, and the scribe wrote them, while the other students would look, listen and transcribe as their own copies. In this way, all learning tasks were accomplished in manageable steps. Rather than doing the tasks for each component of the language knowledge in isolation, as in vocabulary and grammar exercises, the students learned the language patterns and KAL in a meaningful context of the whole texts. Furthermore, knowledge was built and reinforced in a translanguaging way. During this process, as they negotiated the language patterns and knowledge several times in different languages, they can fully understand and master them.

In the interviews, the students commented that the use of metalanguage and the learning of KAL helped them organize and shape their writing, such as terms like Orientation and setting for stages and phases in writing genre structure, thing and quality for components in sentence structure. Text 5-7 shows an example.

Text 5-7　Interviews: metalinguistic terms

S1: 我现在知道记叙文的结构了, 知道先写故事的开头, 再写故事的经过, 最后要有结局才完整, 以前不知道, 写的作文也是不完整的。

S1: Now I know the structure of narrative, and know how to write Orientation, and Complication, then Resolution. I didn't know it before, so my writings before were not complete.

S2: 比以前简单。从句子到段落到整个文章的练习, 我们知道了句子的成分, 也知道了它们怎么构成句子。

S2: (Writing) becomes easier. In the practices from sentence to paragraph to the whole essay, we know the components of a sentence and how to make sentence with these components.

S3: 知道怎样写了。现在知道写故事时句子中的动词要变为过去式, 也知道怎么变换。

S3: (Now I know) how to write. I know verbs in sentences should be changed into past tense when writing a story, and how to change the verb tense.

The students also commented on the benefits in terms of social aspects, such as building multilingual learners' identities, developing a supportive classroom community even sustaining the minority language community. Text 5-8 shows an example.

Text 5-8　Interviews: social aspects

S4: 感觉很好。在课堂上跟同学共同完成任务, 互相帮助, 感觉很好玩。

S4: I feel so good. It was interesting to do the tasks cooperatively and help each other.

S5: 与同学用自己的语言交流, 我变得不害羞了。被老师叫起来也不怕了。

S5: We talked in our own language, and I was not so shy like before. And I was not afraid of being asked in front of the class by the teacher.

S6: 与以前不一样,因为课堂可以很开心。我对班上同学有更多的了解,与朋友也更亲近了。

S6: It is different, because English class was fun! I got to know other students better, and got closer with friends.

From the above, we can see joint construction activities helped the students take control not only of learning knowledge, but also of their agency. The repeated translanguaging practices among L1, L2 and L3 assisted the students in developing deeper understandings and grasping the new languaging more easily. In this way, the students were given the agentive roles to claim language practices. As a result, a democratic and supportive classroom community was constructed, which was a significant step towards an equal and effective teaching and learning.

Other advantages were also observed by involving struggling learners as the scribes. It was often the case that the noisier students were often pointed to fill the roles with the focus of managing classroom. The classroom activities can be also managed by asking the struggling or disengaged students to act the scribe roles, which ensured that every student would benefit from the activities. In both classes, for example, there were many struggling students who wanted to try but did not have the courage, which showed that they were aware of the benefits of being the scribes. In a word, equally distributing the roles as the scribes to the students could maximize both advantages of achievement and management.

To reflect on joint construction activities, one aspect that could be improved is to allow more time for checking and editing after writing. A few grammatical and vocabulary errors were found in the new text because of time limitations for checking. For example, Text 5-6 had errors such as "you can eat bone". These problems can be solved by the ways of the class reading the sentence aloud after it was written and reading the whole text aloud when it was finished, followed by checking and revising.

5.1.5 Towards Iteration 2

Through the first iteration of the TL-R2L cycle, the students have built up knowledge about narrative genre, ideas of field, language devices and discourse patterns that realize the knowledge in texts, and grammar and vocabulary in both Chinese and English. By translanguaging practices in the knowledge exchanges of the learning cycle, the students have fully obtained access to language knowledge in their L1, L2 and L3. At this point, the students have two models of narrative writings in English—the reading text and the jointly constructed one, and numerous translanguaged ideas.

The accumulated knowledge of language and topics provided high level of supports for the next iteration, which started with reading bilingual texts in Dong and Chinese about a Dong folk story (Chinese reading text only for Class 1). The topic was what the students were assigned to write. This is the final iterative cycle before the students write their stories independently, aiming to facilitate students to practice the new languaging ways in English through translanguaging strategies, on the basis of knowledge acquired in the first iteration.

5.2　Iteration 2

Rather than starting with a reading text in English in Iteration 1, Iteration 2 began with bilingual texts in Dong and Chinese (Dong reading text is an ethnic folk story, Chinese reading text is the translated one, see Appendix Ⅲ) for Class 2 and Chinese reading text only for Class 1, because Class 2 are mainly Dong students while Class 1 are not. The learning sequence, from the preceding English-oriented iteration to this mother language iteration, aimed to firstly prepare the students to access the English reading text and then to re-instantiate their own folk stories into high staking English narrative, and moreover, to know Dong written scripts. Since Iteration 1 has thoroughly prepared them with genre and field, together with discourse, grammar and vocabulary through detailed reading, sentence making and joint construction activities, in Iteration 2, more scaffolding in writing based on translanguaging from Dong to English would be provided to prepare for the students' independent writing.

The lesson staging was slightly adjusted to fit the mother-tongue-orientation in Iteration 2. While the language foci on language strata and features remained the same in most steps, the significant change was that one more step was needed, i.e. translating from L1 and L2 to L3, because bilingual reading texts need to be translated in English. In addition, translanguaging strategies were more frequently used in knowledge exchanges, with English involved more in terms of pedagogic discourse.

In this section, two steps of Iteration 2 are the foci of the examinations, i.e. detailed reading and joint construction. For one thing, bilingual reading texts were deconstructed and notes were translated in English in detailed reading, and then reconstructed as English text in joint construction. For another thing, greater incidence of translanguaging practices was found in the two steps than other steps.

5.2.1 Detailed reading

The purposes of detailed reading in Iteration 2 were to identify items and translate them into English. As in Iteration 1, the foci of language strata in detailed reading are also discourse and sentence patterns of the reading text in Iteration 2, but in this cycle the highlighted items were re-instantiated in English. In iteration 1, translanguaging strategies such as code-switching, translation or bilingual instruction were commonly used to provide scaffolding for students to get involved into the lesson activities without semiotic load and emotional stress. Through all activities in Iteration 1, the students were quite familiar with the stages and phases of the learning cycle, the teacher's instruction in each phase, as well as the metalanguage used to refer to the language feature. Thus, in Iteration 2, the instruction in most phases to direct students' task can be conducted mainly in English only, but multilingual instructions were primarily used in the exchange of knowledge such as the Elaborate phase. In addition, translanguaging strategies were mainly used for scaffolding the re-instantiation of L1, L2 into L3.

The lesson sequence of detailed reading in Iteration 2 was Preview, Read sentence—Identify wordings—Re-instantiate wordings in English—Review field, language. It was found that students were quite familiar with the discourse patterns of the interaction so that they can follow the teacher's instruction in English and complete the learning tasks successfully in each phase. In addition, the bilingual texts presented side-by-side assisted students in identifying Dong wordings successfully even though they didn't know the written scripts before.

1. Translanguaging practices in the exchange

In Iteration 2, multilingual practices of the alternative use of L1, L2 and L3 in detailed reading were designed for several purposes (L1 was used only in Class 2, the Dong Class). Firstly, the interplay of L1, L2 and L3 was to ensure the continual success in identifying the wordings in both L1 and L2. Secondly, as they have already been familiar with the discourse patterns and metalanguage of the interactions, L3 could be used more often in this learning cycle. In principle, L3 was used as the main instruction in Prepare and Focus phases, while sometimes language shift was needed to direct students' attention. By this way, the knowledge about English and metalanguage can be reinforced. Moreover, reading bilingual texts and identifying the key terms of the field in L1 and L2 in Class 2 could facilitate Dong minority students to learn one language from another, and ultimately facilitate the learning of two languages. In this case, it was mainly the use of Chinese that promote the learning of Dong written scripts.

Table 5-20 analyzes the typical exchange, taken from Class 1. The class was negotiating the time element in the first sentence of the story. The teacher first focused the students' attention by referring to the sentence of L2 reading text in L3, and prepared the sentence by referring to it in L2, then read it aloud. After the preparation, the teacher specified the students' task in L3, by asking the question "when the story happened". For this kind of question had been done several times in the previous iteration, and they knew well the item to be identified, it was a relatively easy task for them to identify. One student answered it quickly in L2, and the teacher approved it in L3.

Table 5-20 Pedagogic activities, modalities and relations in detailed reading of Iteration 2(1)

Spk	Exchange	Gloss	Phases	Matter	Souring	Sources	Roles	Sts
T	Please look at the first sentence as I read it.		Prepare	sentence	refer L3	L2 text	A2	class
T	这一句。[Reading]很久很久以前,螃蟹的身子并不扁,背上是光滑的,脚也长在肚皮下,行走时是向前爬,而不是横着爬的。	This one. Long time ago, the crab was not flat, and his back was smooth, his feet under his belly, so he walked forward but not across.	Prepare	sentence	refer L2 read L2	L2 text	K1 dK1	class class
T	Please find out when the story happened?		Focus	wording	refer L2	L2 text		
S6	很久很久以前。	Long time ago.	Identify	wording	read L2	L2 text	K2	S6
T	OK, great!		Affirm	approve			K1'	S6

As tasks in detailed reading of Iteration 2 were relatively easy, the target language (L3) was used as more as possible in their already familiar interaction patterns in order to practice and reinforce the ways of English languaging in a natural context. The purpose of translanguaging practices between L2 and L3 in the teacher's role was to ensure that the students could attend to the task of reading sentence as soon as possible, without struggling to interpret the teacher's L3 instruction.

In Class 2, except for identifying items in the Chinese reading text, the students have one more task in detailed reading, i.e. identifying items in the Dong reading text too. The exchange in Class 2 is shown in Table 5-21. As we can see, the students' tasks were to read the sentence and identify items in L1 and L2, so the teacher prepared the sentence in both L1 and L2 by reading it aloud in both languages. The teacher then focused the wording in L3. The students reacted to this question quickly by identifying the Chinese wording, but did not respond to Dong sentence. The teacher then focused the task by asking a code-mixing question in both Dong and Chinese. This time, one student identified the wording in Dong rightly. The teacher affirmed both the Chinese and Dong answers in English.

Table 5-21 Pedagogic activities, modalities and relations in detailed reading of Iteration 2 (2)

Spk	Exchange	Gloss	Phases	Matter	Souring	Sources	Roles	Sts
T	Now I want you to focus on the first sentence. Please look at the sentence as I read it.		Prepare	sentence	refer L1, L2	text	A2	class
T	这一句。[Reading] Xic unv, jih xenp xangh eis biees, ul laic kop kongk, dingl buh beeuv nyaoh dees longc, qamt saengc eis qamt weengc.	This one.	Prepare	sentence	refer L1, L2; read L1	text	K1	class
	很久很久以前,螃蟹的身子并不扁,背上是光滑的,脚也长在肚皮下,行走时是向前爬,而不是横着爬行。	Long time ago, the crab was not flat, and his back was smooth, his feet under his belly, so he walked forward but not across.			read L2	text		
T	Can you find when the story happened? When?		Focus	wording	refer L1, L2	text	dK1	class
S7	很久很久以前。	Long time ago.	Identify	wording	read L2	text	K2	S7
T	Xic nup? (侗语语篇)	When? (in Dong text)					dK1	
S8	Xic unv.	Long time ago.			read L1	text	K2	S8
T	OK, great!		Affirm	approve			K1'	S7, S8

Time phrase is an element of the setting phase at the Orientation stage of the text. This item has been negotiated in the previous iteration so that the students knew it well and could be directly instructed to the learning activities in L3. If the lexical items were new for them, L1 and L2 were used to begin the exchange in Prepare and Focus phases. At last, these items would be re-instantiated in L3 in the Elaborate phase.

In Table 5-22, most students didn't know the item in English, so the teacher directed the task by asking the question in English, and translated it in L1 and L2. This translanguaging strategy was to reduce the students' semiotic load, as well as to prepare for the re-instantiation of L1 and L2 items into L3. The students' task was to identify first the L2 item then the L1 item. So the teacher prepared and focused the task in L1 again. By this way, the students identified the items both in L1 and L2, followed by the teacher's strong praise in L3.

Table 5-22 Pedagogic activities, modalities and relations in detailed reading of Iteration 2(3)

Spk	Exchange	Gloss	Phases	Matter	Souring	Sources	Roles	Sts
T	下一个。 Please focus on the same sentence.	Next.	Prepare	sentence	refer L2 refer L3	text	A2 =A2	class
T	How did the Crab crawl before? 螃蟹从前是怎样爬行的？	How did the Crab crawl before?	Focus	wording	refer L2	text	dK1	class
S9	向前爬。	Crawling forward	Identify	wording	read L2	text	K2	S9
T	Il nup qamt kuenp xic unv?	How did the Crab crawl before?	Focus	wording	refer L1	text	dK1	class
S10	Qamt saengc eis qamt weegc.	Crawling forward, not sideways.	Identify	wording	read L1	text	K2	S10
T	OK, very good!		Affirm	praise				S9, S10

The translanguaging practices in layering the exchange for different linguistic goals took place repeatedly in Iteration 2. Such practices, like the ways of the students' daily communication, assisted them in completing different language tasks easily, and at the same time practicing English languaging and introducing new items in English in a meaningful context. By this way, the whole process in the learning activities went through successfully and quickly, providing well preparations for the task of re-instantiation into L3 in the next Elaborate phase.

2. Re-instantiation in the Elaborate phase

In Iteration 1, translanguaging strategies were used in the Elaborate phase of the learning cycle to build understandings and metalanguage. In Iteration 2, they were used to re-instantiate L1 and L2 into L3, as well as to negotiate meanings in L3.

Table 5-23 shows how L1 and L2 were re-instantiated to L3 in Elaborate phase, following the pronunciation. This exchange follows the exchanges in Tables 5-19 and 5-20, after L1 and L2 wordings were identified, to re-instantiate the time phrase into English. As the time phrase has been previously discussed in Iteration 1, Elaborate in the exchange engaged the students interactively, by the teacher reminding the students the knowledge learned in the previous lesson. The teacher first prepared the wording in L2 and focused the task by asking a question in English and interpreting it in Chinese. The careful preparation helped the students re-instantiate the wording into L3 successfully by recalling knowledge from the prior lesson.

Table 5-23 Pedagogic activities, modalities and relations in detailed reading of Iteration 2 (4)

Spk	Exchange	Gloss	Phases	Matter	Souring	Sources	Roles	Sts
T	故事发生在很久以前。	The story happened long time ago.	Prepare	wording	refer	text	K1	class
T	How to say it in English (用英语怎么说这个时间短语)? 上次阅读和写作中,我们学会了哪些短语?	(How to say in English) What phrases have we learned before?	Focus	wording	remind	prior lesson	dK1	class
S11	In the beginning of years.		Propose	wording	recall	prior lesson	K2	S11
S12	Long time ago.							S12
T	OK, very good!		Affirm	praise	present	knowledge	K1'	Ss
	[Scribing these phrases on board]		Scribe	wording			A1	class
T	Please read "In the beginning of years".		Prepare/ Focus	pronunciation	present	knowledge	dK1	class
Ss	[Pronouncing] In the beginning of years.		Rehearse	pronunciation	recall	knowledge	K2	Ss
T	Well done! In the beginning of years.		Affirm	praise, repeat			K1'	class

After the re-instantiation, the phrase was elaborated by the teacher in terms of spelling and pronunciation, followed by the students' pronunciation in response, and the teacher's affirmation by praising and repeating. The elaboration in English in this exchange not only prepared the students for joint construction in English, but also provided language resources for them in writing English sentences.

In other cases, the students may not have the knowledge about the corresponding L3 wordings of the identified L1 and L2 items, so more support is needed to provide L3 wordings to scaffold them to re-instantiate L1 and L2 into L3. In Table 5-24, the class has just identified the wordings from the bilingual texts "向前爬" and "qamt saengc". The task was to re-instantiate L1 and L2 wordings into L3. The teacher first pointed to them, and re-instantiated them in L3 "crawl forward". She then compared the meaning and structure of this verbal group in L1, L2 and L3, and elaborated it with English pronunciation. The students followed the L3 pronunciation without being commanded. The teacher affirmed it by praising and repeating it.

Table 5-24 Pedagogic activities, modalities and relations in detailed reading of Iteration 2 (5)

Spk	Exchange	Gloss	Phases	Matter	Souring	Sources	Roles	Sts
T	这里讲了螃蟹向前爬, qamt saengc。	*Here, crawl forward.*	Prepare	wording	refer L1, L2	text	K1	class
	向前爬,英语为 crawl forward, crawl 意为"爬",即侗语中的 qamt, forward 指"向前",即 saengc。可见,英语动词短语 crawl forward 词序与侗语 qamt saengc 一致,与汉语"向前爬"语序相反。	*In English, crawl forward, crawl means "爬" in Chinese, "qamt" in Dong. Forward means "向前", namely "saengc". We can see English verbal wording is different from Chinese and the same with Dong.*	Elaborate	wording	present	knowledge	K1	class
T	[Scribing "crawl forward" on the board]		Scribe	wording	present	knowledge	A1	class
T	Crawl forward.		Prepare/Focus	pronunciation	present	knowledge	dK1	class
Ss	[Pronouncing] Crawl forward.		Rehearse	pronunciation	recall	knowledge	K2	Ss
T	Great! Crawl forward.				praise, repeat		K1'	class

Table 5-24 illustrates the significance of translanguaging strategy for managing L3 re-instantiation and learning. As can be seen in the analysis, L3 wording and meaning were negotiated and re-instantiated through the comparison of L1, L2 and L3. The teacher first prepared the meanings of the bilingual wordings by referring to them before presenting the corresponding L3 verbal group, then compared the meaning and grammar of the English wording with Chinese and Dong respectively. The interplay of L1, L2 and L3 provided powerful support for the students to build word meanings and grammar knowledge about English.

3. Reflections on detailed reading

With regard to the translanguaging practices, it can be argued that more practices of using English as the only medium of instruction in the learning cycles of detailed reading was successful in directing the students to complete the learning tasks. The students also kept active in taking part in the learning activities. In the Elaborate phases, they could independently re-instantiate L1 and L2 to L3 by connecting it with their prior learned knowledge. In addition, the translanguaging strategy of comparing different languages assisted the students in accessing English vocabulary and grammar knowledge. In the interviews, the students commented that by comparing the words in different languages, they can easily grasp the new English wordings and recall the English knowledge learned in Iteration 1.

In Class 2, the students made a number of comments on Dong language and their agency. For examples, the reading of bilingual texts assisted them in learning Dong spoken language and written scripts, and the application of Dong language and culture made all students feel included. Moreover, the translation of Dong folk story into English arose their sense of ethnic identification and responsibility to claim for their language and culture. Text 5-8 shows an example.

Text 5-8　Interviews：Dong language

S1：(侗语)方言之间有点不同,如果只听录音都听不懂,对照侗汉语篇,就能听懂了。

S1：The dialects (of Dong) are slightly different. If I only listened to the record, I can't understand. But when I read the Dong and Chinese bilingual reading texts, I can get it.

S2：以前从来没有见过侗文,没有想到就像老师所说的,侗文就像拼音一样这么简单,对照汉语语篇,我就大概能看懂了。

S2：I have never seen the Dong written scripts before, and never thought that the Dong written scripts were so easy, just like Chinese pinyin, as the teacher have told us. If I compared them with Chinese, I can understand them.

S3：很有趣,在英语课上还能够学习侗文,我们自己的文字。很喜欢,有必要学习。

S3：Interesting, we can learn Dong, our own language, in English lesson. I really like it, it's necessary to learn the Dong written scripts.

S4：侗语和侗族故事不仅使我们对英语学习更感兴趣,更重要的是将侗语与英语联系起来,我们觉得学习更有意义。

Dong language and story brought us more interest in learning English. More importantly, the connection between Dong and English made us feel that learning became more meaningful.

S5：应该用侗文,很有意义。我们侗族的故事很有意思,应该翻译出去。

Dong could be used in English, it's meaningful. Our Dong story is very interesting, and it should be translated.

To reflect on detailed reading in Iteration 2, one stage that has been overlooked was the presentation of multilingual notes. To finish the learning cycles quickly, the teacher wrote down only the re-instantiated English notes on the board, but not the identified Chinese and Dong wordings. It can be seen that more emphasis was put on L3 English in Iteration 2. Although the students could compare the Chinese and Dong wordings from the bilingual reading texts with the English notes on the board, to reinforce additive trilingual learning, more time should be allowed to write down multilingual notes on the board, and then compare them and read them aloud.

5.2.2 Joint construction

A notable difference between Iteration 2 and Iteration 1 was that the language resources, i.e. the re-instantiated English notes, have already been presented on the blackboard, so there was no need to negotiate a new field.

1. Lesson activity: Realizing re-instantiation

The goal of joint construction in Iteration 2, different from that in Iteration 1, is to practice writing by rewriting a story directly from the re-instantiated L3 notes and a given field. The stages include Deconstruct model—Using L3 notes for a new text—Review genre, language. At the Deconstruct model stage, the teacher previewed the stages and phases of the story for the jointly constructed text. The core stages for the text are Orientation—Complication—Resolution. The jointly written story in Iteration 2 used the same information resources in bilingual reading texts, and re-instantiated L3 language resources from L1 and L2 in detailed reading.

The lesson activities were almost the same with those in Iteration 1. The teacher first guided the students to discuss the wording and sentence to be written in the new text. After the wording or sentence was approved, the teacher pointed the students to recite and scribe the wording or sentence on the blackboard. The typical lesson activity is presented in Figure 5-4 below.

Figure 5-4　Typical activity in joint construction in Iteration 2

The major difference from Iteration 1 was that the ideas and wordings were already presented as L3 notes in detailed reading. Therefore, the re-construction of a new story and negotiation of the idea choices became the re-expression of bilingual texts into L3 wordings and sentences.

2. Re-expressing bilingual texts in L3

In joint construction, the teacher guided students to re-construct sentences in L3 by referring to the re-instantiated L3 notes. In addition, L3 sentence patterns and grammar were also negotiated and built by inferring to the knowledge learned from the prior lessons. In terms of the language use, by the same way, if the new sentence followed the language patterns learned in the previous lesson or it was relatively simple, more L3 could be used. But sometimes in Elaborate phases, more L2 would be used to support students' understandings and deepen their impressions.

In Table 5-25, the class was making a new sentence by using the L3 notes "flat" and "smooth". The teacher first directed the students' attention by using L2 order, and then prepared the students in two steps. First, she presented the knowledge that the sentence was about the Crab's qualities by referring to the L3 notes, then she reminded them of the wordings of the qualities also by pointing to the L3 notes. As the sentence was relatively simple and the language point has already built in the previous lesson, this preparation was sufficient for the students to propose the new sentence. The teacher affirmed the students' response with praise, and repeated the two students' proposals in a complete sentence by adding a conjunction "and".

Table 5-25　Pedagogic activities, modalities and relations in joint construction of Iteration 2(1)

Spk	Exchange	Gloss	Phases	Matter	Souring	Sources	Roles	Sts
T	现在,请注意听。	Now listen.	Direct	attention	refer	L3 notes	A2	class
T	In this sentence, we talk about the qualities of the Crab.		Prepare	wording	remind	prior lesson	K1	class
T	What was the Crab like and how about his back before?		Focus	wording	point/infer	L3 notes	K1	class
S13	The Crab was not flat.		Propose			prior lesson/ L3 notes	K2	S13
S14	His back was smooth.						K2	S14
T	Well-done! So this sentence is "the Crab was not flat, and his back was smooth".		Affirm	praise/ repeat			K1'	S13, S14

In this exchange, as we can see, because the task was relatively easy, Chinese was only used at the beginning of the learning cycle to focus the students' attention, and English was used to direct all knowledge exchange. As the learning activities in Iteration 1 have provided knowledge foundation for the students, they successfully proposed the sentence "the Crab was not flat, his back was smooth" in English instruction.

Next, the proposed sentence was recited and scribed like the way in Iteration 1. In the following learning cycle in Table 5-26, the teacher reviewed the grammar knowledge by engaging the students interactively. The teacher first prepared the students the grammar knowledge by asking them to recall the knowledge from the prior lesson. One student proposed the wording "and" by referring to the sentence. The teacher then prepared specifically the grammatical function of the word "and" by reminding the students of the knowledge from the prior lesson. Another student proposed the grammatical item in Chinese, followed by the teacher's praise and repeating in both Chinese and English.

Table 5-26 Pedagogic activities, modalities and relations in joint construction of Iteration 2 (2)

Spk	Exchange	Gloss	Phases	Matter	Souring	Sources	Roles	Sts
T	请注意,两个小句之间需要加一个什么词?	*Attention, what word do we need between two clauses?*	Prepare/ Focus	grammar	remind	prior lesson	K1	class
S15	And.		Propose	grammar	refer	sentence	K2	S15
T	"And" 连接两个小句,因此属于什么词?	*"And" links two clauses, so what kind of word is it?*	Prepare	grammar	remind	prior lesson	K1	class
S16	连词。	*Conjunction.*	Propose	grammar	infer	prior lesson	K2	S16
T	Smart! 连词(conjunction)。	*Conjunction*	Affirm	praise/ repeat L2, L3			K1'	S15, S16

The language use in this exchange, different from the previous exchange in Table 5-25, was mainly Chinese with the purpose of relieving the students' semiotic load. Although the grammatical knowledge has already been discussed in Iteration 1, it was still a relatively new way of languaging for the students. Chinese was used to clearly elaborate the language knowledge, so Propose in Chinese was also allowed to ensure the students' understandings. Finally, the item was repeated in both Chinese and English in order to first confirm the Propose and then access the English grammatical term.

From the above, translanguaging strategies were also employed to facilitate learning in joint construction of Iteration 2. Specifically, all students' languages were flexibly used in order to maximize the effectiveness of the lesson activities. As language practices were expanded, such as repeating the grammatical item in bilingual terms, the students' linguistic repertoire has also been expanded.

3. The jointly constructed texts

As could be expected, the joint construction texts in the two classes were quite different although using the same information as a result of their respective discussions during joint construction. As the same with the jointly constructed texts in Iteration 1, the two texts in Iteration 2 were also whole texts that follow the complete stages of story genres, including Orientation—Complication—Resolution. The major difference was that the two texts in Iteration 2 were high staking writings that were expanded with more detailed information as a result of more advanced writing practices.

Both Text 5-10 from Class 1 and Text 5-11 from Class 2 narrated the story of *the Ox and the Crab*. The comparisons of the texts from each iteration showed that joint construction of the Dong story in English is a significant step towards independent rewriting of the Dong story in English.

Text 5-10   The jointly constructed text from Class 1 in Iteration 2

In the beginning of years, the crab was not flat, and his back was smooth, with his feet under his belly, so he walked forward. At that time, the Ox did not listen to the Man, and he did not want to work, and the Man did not know what to do.

One day, the Crab was eating in the river. The Ox did not work and came to the river to take a bath, most excruciatingly idle. Suddenly, the Ox stamped the Crab's back, and the Crab cried with pain. When the Ox moved his feet away, the Crab has been crushed, with a footprint on his back and his feet on the sides. From that day to this, he did not walk forward but sideways. That made the Crab very angry, but he did not know what to do, because he saw the Ox was so big.

Presently, the Ox came to the river to take a bath again. The Crab was waiting behind the stone. When the Ox drank water in the river, the Crab bit the Ox's nose. The Ox cried with pain.

The Man heard the Ox's cry and came to the river. And he saw the Crab bit the Ox's nose, he found the Ox's nose was key to him and put the rope through the Ox's nose. From that day, the Ox began to work for the Man and he learned how to behave.

Text 5-10 was, to some degree, an expansion of the text of joint construction in Iteration 1. The goals of joint construction in Iteration 2, were more than to practice the structure as a whole text, and to practice a high-staking story with the expanded meanings. As Rose and Martin (2012, p. 223) pointed out, "the major difference between speaking and writing is the degree to which meanings are expanded upon", the specific objective of the lesson plan in the program is to practice students' writing step by step, from their everyday speaking experience to school writing, enabling knowledge accumulation as the patterns of semantic waves by Maton (2014).

In Class 2, although the joint construction text in Iteration 2 had different field from that in Iteration 1, it can be also observed that this text was constructed with more details. In this step, more language patterns and resources were provided to support the students to create a high-staking text.

Text 5-11　The jointly constructed text from Class 2 in Iteration 2

Long long ago, the Crab was not flat, his back was smooth, with his feet under his belly, he walked forward but not sideways. The Ox didn't listen to the Man. The man asked him to plough, but his did not want to do, the man didn't know what to do.

One day, the Crab was eating. The Ox didn't work and came to the river to take a bath, most excruciatingly idle. He stamped the Crab's back accidentally. The Crab cried with pain, with a footprint on his back and his feet on the sides. From that day to this, he didn't walk forward but sideways. That made the Crab very angry, but he didn't know what to do, because the Ox was big.

Presently, the Ox came to the river to take a bath again. The Crab was waiting under the stone. When the Ox drank water, the Crab bit the Ox's nose. The Ox cried with pain.

The man heard the Ox's cry and came to the river and knew the nose was the key to the Ox, so the man put the rope through the Ox's nose.

From that day, the Ox began to work for the man. And he learned how to behave.

4. Reflections on joint construction

The students were enthusiastic about joint construction in Iteration 2 and more students actively engaged in scribing on the board. Most students wanted to be appointed as the scribe as they knew the teacher would closely look at their writing. Some students, in Class 2, helped the teacher appoint the students who did not have the chances to be the scribe. Those students who were very quiet in the classroom also realized the benefits of scribing on the board. In the interviews, they commented that this activity helped them not only learn from the teacher and students, but also build their confidence.

Text 5-11　Interviews in joint construction of Iteration 2

S1：大家都上去写,这种氛围让我觉得很放松,我也想试试,以前都不敢。

S1：Everyone wrote (on the board), this learning atmosphere made me very relaxed. So I also wanted to try, and I had never dared to before.

S2：当然有很多好处啦。大家都参与进来这种氛围使我更爱学习英语了。

S2：Of course, there are many benefits. Everyone was involved, this atmosphere made me love to learn English more.

S3：希望能够被老师指导。现在自信多了,能够到黑板上来写给老师和同学们看了。

S3：I wanted to be guided by the teacher. Now I became more confident, and I can scribe on the board to present for the teacher and students now.

One point to reflect in joint construction was that due to time limitation, there was not enough time for the students to take turns scribing the text, so the teacher scribed the last part of the joint construction. Such time limitation constrained the possibility of exploring L3 in more details. Moreover, Chinese was mainly used in the last several lessons to increase the pace, otherwise; L3 could be used more in the discussion, for the students have already been used to the interactive patterns of the learning cycle.

5.3 Summary

This chapter set out to answer the question: "How is the students' whole linguistic repertoire (Dong language as L1, Chinese as L2 and English as L3) used as a resource in the teaching of English, based on the TL-GBP?"

In the intervention program, translanguaging was enfolded in L3 teaching and learning through a process of building up resources. Translanguaging pedagogic strategies like learning multilingual texts, code-switching, translation and using all semiotic resources were employed to facilitate the students to familiarize with the field and the discourse patterns, and to take control of English languaging. In brief, the intervention program provided scaffolding by carefully shifting the discourse towards L3.

As discussed in this Chapter, L1 and L2 were used as a scaffold at the beginning of the intervention, and this scaffold was gradually withdrawn as the students' resources were expanded. At the level of the curriculum sequence, L1 and L2 were used to assist the student in accessing L3 reading text that was first introduced to provide language resources in Iteration 1. Bilingual texts in L1 and L2 were then adopted as curriculum resources to re-instantiate L3 resources in Iteration 2. These translanguaging activities provided solid foundation for the students' independent construction. In independent construction, L1, L2 and L3 resources were all at the students' disposal at every stage of their writings to help them develop and organize their thoughts. At the level of classroom discourse, code-switching and translation among L1, L2 and L3 were used to deepen their understandings, and L3 was first introduced in Evaluate phases, then in the Elaborate phases, and finally in the Prepare and Focus phases of the learning cycles.

With regard to KAL, KAEL terms were primarily used, and sometimes knowledge about Chinese language (KACL) terms were also used to compare with KAEL. As the TL-GBP program is a reading oriented pedagogy, KAEL provided a way of deconstructing the reading texts and reconstructing a new text by explicitly and implicitly using metalinguistic terms. In deconstructing the reading texts, KAEL terms were provided by explicit instruction to label the name of genre and the generic structure of the reading texts and some traditional grammar terms like verb group and tense. Meta-discourse in the forms of commonsense terms (time, place) and exophoric reference (that and this) was also applied in the iterations, which facilitated the students to identify what the teacher was referring to. In reconstructing a new text, particularly in joint construction, KAEL terms were used to talk about how to create a new text, identifying what was required in a text or a sentence and what to re-instantiate.

CHAPTER SIX
STUDENTS' WRITING DEVELOPMENT IN ENGLISH

The students' L3 writing development in both classes will be firstly traced. Therefore, the students' writing texts will be reviewed in details following three different phases of the intervention: before, during and after the intervention, with the specific consideration of the pedagogic impact. Before the intervention, the students were assigned to write their pre-texts, which served as the base-line investigation to measure their literacy level, and to provide evidence of the challenges they met in L3 writing. During the intervention stage, which involved two iterations, the students' writing texts in Iteration 1 were collected to provide information about the impact of the particular pedagogic activities planned to address the challenges. Finally, at the end of the intervention stage, the students' post-texts were used to demonstrate the results of the intervention program, i. e. to what extent the students take control of L3 written language. Accordingly, texts at all stages of the program will be analyzed in the following sections to examine and interpret the development trajectory of the students' L3 writing.

6.1 Writing Assessment Criteria

R2L methodology has been elaborated in Chapter 2 (Section 2.3). Here the writing assessment criteria will be explained in more details, and some additional criteria developed by the research will be explained too, with the purpose of assessing and scrutinizing all L3 texts produced specifically by multilingual students at all stages of the intervention program.

6.1.1 R2L assessment criteria

The assessment developed in R2L program was in conjunction with the model of context and language in SFL, with totally 14 criteria concerning all aspects of context and language patterns that realize them. Context includes genre and register; and language includes discourse semantics, lexico-grammar, and graphology. The R2L assessment was designed to accurately analyze the language resources that students brought to in their writing task, comparing to expected writing exemplars at each school year level.

In the assessment, each criterion is given a score from 0-3 (0=absent; 1=present but weak; 2=good; 3=excellent), thus the total score is 42. Students' writing texts are measured against the writing standard in the exemplar for each stage of school. Guiding questions with different focus for each genre family are provided for each criterion to assist teacher in judging the students' texts. The R2L assessment tool for story genre family is outlined in Table 6-1 (Rose & Martin, 2012, p. 282). At the level of genre, evaluation focuses on the social purpose of the text, and its organization of Staging and Phases within each stage. At the level of register, it focuses on the text's Field, Tenor, and Mode. At the discourse level, Lexis, Appraisal, Conjunction and Reference are identified. At the grammar level, grammatical variety and accuracy are evaluated. In terms of graphic features, Spelling, Punctuation and graphic Presentation are marked. A general direction is provided in each part, followed by more focused directions for the score to judge.

Table 6-1　R2L marking criteria for story texts

Criteria	Guiding questions	Score
CONTEXT	*What is your quick first impression of the text? Does it attract the readers?*	
Purpose	Is the story genre appropriate and well-developed for the writing purpose?	0-3
Staging	Does it go through appropriate stages for the genre and field?	0-3
Phases	Is each stage organized in appropriate sequence of phases?	0-3
Field	How well does the writer construct the plot, settings and characters?	0-3
Tenor	How well does the writer engage the reader?	0-3
Mode	Is there an appropriate use of literacy language of written stories?	0-3
DISCOURSE	*Mark the discourse criteria in the text and give an accurate measure*	
Lexis	Is the field well-constructed by the plot and literacy language?	0-3
Appraisal	Are there any appraisal resources in text? How well is appraisal used to engage, persuade and evaluate reader and characters?	0-3
Conjunction	Is there any logical relation between all sentences?	0-3
Reference	Is it clear who or what is referred to in each sentence?	0-3
GRAMMAR	*Grammar and graphic criteria are judged overall rather than one-by-one* Are the grammatical conventions of written English used accurately? Is there an appropriate variety of sentence and word group structures for the school stage, or is it too simple?	0-3
GRAPHIC FEATURES	*Make quick judgments about the grammar and graphic criteria*	

Table 6-1 (Continued)

Criteria	Guiding questions	Score
Spelling	How accurately spelt are core words and non-core words?	0-3
Punctuation	How appropriately and accurately is punctuation used?	0-3
Presentation	Are paragraphs used? How legible is the writing? Is the layout clear? Are illustrations/diagrams used appropriately?	0-3

6.1.2 Considerations in assessing L3 writing texts

Since L3 learning is greatly different from L1 and L2 learning, its particular characteristics were carefully taken into considerations in the program. Two issues to note in L3 learning were translanguaging and cross-linguistic influence. Translanguaging in the students' writing will be discussed next in Chapter 7. In this section, the focus is cross-linguistic influence on L3 writing, which was taken into account in the R2L assessment.

Cross-linguistic influence refers to the complex mechanism of multilingualism. Specifically, in the process of learning L3, both L1 and L2 will influence third language acquisition, especially at early stage, easily resulting in substitution, borrowing, alternating target language, excessively utilizing or simplifying, and misunderstanding. In the program, cross-linguistic influence among Dong, Chinese, English, particularly the negative influence the students had in learning English as their L3 were carefully examined. Two language strata were focused: lexis and grammar.

Since three languages were inter-played in the intervention, the differences of literature language between L1 or L2 and L3 posed great challenge for students. This was particularly true when students looked up a dictionary for constructing meaning or re-instantiating terms. As students constructed a new field in L3, they would borrow L1 or L2 language resources or literally translate L1 or L2 into L3. This would be closely examined in assessing lexis by the researcher, who took advantages of understanding L1, L2 and L3.

In R2L assessment criteria, the grammar focus is on its accuracy in narrating stories. L3 grammar knowledge has been built during the intervention, but its use by students in their writing can be also inaccurate as a result of cross-linguistic influence. For example, sometimes even the right or proper L3 wordings were used in a sentence, the sentence structure may be somewhat inappropriate. The phenomenon of cross-linguistic influence in this research was not taken as negative, instead it was observed as information related to the development of students' grammar knowledge. Specifically, to examine whether the influence was less visible can provide information about the impact of the intervention program on students' L3 development. Except for lexis and grammar, other strata could also provide a large amount of relevant information.

Cross-linguistic influence in terms of lexis and grammar was used as a basic factor to examine L3 writing development. These considerations, though not the main concerns, extended two criteria in the R2L assessment, marked by adding a question for each shown in bold font in Table 6-2.

Table 6-2 R2L assessment with additional criteria for L3 in lexis and grammar

Criteria	Guiding questions	Score
CONTEXT	*What is your quick first impression of the text? Does it attract the readers?*	
Purpose	Is the story genre appropriate and well-developed for the writing purpose?	0-3
Staging	Does it go through appropriate stages for the genre and field?	0-3
Phases	Is each stage organized in appropriate sequence of phases?	0-3
Field	How well does the writer construct the plot, settings and characters?	0-3
Tenor	How well does the writer engage the reader?	0-3
Mode	Is there an appropriate use of literacy language of written stories?	0-3
DISCOURSE	*Mark the discourse criteria in the text and give an accurate measure*	
Lexis	Is the field well-constructed by the plot and literacy language? **Is the literacy language used appropriately?**	0-3
Appraisal	Are there any appraisal resources in text? How well is appraisal used to engage, persuade and evaluate reader and characters?	0-3
Conjunction	Is there any logical relation between all sentences?	0-3
Reference	Is it clear who or what is referred to in each sentence?	0-3
GRAMMAR	*Grammar and graphic criteria are judged overall rather than one-by-one* Are the grammatical conventions of written English used accurately? Is there an appropriate variety of sentence and word group structures for the school stage, or is it too simple? **Is there any cross-linguistic influence?**	0-3
GRAPHIC FEATURES	*Make quick judgments about the grammar and graphic criteria*	
Spelling	How accurately spelt are core words and non-core words?	0-3
Punctuation	How appropriately and accurately is punctuation used?	0-3
Presentation	Are paragraphs used? How legible is the writing? Is the layout clear? Are illustrations/diagrams used appropriately?	0-3

6.2 Assessing Pre-intervention Text

We collected 48 pre-intervention texts from two classes—23 from Class 1, and 25 from Class 2. Scores in both classes were very low in general. The average level of the pre-writing texts was 8 (out of 42) for Class 1, the average score was even lower in Class 2, only 7. From the assessment of the students' texts, we can see that these students evidently did not grasp the way of English languaging, especially in terms of written language. Mistakes can be found in nearly every text, and some students even cannot write a complete sentence in their pre-texts.

Six students' pre-texts were selected from two classes as examples. The original texts were firstly presented, and typed, then laid out with each clause on a separate line. The texts will be analyzed with the consideration of the following levels of realization: genre and register, implying the extent to which the texts realized their purposes, organizing tenor, field and mode; discourse and grammar, mainly including the appropriateness or accuracy in terms of lexical and grammar use, and cross-linguistic influence from L1 or L2; as well as graphology and punctuation, seen as more "mechanical" dimensions of the texts.

6.2.1 Genre and register

For the pre-text writing task, the students in both classes were asked to write a narrative about an unforgettable experience, which can be a thing, day, lesson or other things. Rose and Martin (2012, p. 50) outlined the schematic structure of narratives as Orientation—Complication—Evaluation—Resolution. The Orientation stage provides the setting of the events, then a series of complicated problems are described at Complication stage, and sometimes the characters' reaction may be expressed by an extra Evaluation stage, at last the problems are resolved at Resolution. In short, a narrative is to build tension and then relieve it. Before writing, students were not given any instruction about how to write a narrative.

Many students wrote the texts as narratives, although their texts were usually too short and simple, most of them in one or two paragraphs, being made up by short sentences. Few texts were another genre, recount. The reason may be that the students were affected by ways of Chinese languaging, in which recount and narrative are regarded as the same genre. As their pre-texts were too short, genre and register can be hardly realized, lacking clear stages and phases. As a result, the purpose of writing a narrative was not effectively achieved because of the short length of the text. Field, tenor and mode were mostly realized by everyday and commonsense oral language of the topic, and in some cases these cannot be effectively realized because of their poor English.

Text 6-1 presents the pre-text written by Student 1 from Class 2. Text 6-1 is an example of a pre-text with only several short sentences in spoken mode, lacking some stages and phases. As we can see, the grammar was congruent and the text cannot be well organized. Conjunctions were used but not in appropriate ways. As this text only realized simple Orientation (two sentences) and Coda stages (one sentence), lacking Complication stage, thus it can be developed as a narrative or recount. Hence, the purpose was not clearly achieved. Besides, not a sentence was correctly constructed in an accurate grammatical structure. Errors were found in terms of spelling and punctuation. Thus, the text can only get 5 points.

Text 6-1　Pre-text 1

Today, I'm and feind eat Practice jump dance but the body is very tired.
So I'm is pleasure.

[Text 6-1]

Stages

1	Orientation	Today, I'm and feind eat Pratice jump dance
2		but the body is very tired.
3	Coda	So I'm is Pleasure.

At the Orientation stage, clauses 1 and 2 simply told the setting, including character, problem and reaction. Clause 3 concluded the text in Coda by expressing her feeling about the event. This text lacked the core parts of the narrative, i. e. Complication and Resolution stages, thus the text was not well organized. In addition, the tenor is entirely simple personal evaluation.

Text 6-2 presents the pre-text written by Student 2 from Class 1. Text 6-2 was relatively better organized than Text 1, but still weak at all language levels. There were three stages in the text, i. e. Orientation, Complication and Resolution, but each stage was realized by only one or two sentences. Besides, the text was presented by only one short paragraph. The text also got a low score of 8.

Text 6-2　Pre-text 2

Yesterday is an unforgettable, because in the yesterday we have dancing lessons, So we are very tired, Is the teacher called yatui, But I now No pain, no gain!

[Text 6-2]
Stages

1	Orientation	Yesterday is an unforgettable,
2	Complication	because in the yesterday we have dancing lessons,
3		So we are very tired,
4		Is the teacher called yatui,
5		But I now No pain, no gain!

Text 6-2 provided a specific event, compared with Text 6-1. The Orientation told that the unforgettable day was yesterday. The Complication then described the specific event was having dancing lessons by presenting what they were doing, which showed translanguaging between English and Chinese. The conclusion was the writer's feeling about the dancing lessons.

Whether there are problems and resolutions are the major factors that distinguish narrative from recount, as its goal is to entertain people by disturbing then restoring equilibrium. Whereas recount tends to share feelings about the unproblematic events, narrative tends to create problems and then solve them. The following texts are examples of narratives found in pre-texts.

Text 6-3 presents the pre-text written by Student 3 from Class 2. Text 6-3 had relatively clear stages, i. e. Complication—Resolution, and can be taken as a narrative. In Text 6-3, the writer described the problem in the supermarket and its resolution.

Text 6-3　Pre-text 3

One day, I'm went shopping with my students. After. I'm forget book in supermarket. When I'm come back. My book wasn't there. So, I'm feeling sad.

As can be seen in [Text 6-3] below, clauses 1 and 2 described the writer's problem—forgetting her book in the supermarket. Clauses 3 and 4 were Resolution, that is she didn't find her book. Clause 5 was her reaction to this event: she felt very sad. The text was also a simple paragraph in a spoken mode without so much detailed information. There were some simple conjunctions and references, but some improper and wrong use of grammar, lexis and punctuation. Accordingly, the score of this test was 10.

[Text 6-3]

Stages

1	Complication	One day, I'm went shopping with my students.
2		After. I'm forget book in supermarket.
3	Resolution	When I'm come back.
4		My book wasn't there.
5		So, I'm feeling sad.

Text 6-4 presents the pre-text written by Student 4 from Class 1. Text 6-4 was a better organized narrative, including Orientation, Complication, Resolution, although they were realized in short paragraphs with each having one simple sentence.

Text 6-4 Pre-text 4

Yesterday was very an unforgettable day. I've been studying all afternoon. I finally learned how to ride a bike. I very happy.

[Text 6-4] below outlines the genre and register analysis, using a double slash (//) to indicate the end of a paragraph. Clause 1 introduced the Orientation of the narrative: the unforgettable day was yesterday. Clause 2 told us the event was studying, but the Complication was too simple so that the readers cannot find what she has been studying and the whole process. In clause 3, from the Resolution, we can know she studied riding a bike and finally she learned it. The text had only several short sentences like the above texts, but it was well performed in terms of grammar, punctuation, so it was scored 12 points.

[Text 6-4]

Stages

1	Orientation	Yesterday was very an unforgettable day. //
2	Complication	I've been studying all afternoon. //
3	Resolution	I finally learned how to ride a bike. //
4		I very happy. //

Text 6-5 presents the pre-text written by Student 5 from Class 2. Text 6-5 was also a narrative that had the same topic with Text 6-4, i.e. learning riding a bike, but it expressed in more details as more information was added. The writer also added an equivalent Chinese version to help express meanings.

Text 6-5　Pre-text 5

I remember, in weekend. I want study by bike. But I don't. And My Sister very Peatice teach and encourage me. I spent time the practice by bike. Finally I learn by bike. I very happy and unforgettable.

翻译：我记得，有一个周末，我想学习骑自行车，但是我不会。然后我的姐妹非常有耐心地教和鼓励我，我花费了时间去练习单车。最后我学会了骑单车，我非常开心和难忘。

Text 6-5 provided more information than Text 6-4. Clause 1 specified the setting: the time was weekend, and the event was to study riding a bike. Clause 2 described the problem she met: she didn't. Clauses 3 and 4 were Resolution. The solution to the problem was her sister helped her, and finally she learned how to ride a bike. Clause 6 expressed her feeling about this experience. Some literacy words were used like "patient" and "encourage", but the spelling and grammar errors were also found. The writer may realize this and added the Chinese re-instantiation of the writing. The text was relatively better organized, but still lacked enough detailed information to make it attractive. Its total score was 14.

[Text 6-5]
Stages

1	Orientation	I remember, in weekend. I want study by bike.
2	Complication	But I don't.
3	Resolution	And My Sister very Peatice teach and encourage me.
4		I spent time the practice by bike.
5		Finally I learn by bike.
6		I very happy and unforgettable.

Text 6-6 presents the pre-text written by Student 6 from Class 1. Text 6-6 presents another example of better organized narratives, including Evaluation stage. In this text, equivalent Chinese translation was also provided. This pre-text, however, also showed some grammatical and graphic mistakes both in English text and its Chinese translation.

Text 6-6　Pre-text 6

One day, I and my mother outside to buy thing.
一天，我和我的妈妈到外面买东西。

Forget to pay, then everyone very embarrassed.
忘了付钱,后来大家都很尴尬。
But the boss forgave us accidentally, we didn't mean to.
但是老板原谅了我们的无意,我们不是故意的。
It makess me very unforgettable. is also a lesson
这件事情让我很(难)忘,也是一个教训。

As we can see in [Text 6-6] below, clauses 1 and 2 outlined the event and problem. Then clause 3 evaluated the event: everyone felt embarrassed. Finally, the solution to the problem was that the boss forgave them in clauses 4 and 5. Clauses 6 and 7 expressed her feeling about this event. The evaluation can engage the readers and facilitate the achievement of the purpose. However, because there were some grammatical, spelling and punctuation errors in this text, the total score was 15 points.

[**Text 6-6**]

Stages

1	Complication	One day, I and my mother outside to buy thing.
2		Forget to pay,
3	Evaluation	then everyone very embarrassed
4	Resolution	But the boss forgave us accidentally,
5		we didn't mean to.
6		It makess me very unforgettable.
7		is also a lesson

From the above, we can see two genres were found in the pre-texts, i.e. recount and narrative. They both belong to story genre family (Martin & Rose, 2008), "to interpret life's chaos and rhythms, to evaluate each other's behaviors, and to educate and entertain our children, moreover, to draw the children's attention and ignite their imagination" (Martin & Rose, 2008, p. 49). Learning these genres lays foundation for cultivating minority students as inheritors to transmit ethnic culture.

The schematic structures in the pre-texts yet can hardly meet the standard. In most cases, the stages and phases were not well-arranged. Some texts were too short to identify the genres. In some texts, the stages cannot be well realized because of the simple sentences and inaccurate English expressions. For example, the evaluations or reactions were placed at the end of the text after the resolution, which may be influenced by Chinese narratives.

With regard to register, the texts were far from literary expressions in terms of field, tenor and mode. The texts reflected the commonsense understanding about the field, involving simple personal knowledge. The language mode was too spoken for the junior college standard. Furthermore, the texts showed little ways of English languaging but Chinese languaging that were probably literally translated into English, which can be seen in the bilingual writings such as Texts 6-5 and 6-6.

6.2.2 Discourse and grammar

The students' discourse and grammar resources were assessed by comparing them with the appropriate use of words and structure in written English (Rose & Martin, 2012; Rose, 2015a). In the pre-texts, accurate expressions and congruent grammar were evaluated. In addition, cross-linguistic influence from their L1 and L2 was another area of interest. Congruent grammar is usually the oral language pattern that uses simple short sentences, in which, Participants are realized by simple nominal groups and Processes are mainly realized by simple verbal groups. In the pre-texts, most of the clauses were this type, such as clause 2 in Text 6-2.

[**Text 6-2**]

2	because	in the yesterday	we	have	dancing lessons
		Environment	Actor	Process	Goal

In the clause, the Participant was realized by nominal group "we" and "dancing lessons"; the Process by simple verbal group "have". Some clauses had expanded structures to realize Participants. Clause 3 in Text 6-4 is an example of this type.

[**Text 6-4**]

3	I	finally	learned	how to ride a bike.
	Actor	Environment	Process	Goal

The Goal in clause 3 was realized by a clause rather than a simple nominal group. In some texts, the writers were also likely to use incongruent grammar structure, but their limited English competence resulted in the inaccurate expressions, as can be seen by comparing their English text with its parallel Chinese one. Their English texts, conversely, indicated the ways of thinking in Chinese.

Therefore, cross-linguistic influence in terms of grammar was an important factor. The influence occurred to various degrees, particularly greater in word groups and sentence structures. One problem was word for word translation. The English words were arranged by the order of Chinese languaging, so they may not construe the same experiential meanings in English. Most clauses in Texts 6-1 and 6-2 showed examples of this type of cross-linguistic influence. These clauses cannot express clear meaning in English, so the readers can hardly get the meanings. Clause 4 in Text 6-6 shows another example.

[Text 6-6]
4   But the boss forgave us   accidentally

Clause 4 was to construe the meaning—"their carelessness was forgiven", while it actually expressed the meaning—"they were forgiven by accident". The equivalent meaning construed in English is showed in the following 4a.

English equivalent of clause 4 in [Text 6-6]
4a   But   the boss   forgave   our carelessness
            Senser   Process   Phenomenon

In clause 4, however, instead of using "our carelessness" as Phenomenon, the writer expressed the Phenomenon as us, and the word "accidentally" becomes the Manner. This meaning was totally not the writer's purpose and must mislead or confuse the readers as a result of the improper literal translation of "我们的无意". The reason was that the writer didn't know well the English way of languaging and was influenced by the way of her own language knowledge. Word inflexions in English usually occur to indicate differences between word classes or grammar structure, while in both Chinese and Dong there are no such inflexions, instead these differences are shown by adding another wording. The writer thus used the word literally without noticing its right grammatical form.

In some cases, the sentence grammar may follow the Chinese grammar structure, namely, to put the English words into the order of Chinese clause. The influence of Chinese clause can be seen when the clause is compared with its right equivalent in English. Clause 1 in Text 6-6 shows an example.

[Text 6-6]
1   One day,   I and my mother   outside   to buy   thing.
     Location   Actor   Location   Process   Goal

Apparently, clause 1 showed the Chinese interference. It would have meant the writer and her mother went shopping outside. In English, the process is the core element of the clause (Rose & Martin, 2012). In this simple clause, a verbal group that realized the Process should follow the Actor, thus the use of the adverb *outside* following the Actor without a verbal group was wrong.

To demonstrate the interference, the revised equivalent of clause 1 in English is presented in 1a.

Equivalent clause in English

1a	One day,	my mother and I	went	shopping	outside.
	Location	Actor	Process	Goal	Location

The equivalent clause in Chinese is provided in 1b to reveal the influence of Chinese.

1b	一天	我和我的妈妈	到外面	买	东西
	One day,	I and my mother	outside	to buy	thing.
	Location	Actor	Location	Process	Goal

The equivalent clause showed the evidence of the word for word translation from Chinese to English. It can be seen that the Location "outside" in Chinese "到外面" closely followed the Actor, the Process "buy" was realized by a propositional phrase rather than a verbal group. In Chinese, as a parataxis language, the word order in a sentence is not so strictly set like that in English, so "到外面" (outside) can closely follow the Actor. It was likely that students wrote inaccurate sentence by following Chinese structure.

Another point to note in terms of Chinese interference concerns conjunction, as it plays an important role in organizing a text, especially in story genres. It is an important resource to construe series of events. In Chinese, conjunction is construed differently from English. Two conjunctions for the same purpose can be used in a sentence in Chinese. Clauses 2 and 3 in Text 6-2 show examples of this type of influence.

[Text 6-2]
2 because in the yesterday we have dancing lessons,
3 So we are very tired,

However, there should be only one conjunction to link two clauses in a sentence in English, which can be revealed by the equivalent sentence in English as in 2+3a below.

English equivalent of clauses 2 and 3

2+3a   Yesterday we had dancing lessons, so we were very tired.

The equivalent of sentence (2+3b) in Chinese presents that two conjunctions in a sentence are reasonable.

Chinese equivalent of clauses 2 and 3

2+3b   因为昨天我们有舞蹈课，　　　　　　所以我们很累。
        because in the yesterday we have dancing lessons, So we are very tired,

Apart from cross-linguistic influence in terms of grammar, it is also crucial to consider English resources that are needed to construct stories. The main resources are verbal groups that construe the process of the event and nominal groups that refer to the participants. Chinese grammatical forms of verbal groups and nominal groups in clauses are different from those of English, so the students have to learn these to construe meanings in different ways.

Table 6-3 presents some examples of cross-linguistic influence in terms of the use of verbal groups and nominal groups in the clauses, which were selected from a number of the pre-texts. These resources construe experience and track participants.

Table 6-3   Elements of cross-linguistic influence in the pre-texts

No.	Elements of cross-linguistic influence	Clauses	English equivalents
1	Lack of verbal groups	I very happy.	I was very happy.
2		then everyone very embarrassed.	Then everyone was very embarrassed.
3	Redundant use of verbal groups	I'm went shopping with my students.	I went shopping with my classmates.
4		I'm is pleasure.	I was pleased.
5	No tense change for verbal groups	So we are very tired.	So we were very tired.
6		Our class have a dance lesson.	Our class had a dance lesson.
7	Tracking participants (no nominal groups)	Forget to pay.	We forgot to pay.
8		is also a lesson.	It was also a lesson.
9		Music and dance very favorite.	Music and dance are my favorite.

In Chinese, relational clauses do not always have a Process. In the attributive mode, a Process realized by a verbal group is not involved, and in the identifying mode, the Process is optional. Clause 1 in Table 6-4 provides a typical example of this type of influence from Chinese, while the equivalent clause in English (1a) illustrates the linking verb "was" is an indispensable part in the clause.

English equivalent of clause 1

1a　　I　　　　was　　　　very　　　　happy.
　　　Carrier　Process　　Manner　　Attribute

The equivalent Chinese of clause 1 (1b) illustrates that the Process in a relational attributive clause is unnecessary in Chinese.

Chinese Equivalent of clause 1

1b　　我　　　　非常　　　　开心。
　　　I　　　　very　　　　happy.
　　　Carrier　　Manner　　Attribute

In Dong, a large number of words end with the nasal consonants "m" or "n", such as "qamt kuenp" (walk). Therefore, Dong students usually have the habit of ending a word with the nasal consonants, which would influence their English writings. Clause 3 shows an example of this interference. The writer habitually put a "m" after the Actor and before a verbal group, resulting in the redundant use of verb groups in a clause. The equivalent clause in English (3a) below shows that there is no need of a "m" there.

English equivalent of clause 3

3a　　I'm　　　went　　　　shopping　　with my students.
　　　Actor　　Process　　Goal　　　　Manner

Another type of interference from L1 and L2 is the form of verbal groups in a sentence. In English, the Finite element is needed to circumscribe the proposition, which is expressed by a temporal or modal verbal operator. While in both L1 and L2, the proposition is not necessarily defined by a verbal operator, instead it is usually realized by other types of word groups. In a story, the events are usually located by primary past tense of the verbal groups, so to change a verbal group into past tense in a story is needed. The students, however, did not know or forgot to change the tense form of the verbal groups. The English equivalent of clause 5 (5a) shows an example of the verbal tense change.

English equivalent of clause 5

5a   So   we   were   very   tired.
          Carrier   Process   Manner   Attribute

In Chinese, especially in the spoken form, Participant is not necessarily construed in responding move in an exchange, for once the Theme has been built in the beginning move, the key point is to deploy the Predicator to negotiate the proposition or proposal in play. Therefore, the Participant was usually absent in this case in the pre-texts. The type of interference can be seen in clauses 7 and 8 from Text 6-6, lacking the Actor or Token. The Participants of clause 7 are the writer and her mother, who have been introduced in the previous clause that described they bought something outside. Clause 8 is to evaluate the event. They are shown below:

[Text 6-6]

7   Forget to pay
8   is also a lesson

Since the Themes of both clauses have previously introduced, it is assumed that they can be omitted in Chinese. However, as for English grammar, it is ambiguous or even wrong not to have subject at the beginning of the sentence. The English equivalents of clauses 7 (7a) and 8 (8a) show that the subjects are necessary in English.

English equivalents of clauses 7 and 8

7a   We forgot to pay.
8a   It was also a lesson.

In sum, this sub-section presents cross-linguistic influence in terms of discourse and grammar in the pre-texts that the students experienced in their L3 writings. For the teacher, the influence can provide information in assessing students' language knowledge about L3 writing. For the students, this influence can be viewed as a result of their translanguaging learning strategy. Most multilingual learners may naturally draw from their linguistic repertoire as the readily available semiotic model for writing in the target language. The translanguaging strategy help with their thinking and self-regulation in leaning, while the interference can be minimized by comparing and contrasting their L1, L2 and L3, and by providing the students with more languaging practices in L3.

6.2.3 Graphic features: spelling and punctuation

Graphology is an essential part in L3 writing, which indicates to what extent the students obtained the written language resources. Spelling in English writing is a great challenge for students, for it hugely varied from the graphology system in Chinese. Chinese is hieroglyphic, while English is phonemic. In Chinese, the spoken system is arguably different from the written system, so students seldom make connections between the spoken and written form when learning to spell English words. Furthermore, they have little knowledge about English graphology knowledge. Punctuation in English is also differently used from that in Chinese, thus it was sometimes mistakenly used in the students' L3 writings.

Poor spelling was apparent in the pre-texts, even though the texts were very short and simple, which indicated the students have learned little about English written language. Particularly for some week students, misspelling occurred commonly in their texts, even in very simple words, such as "an". Text 6-2 shows an example as presented in Table 6-4.

Table 6-4 Misspelling from Text 6-2

Clause	Misspelt word	Correct spelling
1	au	an
2	mast	most
3	no't	don't
4	unforgettable	unforgettable

Punctuation is also an important graphic feature in written mode, which is also a challenge for some students, particularly the use of comma and full stop. Some mistakes were found in the pre-texts. In Text 6-3, for example, there was misuse of full stop in clause 1 "One day. I'm went shopping with my students."—a full stop was used after a word group as if it was a sentence. The punctuation in Text 6-2 was seriously mistaken, which only used commas to separate clauses and one exclamation mark in the last clause, and no full stops in a text.

Text 6-2

> Yesterday is an unforgettable, because in the yesterday we
> have dancing lessons, So we are very tired, Is the teacher
> called yatui, But I now No pain, no gain!

In some cases, the texts were arranged just into one paragraph, which was not odd considering the fact that the texts were usually very short. However, evidence from the analysis of the pre-texts shows that there is a need for the students to learn about paragraphing, for it is necessary for longer texts.

6.2.4 The students' linguistic competence in the pre-texts

From the above, we can see the students' literacy skills were very week. They knew little about the basic components of English written language. Some students cannot write more than one or two sentences. Some even had never written before. Generally, their performance cannot meet the standard of their grade level.

In the pre-texts, their language resources, regardless of the scores, were drawn from the commonsense discourse in their daily lives. Most texts used simple sentences to construe experiences. Hardly were any literacy linguistic resources and devices employed so that no tensions were built and resolved in stories. Their scarce language resources suggested the results that the texts were prosaic, so they did not achieve the purposes.

In terms of genre and register, the students may also draw on their linguistic repertoire, shown by the fact that their texts did not follow the standard stages and phases. The reason for this is probably that the students had no access to the mode of English written language. If the students had been exposed explicitly to the knowledge about the linguistic properties, or to the new ways of English languaging, they would have organized the structure better and written longer texts.

These findings are not surprising, for the students had poor performance in the entrance examination, which indicates that they have learned little about English knowledge in their secondary schools. After they entered the college, they were taught only simple oral English like dialogues and short readings. This case is commonplace in colleges of Guizhou minority areas, particularly for junior college students.

As students graduated from middle school, they were expected to write a more expanded story with a series of Complications and Resolutions by acquiring and employing more language resources, like a good control of grammar, lexical metaphor, repeated sentence patterns and literacy devices. Their pre-texts, however, suggested the similarity with writing level of the primary school as early L1 English writers (Rose, 2015c).

It is assumed that the writing development of an additional language follows the same trajectory of L1 writing (see Emiliar & Christie, 2013; in Christie, 2012). In this vein, the intervention program designed and implemented a TL-GBP pedagogy based on the principles that effective learning involves providing learners with explicit knowledge about the language, while incorporating translanguaging on the principle of drawing on multilingual learners' whole linguistic repertoire. In so doing, the goal is to promote L3 writing so that the multilingual writers' L3 literacy level could approximate that of L1 learners.

6.3 Assessing Individual Construction

At the end of Iteration 1, the students were asked to complete an individual construction, i.e. to construct a new story with language resources negotiated in the learning cycle. The main purpose of the task in individual construction was to practice the skills they had learned in the previous steps. The characters and results of the individual construction activities can be viewed by looking closely at the learning tasks and the writings produced. Evidence of the expansion of the linguistic resources was found in the individual writings.

6.3.1 The learning task in individual construction

Individual construction is a lesson step that the students carry out individually following the joint construction, resulting in a written text. Individual construction lies in the outmost layer of the R2L cycle, which primarily considers the management of the overall structure and the field, while emphasizing the reconstruction of discourse, grammar and graphology, as these are closely linked with the writing development and assessment.

In stories, individual construction aims to "attempt a text following the same patterns of the original reading text and the joint construction one, together with the ideas that have previously listed on the board" (Rose & Martin, 2012; p. 147). At this point, the students were not required to write a completely new story for it was still a challenge for them. Its main function was to "practice using the same narrative devices as the teacher guided them to use in joint construction" (Rose & Martin, 2012; p. 147).

The discourse was reconstructed by using the same language patterns in detailed reading and joint construction, but with a new field, such as new characters or settings, and some similar elements can be also used, particularly for the weak students. By this way, graphology was also reconstructed by practicing rewriting the same key words. Thus, handing over the control of English language knowledge about grammar and graphology (lower strata) to students would be the focus of the activities of individual construction. The main activity was to apply the sentence patterns to a new field, by the way of replacing some key elements of the sentence while maintaining its grammatical structure.

Translanguaging as a tool was encouraged at any stages of individual construction in order to assist students in creating ideas, developing thoughts, and expanding language resources, etc. Some translanguaging strategies for individual construction were: (1) translanguaging in Planning: using multilingual repertoire and multimodal resources to organize thoughts. Students can use any languages or draw on any modalities, like drawing, diagram, graphs to create ideas of their writings; (2) translanguaging in Drafting: glosses. The students can use any familiar words and expressions or make graphs when drafting, or they can transform them into English texts; (3) translanguaging in final product for rhetorical purpose. In their writing of ethnic folk stories, some linguistic and semiotic resources can be applied in their final products to highlight some ethnic objects or literacy characters. In addition, in the process of individual construction, the discussion in their familiar languages was also taken as a translanguaging tool to ensure clear and deep thought.

In the intervention, although it was the students' main task to carry out individual construction, the activity was done in the classroom. The students firstly copied ideas and words listed on the board and the jointly constructed text with its labels on their notebooks. Meanwhile, the teacher instructed them to use translanguaging strategies in writings. In addition, the teacher provided support for students whenever they consulted with the teacher, or needed new resources in writings.

6.3.2 Writing production in individual construction

The students' individual writing texts were the final products of Iteration 1. The production in individual construction played an extremely important role in checking the effectiveness of the teaching and learning in Iteration 1. In Iteration 1, the texts of individual construction were based on the texts of detailed reading and joint construction. In joint construction, two classes created two different stories; the text of Class 1 was about the story of the Ox and the Crab, and the text of Class 2 about the story of the Ox and the Bird. Both texts were relatively simple and short, for the main purpose of joint construction in Iteration 1 was to practice the basic skill of writing a whole text in consideration of the students' insufficient language resources.

1. Individual construction in Class 1

Text 5-5 (repeated below) is the text of joint construction written together by Class 1. It thus, together with the reading texts, served as a model for the students' individually constructed texts in Class 1.

Text 5-5　Jointly constructed text of Class 1 [repeated]

Long time ago, when the world was brand new, there was an Ox, and he lived on the edge of the river, because he did not want to work. He liked to take a bath, most excruciatingly idle.

One day, the Ox did not want to work, and he went to the river to take a bath. And he stamped the Crab accidentally. The Crab cried with pain. That made the Crab very angry.

Presently, the Crab nipped the Ox's nose. The Ox cried with pain.

The Man came to the river, and he put the Crab in the river, and put the rope into the Ox's nose.

Most students in both classes can write a successful whole text, although their stories were still quite simple. Text 6-7 written by Student 4 is a representative of the individually constructed texts in Iteration 1 from Class 1. It reveals the student's good control of the target generic structure.

Text 6-7　Representative of individual construction text from Class 1

Long long ago, when the world was brand new, there was a Horse, and he live on the edge of the grass land, because he did not want to work. He liked to take a bath, and liked to eat grass, most excruciating idle.

One day, the Horse did not want to work, and he went to the grass land and trot. And a man play Horse tail, That made the Horse very angry, play（踢）the man.

The man came to the grass land, and said the man, sorry, I'm sorry for you. And from that day to this, the Horse began to work for man.

As we can see, Text 6-7 was well organized, following the generic structure of joint construction. It also showed good use of language resources from the jointly constructed text and reading text and control of English grammar, except for a few errors in terms of the use of verbal tense. In terms of graphic features, the text was well presented with right spelling, punctuation and appropriate paragraphing. Thus, its total score was 25, greatly promoted compared with the pre-text.

To examine Text 6-7, the language resources that the student used in constructing a new field was the primary focus, involving comparing the text with the joint construction text by examining the sentences used. Table 6-5 presents the comparison of sentence patterns at the Orientation stage of the two texts.

Table 6-5 Tracing the use of language patterns at the Orientation stage in Text 6-7

No.	Joint construction text	No.	Individual construction text
1	Long time ago, when the world was brand new,	1	Long long ago, when the world was brand new,
2	there was an Ox,	2	there was a Horse,
3	and he lived on the edge of the river,	3	and he live on the edge of the grass land,
4	because he did not want to work.	4	because he did not want to work
5	He liked to take a bath, most excruciatingly idle.	5	He liked to take a bath,
6		6	and liked to eat grass, most excruciating idle.

Table 6-5 shows that the student appropriately applied the language patterns of jointly constructed text to construct a new field with just the replacements of some key elements. In clause 2, for example, she followed the same "there be" sentence pattern, but substituted the Participant "Horse" for "Ox"; thus a new character was built. In the next clauses, the lexis for other elements like Process and Environments were also replaced, thus new events and settings were built too. Furthermore, the student expanded the sentence by adding a new clause, making a distinction of her writing from joint construction text. The use of language resources in Text 6-7 is showed in Table 6-6 by underlining the replaced parts and outlining the added clause by a box.

Table 6-6 Highlighting the replaced and new elements in Text 6-7

Joint construction text	Individual construction text
Long time ago, when the world was brand new,	Long long ago, when the world was brand new,
there was an Ox,	there was a Horse,
and he lived on the edge of the river,	and he live on the edge of the grass land,
because he did not want to work. =	because he did not want to work
He liked to take a bath, most excruciatingly idle. // =	He liked to take a bath,
	and liked to eat grass, most excruciating idle. //

The student built a new field by re-constructing the sentence patterns with new elements, showing that she has learned to construe different experiential meaning through the same language patterns.

Text 6-7 is a typical example of individual construction in Class 1, and most students have the similar performance. Although there were a few problems, their performance was affirmed by the teacher in both written and oral form. The text returned to the student for revision after assessment, showing that (1) stages and phases were well organized; (2) a few words and phrases were revised or annotated. Such assessment provided sufficient support for students to revise their individual writing. A few students still had difficulties in doing this task. They could be assisted through discussing and providing the elements in the process of writing. Due to time limitation, a few weaker and slower students did not write complete texts though they had a good beginning. Text 6-8 written by Student 7 serves as an example.

Text 6-8   An unfinished individual construction text from Class 1

Long time ago, when the world was brand new, there was a Dog, and he lived on the Dong house, because he did not want to work. He liked to sleep, most excruciatingly idle.

On day, the Dog did not want to work, and he went to the Dog house to sleep. And he bite the man. The man cried with pain. That made the man very angry.

Presently, the Dog

It can be seen that the text was not complete but this may probably not be the students' intention. She made a good beginning at the Orientation stage and construed part of the Complication, properly using the language patterns. She also took good control of English grammar for there were only a few errors of verbal tense in her text. If she could have continued to complete her text, she would have got a relatively high score. But in this case, her text was only scored as 19 points.

As we can see, cross-linguistic influence occurred less in individual construction. The students presented right expressions by using the previously learned language resources, but a few awkward Chinese language patterns were found in their independent writings. Text 6-9 written by Student 8 reveals problems resulting from interference in terms of Chinese sentence patterns.

Text 6-9 An individual construction text with interference from Class 1

In the beginning of years, when the world was brand new, there was a cat, and he lived on the river, because he did not want to work. He very like eat fish.

One day, the cat did not work, and he went to the river. he every day on the river see fish. Because he think eat fish have fish he every day very happy!

But at the end of the day, cat think time is money, I didn't not work. But the cat eat fish. Cat think no pain, no gain.

So we every day Do what you say, say what you do!

Text 6-9 revealed the student's good control of the generic structure shown by successful stages and phases and right language patterns. She was able to apply some learned sentence patterns to construe new meanings, but some use of language resources was clumsy. For example, the basic sentence structures and meanings in some clauses were confused:

"he every day on the river see fish."

"Because he think eat fish have fish he every day very happy!"

Arguably, the two sentences were created by the writer herself without referring to the similar language patterns in English. She attempted to build richer plots, but unfortunately, as there were no similar language patterns taken as references, she had to draw on her own linguistic repertoire. The former clause, equivalent to "He looked for fishes by the river every day", put the Environment mistakenly behind the Actor. It was obviously a potential source of interference from Chinese, since in Chinese the Environment that locates the Actor's experience is closely put after it. However, the use of verb "see" was not the literal translation of Chinese but the misuse of her English repertoire. The latter, equivalent to "Because he thought of eating and having fishes, he was very happy everyday", was a literal transfer from Chinese, since in Chinese, (1) there is no inflexion of word, and (2) as discussed above, the Environment can be flexibly placed, usually near the Actor. As a result, it was difficult for the students to change the verb forms for different grammatical functions.

2. Individual construction in Class 2

Text 5-6 (repeated below) was the text of joint construction written together by Class 2. It thus, together with the reading texts, served as a model for individual construction in Class 2.

Text 5-6　Jointly constructed text of Class 2 [repeated]

　　In the beginning of years, when the world was so new, there was an Ox, and he lived on the edge of a river, because he did not want to work. So he ate grass. He liked to take a bath and he was happy every day.

　　Presently the Dog came to him, with a bone in his mouth, and said, "Come and fetch and you can eat bone".

　　The Ox said 'Moo' and stamped the Dog. That made the Dog very angry.

　　Presently, the Dog called the bird to bite the Ox's nose. And the Ox cried with pain. The Man heard the Ox's cries and came to him. He put the rope into the Ox's nose.

　　And from that day to this the Ox always wears a rope. And he began to work for Man.

The individual construction texts from Class 2 in Iteration 1 also presented clear stages and phases, revealing the students' good control of the genre knowledge. Furthermore, the texts generally included more specific phases with detailed information. The reason for this may be that joint construction text used as a reference in Class 2 was longer with more phases than that of Class 1. Text 6-10 written by Student 5 was a representative of individual texts from Class 2.

Text 6-10　Representative of individual construction text from Class 2

　　In the beginning of years, when the world was so new, there was an Sheep, and he lived on the edge of a plain, because he did not want to work, so he ate grass, and he was happy every day.

　　Presently the Ox came to him, with the yoke on his neck and said, "Come and plough like the rest of us."

　　The Sheep said "baa" and stamped the Ox. That made the Ox very angry.

　　Presently the Ox carried the fly to the Sheep's nose.

　　And the Sheep cried with pain. The man heard the Sheep's cries and came to him. He put the rope into the Sheep's nose.

　　And from that day to this, the Sheep always wears a rope. And he began to work for Man.

Text 6-10 shows good control of stages and phases and relevant language patterns. For example, new events were construed by using appropriate nominal groups and process types from the previously learned sentence patterns, some of which were incongruent grammatical structure to expand the experiential information, and good thematic choices to progress the text forward. In terms of language strata, there were only a few grammatical and spelling errors in Text 6-10 so that its total score was 28 point, going up to the standard.

Table 6-7 outlines the Complication stage of Text 6-10, indicating the use of different elements in the same sentence patterns of joint construction.

Table 6-7 Tracing the use of language patterns at the Complication stage in Text 6-10

No.	Joint construction text	No.	Individual construction text
1	Presently the Dog came to him, with a bone in his mouth,	1	Presently the Ox came to him, with the yoke on his neck,
2	and said, "come and fetch and you can eat bone".	2	and said, "come and plough like the rest of us".
3	The Ox said "Moo"	3	The Sheep said "baa"
4	and stamped the Dog.	4	and stamped the Ox.
5	That made the Dog very angry.	5	That made the Ox very angry.

In clause 1, the Participant and Environment were changed within the same sentence pattern, resulting in building a new plot. In clause 2, one process was changed and the sentence pattern was partially different by changing a clause into Environment, following the relevant pattern of the reading text. The different event was then constructed. In clauses 3 and 4, various Participants were used to present new characters "Sheep" and "Ox" in the student's individually constructed text. The replaced elements are highlighted in Table 6-8.

Table 6-8 Highlighting the replaced and new elements in Text 6-10

Joint construction text	Individual construction text
Presently the Dog came to him, with a bone in his mouth,	Presently the Ox came to him, with the yoke on his neck,
and said, "come and fetch and you can eat bone".	and said, "come and plough like the rest of us."
The Ox said "Moo"	The Sheep said "baa"
and stamped the Dog.	and stamped the Ox.
That made the Dog very angry.	That made the Ox very angry.

Texts like Text 6-10 were commonly found in both Class 1 and Class 2, which reveals the result of individual construction—the students took a good control of stages and the previously learned language patterns. Comparatively, students in Class 2 had a better grasp of phases and wrote the stories with more detailed plots. Moreover, they used the language patterns more flexibly. For example, some students alternately used the language resources from the joint construction text and reading text, as manifested in clause 2 of Text 6-10. Text 6-11 written by Student 9 shows another example of more flexible use of language resources.

Text 6-11   An individual construction text with flexible language use from Class 2

In the beginning of years. When the world was so new and all, there was an Horse, and he lived in the middle of a grassland, because he did not want to work, so he ate grass, He liked to take a trot. So he was most excruciatingly idle.

Presently, the cow came to him, with a grass in his mouth, and said "Come and have milk, and you can eat grass."

The Horse said "neigh" and stamped the cow. That made the cow very angry. Presently cow cries the man and came to him, the Man put with a saddle on his back and a bit in his mouth.

And from that day to this the Horse always wears a rope. And, he began to work for Man.

Text 6-11 had flexible use of various language patterns. For example, at Complication stage, each clause followed the parallel pattern of jointly constructed text, while substituting some new elements for the original ones. At Resolution stage, however, the clauses did not follow the same order of the model. Clauses 6 and 7 followed the patterns of clauses 7 and 9 but with some modifications. Next, the student created a new sentence by combining the phrase pattern in clause 1, aiming to build a new resolution for her story. Table 6-9 presents the use of language patterns in Text 6-11 by highlighting the rearranged sentence patterns in boxes and pointing the reference sentence patterns with arrows.

In Text 6-11, the student flexibly used the language resources to build a new field. Rather than following the sentence patterns clause by clause, she employed every resource at her disposal to realize her intention of construing meanings. For example, in clause 6, she used the resource of Environment in clause 6, and the resource of Process in clause 7 of joint construction. In clause 8, she reorganized the Environment of clause

1 at Complication stage as the Participant in clause 8 in her Resolution. Although some errors or interferences were found in her reorganizations of language patterns, which was addressed by the teacher's feedback, her writing showed how she used translanguaging to construe experiential meaning through various realizations.

Table 6-9 Highlighting the use of language patterns in Text 6-11

Stages	No.	Joint construction text	Individual construction text
Complication	1	Presently the Dog came to him, with a bone in his mouth,	Presently, the cow came to him, with a grass in his mouth,
	2	and said, "Come and fetch and you can eat bone".	and said "Come and have milk, and you can eat grass"
	3	The Ox said "Moo" and stamped the Dog.	The Horse said "neigh" and stamped the Cow.
	4	That made the Dog very angry.	That made the Cow very angry.
Resolution	5	Presently, the Dog called the bird to bite the Ox's nose.	Presently cow cries
	6	And the Ox cried with pain.	the Man and came to him
	7	The Man heard the Ox's cries	the Man put with a saddle on his back and a bit in his mouth.
	8	and came to him.	
	9	He put the rope into the Ox's nose.	

Problems were found in some texts. The common one concerned with the change of verbal tense, which was not unexpected. Although we have had numerous practices of changing verbal tense, the students were deeply influenced by Chinese way of languaging. Text 6-12 written by Student 10 presents an example of a text with such type of cross-linguistic influence.

Text 6-12 An individual construction text with interference from Class 2

In the beginning of years, when the world was new and all. Dog was the best friend of man, people liked it very much, dog can help people with look at home. But one day it won't work for people anymore, most excruciatingly idle. So the Cat and the rabbit went to play on it.

The dog is very angry, chase them two runs, the Cat and the rabbit caught hold of its tail. The dog jumped up, humans see here that the dog's weakness was its tail, from now on, the dog can only work for human.

Text 6-12 also presents the student's flexible combination of her previously learned language patterns and own linguistic repertoire; as well as her translanguaging strategy. One problem to note in the text was the change of verbal tense. The student actually knew the rule, but she would habitually forget to change the verbal tense. This can be seen from the fact that in some clauses she changed the verbal tense into past tense, such as "when the world was new and all" and in some clauses she did not, such as "Dog is best friend of man".

Other problems found in some texts included the incomplete text lacking stages or phases, interference from L1 sentence pattern, and spelling errors. Several texts in Class 2, like those in Class 1, made a good beginning, while lacking Complication stage or Resolution stage, leaving the text incomplete. The interference by the way of Chinese languaging was shown by the confused or awkward sentences the students made. For example, the clause "chase them two runs", equivalent to "chased them", was the literal translation of Chinese. All in all, the errors and problems of the texts in individual construction dramatically decreased compared with the pre-tests, which were coped with by the feedback from the teacher researcher.

In sum, the texts in individual construction of both Class 1 and Class 2 fulfill the basic expectations of the learning task by taking a good control of the stages and phases, and flexible use of language patterns. The students have gradually developed the ways of English languaging in their writings, such as, in the use of accurate clause patterns, nominal groups and process types. Comparatively speaking, the texts in Class 2 presented more flexible use of language resources. In writing the texts, the students in Class 2 used any language resources to construct meanings, by combining the reading text with joint construction text, the beginning with the ending, English with Chinese. However, their use of grammar and lexis to some extent was cross-linguistically influenced. The reason may be that English languaging was still new for them. When there were no relevant English resources, they would resort to their previously acquired ways of languaging. Even they have learned new ways of English languaging, they may forget to use them at times. Therefore, more English resources and languaging practices are needed to help take control of the basic English language in low language strata.

6.3.3 The role of individual construction

Individual construction was a significant step for both the teacher and the students.

For the teacher, it provided an insight into the students' learning progress as reflected in their writing results, which was helpful for them to prepare the next lesson. For example, which language aspects should be emphasized?

The individual construction activities assisted the students in practicing the writing patterns which had been explicitly scaffolded for them. As the genre and register have been set, the students could focus on developing low language strata, i.e. grammar and graphology. Since the language patterns were provided and practiced in sentence making and joint construction steps, the students practiced constructing a new field with the language patterns. In particular, the struggling learners obtained opportunities to practice spelling and punctuation by repeating the same language patterns.

The individual construction task thus played an important role in promoting students' developmental trajectory in their writing. As the comparison with the results of pre-texts showed, individual construction was a crucial step towards the final assessment task. The genre and language resources were reconstructed in each step through all learning activities incorporating translanguaging in meaningful contexts. Although individual construction was mainly carried out by students individually, translanguaging as a supportive tool was encouraged to recognize their thoughts or to discuss with other students or the teacher. In addition, the teacher also provided language supports or feedback to assist students in completing a successful whole text.

6.4 Assessing Post-intervention Text

The total 44 texts were collected in post intervention from two classes: 22 from Class 1 and 24 from Class 2. The average score for Class 1 was 25 (out of 42); the highest score was 34, the lowest was 14. The average score for Class 2 was 23 (out of 42); the highest was 34, the lowest 12.

8 examples from the post-texts were selected and analyzed below, following the same steps as introduced in Section 6.2. The original texts were firstly presented, then typed as a whole text and laid out clause by clause. In the following discussion, several levels of realization were considered: (1) genre and register, examining to what extent the text achieved its purpose, constructed field, enacted tenor and formed mode; (2) grammar, including aspects of appropriate language structure, literacy language device, and the incidence of low rank cross-linguistic influence; (3) lexis, checking the appropriate use of entities in English, and graphic features, covering spelling and punctuation.

6.4.1 Independent writing task

After two iterations of the intervention program, the students were asked to do the independent writing task. This task was to write an ethnic story they had heard before, or to expand their independent construction text. The task challenged the students in two ways. The first, their stories were mostly told by their ethnic language or Chinese, but they had to re-instantiate information from their languages into English. The second, as the students had relatively poor English resources, the expansion of literacy language was still a challenging task for them.

In their independent writing, the students adopted the strategies modeled in the sentence making and joint construction steps. In addition, translanguaging strategies were also encouraged. Firstly, the students could use all resources that they have accessed to, including all reading texts and joint construction texts, re-instantiated resources and resources negotiated for ideas. Secondly, the students could use translanguaging at any writing stage, such as recognizing ideas, planning, drafting, to integrate every language resource with their own linguistic repertoire in order to construe their experimental meanings.

The individual writing task for the post texts was also carried out in the classroom. The students can consult with the teacher or discuss with their classmates at any point and in any language. After they finished the texts, their post-texts were collected as the sources for assessment of the result of the iterations.

6.4.2 Narrative for ethnic stories

The post texts served as sources for investigating the writing promotion after the iterations. The impact of the iterations on the students' writings was then explored to investigate how the stories were organized, how the plots were constructed, how language resources were developed, according to the assessment principle described in Section 6.1. In particular, genre and register, lexical resources, and grammar and graphic features will be the foci.

1. Genre and register

The genre modeled in the intervention program included stages and phases of narratives. During the intervention, only the core stage was introduced without too much detailed information in Iteration 1. In Iteration 2, there were more additional phases, including a series of problems and solutions.

In terms of genre and register, the post-texts demonstrated great development. Most texts were organized following the structure of narratives. The field was successfully constructed by more specific phases with clear settings and plots. The tenor was enacted by rich evaluations, and the mode presented the written resources. The promotion can be testified by making a comparison with both low and high scored texts in the pre-texts.

Text 6-13 presents the post-text of Student 1, the writer of Text 6-1 from Class 2. Text 6-13 shows an example of progress for a low scoring pre-text student.

Text 6-13　Post-text 1

In the beginning of years, when the world was so new. There was an Dog, and lived on the Living in an house, because he did not want to work, so he ate farmer's bone and meal, and he was happy every day.

Presently, the Horse came to him, with the saddle on his back and a bit in his mouth, "Dog, O, Dog, come out and trot like the rest of us."

The Dog said "accumulate" and stamped the Horse went away and told the Man, and the Ox very angry.

Presently the Horse called the fly to the Dog's chief. And the Dog cried with pain. The Man heard the Dog's cries and came to him.

And from that day to this the Dog alway House the house for the farmer.

Text 6-13 is a story about how the Dog worked for the Man. The Dog is one of the favorite live stocks in the Dong area. The text first described the setting of the story, including time, place, character; then the Complication with a series of problems, including the Dog's unwilling to work and the conflict between the Dog and the Horse. At the Resolution stage, the tension was released by the re-setting and solution phases.

Compared with Text 6-1, Text 6-13 shows great progress. Text 6-1 was more like a short recount with no Complication (discussed in Section 6.4.2), while Text 6-13 was a narrative with complete stages, and each stage was well developed than Text 6-1 in that Text 6-1 had only three sentences in a paragraph, while in Text 6-13, several paragraphs were used to indicate different phases. In Text 6-13, more accurate written language resources were used too. For example, the writer used the inaccurate expression in clause 2 of Text 6-1: "but the body is very tired", and she can express this pattern in clause 6 of Text 6-13: "he was happy every day". Table 6-10 presents the comparison of the stages and phases between Texts 6-1 and 6-13.

Table 6-10 Comparison of stages and phases between Texts 6-1 and 6-13

Stages	Phases	Text 6-1 (Pre-text)	Text 6-13 (Post-text)
Orientation	Setting	Today, I'm and feind eat Practice jump dance.	In the beginning of years, when the world was so new. There was an Dog,
	Problem	but the body is very tired	and lived on the Living in an house, because he did not want to work,
	Solution		so he ate farmer's bone and meal,
	Reaction		and he was happy every day.
Complication	Problem		Presently, the Horse came to him, with the saddle on his back and a bit in his mouth, "Dog, O, Dog, come out and trot like the rest of us." The Dog said "accumulate" and stamped the Horse went away and told the Man, and the Ox very angry.
	Problem		Presently the Horse called the fly to the Dog's chief. And the Dog cried with pain. The Man heard the Dog's cries and came to him.
Resolution	Solution	So I'm is pleasure.	And from that day to this the Dog always House the house for the farmer.

The post-text developed rich plot by setting a series of problems and then resolving them, which reveals the student's progress of using various language resources to build a new field.

This progress was also quite evident for low-scoring students in the pre-texts from Class 1. Another example to show the progress is Text 6-14, written by Student 2 whose pre-text was Text 6-2.

Text 6-14   Post-text 2

[Orientation]

setting

In the beginning of years, when the world was brand new. there was a Cat, and he lived on the river, because he did not want to work, He liked eating fish.

[Complication]

problem

One day, the Cat did not work, and he went to the river. At the time running a Dog, The dog said what are you doing. Cat said I thought eating fish. Dog very angry, He said fish? Fish is my, Cat said the we come river catch, after a time, dog said, I not fish, you eating. I throw in the towel. Cat very happy!

[**Resolution**]

But we call it "Dog" now, not to hurt his feelings. The Cat said give you eating.

At The time, Cat and Dog peace, His become good friend.

Text 6-14 is a story about the Cat and the Dog, two most common domestic animals. There is a saying in the Dong community: "The Cat can't see the Dog, and the Dog can't see the Cat", which means the Dog and the Cat are born enemies, and if they see each other they must fight. Text 6-14 described the problems between the Cat and the Dog and the resolution. The Orientation stage told the time, place and characters.

At the Orientation stage, the student appropriately applied the learned language resources to introduce the setting: the time, the character Cat, where he lived, and what he liked to do. At the Complication stage, she developed the plot of the story: the Cat and the Dog quarreled for a fish. At the Resolution stage, the solution was they lived in peace. As we can see, the genre and register were well developed. The Complication and Resolution stages show the evidence that the student learned to combine his own linguistic resources with the newly learned patterns, though there still existed a few inappropriate and inaccurate language use. For these reasons, the total score of Text 6-14 is 25 points, 17 points higher than 8 points of her pre-text.

The progress in terms of genre and register was also presented in the post-texts of the students whose pre-texts are medium scored. Text 6-15 was the post-text of Student 3 whose pre-text was Text 6-3 from Class 2.

Text 6-15 reorganized the story of the reading text by using most of the resources negotiated in the previous activities and some new resources. It was also structured as stages of Orientation—Complication—Resolution. The Complication stage in Text 6-15, compared with Text 6-3, was well developed with more detailed information, composed of three paragraphs to elaborate three problems. Its genre analysis is presented below.

Text 6-15　　Post-text 3

[**Orientation**]

setting

In the middle of a Howling Desert, there's an animal that did not want to working. he name's camel.

[Complication]

problem 1

One day the Camel were walking. there's a dog came to him and said "How the camel got you hump?" The Camel's said, because I didn't want to work, HA HA HA! dog said, "At that time, you have to work or not, now you should be punished." Humph! Said the Camel, and went away.

problem 2

Presently, the Horse came to him and as usual with a saddle on his back and a bit in his mouth, and said "Oh! Camel how the camel got you hump?" said the Camel, very angry, you went out! you guys were so annoying. I didn't want to tell you. the Horse said: "Camel, you're very lazy to back to grow up the hump, and went away."

problem 3

Presently the Ox came to him and said: "Camel O Camel! how the Camel got you hump?" The Ox was very surprised to say, the Camel were starting to be unhappy again and said: "Were you here to laugh at me? the Ox said: HA HA! No, not really, I just feel like you are so lazy, that's the way it is, the Camel was angry and said" Humph! and went away.

[Resolution]

solution

In the end, the Camel had not become so diligent. So Man always find a way to punish him. He wouldn't be so naughty.

Text 6-15 rewrote the topic of the reading text, i.e. the lazy Camel. It inevitably employed the language resources in the reading text. Moreover, the student expanded the plots by adding her linguistic repertoire into three paragraphs at the Complication stages, presenting a vivid picture that how three animals: the Dog, the Horse and the Ox coped with the lazy Camel. The text was adequately organized in genre and phases. Some inappropriate and inaccurate use of grammar patterns and punctuation were found, so the total score is 27 points, 17 points higher than the pre-text.

Text 6-16 shows another example of the progress with a more engaging story in the post-text by Student 4 from Class 1, whose pre-text (Text 6-4) was at medium level. The pre-text was also a narrative that recounted the event of learning to ride a bike, but it had only four simple sentences without any meaning expansions. The post-text was a narrative about a story of the Man and the Horse, and tensions between them were built in the story, successfully realizing the purpose of engaging readers.

Text 6-16　Post-text 4

[Orientation]

setting

In the beginning of years, when the world was brand new, there was a Horse, and he lived on the edge of the grass. he did not want to work. He liked came to the river to take a bath, and like to ate grass, most excruciatingly idle.

[Complication]

problem 1

One day, the Horse did not want to work, and he went to the grass land and trotted. And a Man played Horse tail, That made Horse the very angry, play the Man. The Horse mater came to the grass land, see the scene.

problem 2

Presently the Horse came to the river to take a bath. The Horse mater heard the Horse's cry and came to the river. And he saw a man pulling the tail of a horse. The horse was angry. The Horse mater said to the Man, the tail was the Key. He found the Horse tail was key to him. And said sorry.

[Resolution]

solution

And from that day to this, the Horse began to work for Man.

Text 6-16 was also a whole story with adequate stages and phases. There were only a few errors in terms of grammar and spelling, thus its total score was 30 points, 18 points higher than the pre-text.

The post-text was in fact the expansion of the student's individual construction text (Text 6-7) in Iteration 1. As the main focus of Iteration 1 was the genre, i. e. how to write a whole text, and the emphasis of Iteration 2 was the expansion of the story, i. e. how to write an engaging story, the text expanding was also encouraged. Text 6-16 was a typical example of the writing expansion. It mainly expanded the Complication stage by adding new plots. The comparison of the Complication stage between Texts 6-7 and 6-16 is presented in Table 6-11.

Table 6-11   Comparison of the Complication stage between Texts 6-7 and 6-16

Phases	Pre-text	Phases	Post-text
problem 1	One day, the Horse did not want to work, and he went to the grass land and trot. And a man play horse tail, That made Horse the very angry, play the Man.	problem 1	One day, the Horse did not want to work, and he went to the grass land and trotted. And a Man played Horse tail, That made Horse the very angry, play the Man.
solution	The man came to the grass land, and said the Man, "sorry, I'm very sorry for you."	solution	The Horse mater came to the grass land, see the scene.
		problem 2	Presently the Horse came to the river to take a bath. The Horse mater heard the Horse's cry and came to the river. And he saw a man pulling the tail of a horse. The horse was angry. The Horse mater said to the Man, the tail was the Key.
		solution	He found the Horse tail was key to him. And said sorry.

Text 6-16 expanded the Complication stage by adding a problem and a solution phase, and the previously learned language patterns were more accurately applied. In addition, the writer also demonstrated her knowledge about combining new resources with the old ones.

As the students' control of genre and register developed, some of them characterized the plots by using phases more than resources negotiated during the iterations. The discussion mainly covered the problems of a lazy or idle animal (for the Complication stage) and the solution that the animals began to work for the Man (for the Resolution stage). Some students developed their stages following the same phases and language patterns as taught during the iterations, demonstrated by Texts 6-14, 6-15, 6-16. Some expanded the phases and constructed various interesting stories, with rich plots unconfined by the models.

Text 6-17 written by Student 11 from Class 2 and Text 6-18 written by Student 12 from Class 1 can be taken as examples. The generic structure of both texts are presented below, with the stages and phases annotated.

Text 6-17   Post-text 5

[Orientation]

One day, the son of a king mouse was very hungry, and he went to the rice house of the cat's master's house.

[Complication]

The cat found the cat and ate him. The king was angry and wanted revenge.

[Resolution]

The next day, the king mouse called his good friend the dog to cheat the cat to kill a place that nobody knows, how is the dog deceived? The dog went to the river by the river to hang a fish, and he took the cat and killed the cat.

The problem at the Complication stage described the plot that the cat ate the son of the mouse king, and the solution at the Resolution stage was that the mouse king asked his friend dog to kill the cat.

Text 6-18   Post-text 6

[Orientation]

In the beginning of years, there had a cat, he was sleeping every day. He did not want to work and he like to eat. Most excruciatingly idle.

[Complication]

One day, the cat was sleeping on the flowed, then he saw a little mouse in the kitchen, the mouse was eating rice. The cat came to the kitchen. He caught the mouse' head. The cat was hungry, then the cat ate the mouse.

The man came to the kitchen. He saw the cat was eating the mouse. The man was praised the cat.

[Resolution]

From that day, the cat began to work the man.

Text 6-18 followed the Orientation and Resolution stages taught in the iterations, but the plot at the Complication stage was creative. It was about how the cat caught the mouse.

Both Texts 6-17 and 6-18 followed the same stages and phases of the narratives of the models, but their fields and plots were innovative. The innovative compositions served as an indicator of the students' confidence and control over relevant KAEL.

2. The expansion of language resources

Literacy language is an important part in the assessment of narrative, since such kind of language resource construes the field of stories to engage readers. Those language resources realize the key elements that construe a series of plots. Analyzing the use of language resources in the post-texts showed that whether the students were able to construct a series of events in the way of English languaging.

The most apparent progress they made was the meaning expansion in the post-texts, involving more language resources. The pre-texts generally consisted of several short sentences, mostly involving the students' speaking language in daily life. Obviously, the key elements were usually lacked, so the stories were more often incomplete or monotonous. The wordings that expand meanings are related to the key elements in stories, which assists in building tensions in stories. Table 6-12 compares the wordings at different stages between Texts 6-1 and 6-13.

Table 6-12 Meaning expansions in Text 6-13 compared with Text 6-1

Stage	Word groups	Text 6-1(Pre-text)	Text 6-13(Post-text)
Orientation	time	today	In the beginning of years, every day, the world, an Dog, he
	people/thing	I'm and feind, dance, the body,	farmer's bone and meal
	process	eat, practice, jump	was, lived, did not want to work, ate, was
	place		in an house
	quality		so new, happy
Complication	time		Presently
	people/thing		the Horse, him, Dog, the Man, fly, Dog's chief, /cries, "accumulate"
	process		came to, come out, trot, said, stamped, told, went away, called, cried, heard
	quality		with the saddle on his back, a bit in his mouth, like the rest of us, angry, with pain
Resolution	time		And from that day to this
	people/thing	I	the Dog, the house, the farmer. /House
	process	am	
	quality	pleasure.	Always

The wording comparison shows more use of literacy language in the post-text. The expanded wordings indicate that the student's progress going beyond her personal experience to employ rich language resources to construe rich and meaningful experience. Table 6-13 indicates how the language resources in Text 6-13 realized various elements, construing rich experiential meanings.

CHAPTER SIX STUDENTS' WRITING DEVELOPMENT IN ENGLISH

Table 6-13 Wordings in Text 6-13

No.	Stages & Phases	Clauses	Word groups	Wordings
1	[Orientation] setting	In the beginning of years, when the world was so new.	time	In the beginning of years, every day
2		There was an Dog,	people/ thing	the world, an Dog, he
3		and lived on the Living in an house,	thing	farmer's bone and meal
4	problem	because he did not want to work,	process	was, lived, did not want to work, ate, was
5	solution	so he ate farmer's bone and meal,	place	in an house
6	reaction	and he was happy every day. //	quality	so new, happy
7	[Complication] problem 1	Presently, the Horse came to him, with the saddle on his back and a bit in his mouth,	time	Presently
8		"Dog, O, Dog, come out and trot like the rest of us."//	people/ thing	the Horse, him, Dog, the Man, fly, Dog's chief, cries, "accumulate"
9		The Dog said "accumulate"	process	came to, come out, trot, said, stamped, told, went away, called, cried, heard
10		and stamped		
11	reaction	the Horse went away	quality	with the saddle on his back, a bit in his mouth, like the rest of us, angry, with pain
12		and told the Man,		
13		and the Ox very angry. //		
14	problem 2	Presently the Horse called the fly to the Dog's chief.		
15		And the Dog cried with pain.		
16	reaction	The Man heard the Dog's cries		
17		and came to him. //		
18	Resolution solution	And from that day to this, the Dog alway House the house for the farmer.	time	And from that day to this
			people/ thing	the Dog, the house, the farm
			process	House
			quality	always

At the Orientation stage, time and place groups served as the key elements that construe the setting, and people and thing groups presented the problem, whereas the process groups constructed a series of events, and quality groups pointed out both the reaction and setting. At the Complication stage, these types of word groups composed of 11 clauses that built a series of problems and reactions. At the Resolution stage, they demonstrated the solution. It can be seen that the use of rich language resources expanded the experiential meanings, assisting the student in constructing a successful and meaningful whole story.

The post-texts also provided evidence of the promotion of the re-instantiation skills. In L3 writing, re-instantiating wordings from mother language to English can be a great challenge, as descriptions of various events involve lexical items or elements that they may have never accessed before. Many post-texts showed re-instantiations from their folk stories as they constructed various fields or plots by using new items in the sentence patterns from previously negotiated texts. Text 6-13, for example, applied a number of sentence patterns, such as in clause 5, using the new items "bone and meal" in the model "so he ate...". The text was successful in reconstructing the ideational meaning of appropriate lexical items.

Some other texts, however, did not use accurate or appropriate word items when re-instantiation happened. In Text 6-14, there were some awkward use of items: "my" in clause "fish is my" and "give you eating". These two items were instantiated from "我的"(mine) and "给你吃"(give you fish) in Chinese. The first one indeed means "我的鱼" in Chinese, and the proper English word should be the noun possessive pronoun "mine". The reason for the error may be that there are not possessive cases of noun in Chinese. The equivalent English of the second item should be "give you fish". Since most Chinese sentence patterns are different from those of English, when there were no equivalent English language resources in the students' repertoire, they tended to draw from their familiar Chinese patterns.

Literal translation in the post-texts was nevertheless a part of L3 writing development, especially for multilingual learners. It showed the development of their linguistic awareness, which was a step beyond what they actually produced.

3. Grammatical development

In terms of grammar, the students made progress to various extent depending on the challenge shown in their pre-texts. Generally, the grammatical development mainly involved more appropriate grammatical structure for story writings, and less cross-linguistic influence in their post-texts. Progress in grammar can be explored through the appropriate use of sentence patterns, nominal groups, verbal groups and conjunctions.

The development of nominal group and verbal group forms was evident when comparing the low-scored pre-texts with the post-texts. Text 6-1 was marked as one of the lowest scores by a weak learner, but Text 6-13 showed great progress. The comparison is presented in Table 6-14.

Table 6-14 Grammar comparisons between Texts 6-1 and 6-13

Text 6-1	Text 6-13
Clauses	Clauses
1. Today, I'm and feind eat practice jump dance. 2. but the body is very tired. 3. So I'm is pleasure	1. In the beginning of years, when the world was so new. 2. There was an Dog, 3. and lived on the Living in an house, 4. because he did not want to work, 5. so he ate farmer's bone and meal, 6. and he was happy every day. // 7. Presently, the Horse came to him, with the saddle on his back and a bit in his mouth, 8. "Dog, O, Dog, come out 9. And trot like the rest of us."// 10. The Dog said "accumulate" 11. and stamped 12. the Horse went away 13. and told the Man, 14. and the Ox very angry. // 15. Presently the Horse called the fly to the Dog's chief. 16. And the Dog cried with pain. 17. The Man heard the Dog's cries 18. and came to him. // 19. And from that day to this the Dog alway House the house for the farmer.

As discussed in Section 6.2.2, Text 6-1 had simple and congruent grammar, showed by using simple clauses with simple nominal group structures like "I", "the body". It also showed that the writer cannot control the grammatical knowledge well, which was indicated by the grammatical problems with Participants (e.g. "I'm and feind" in clause 1, "the body" in clause 2), Processes (e.g. "eat practice" in clause 1), Attribute (e.g. "pleasure" in clause 3).

In Text 6-13, the development of grammar was evident. The sentence structures were expanded and incongruent grammar was used. For example, in clause 7, there was an expanded Environment "with a saddle on his back and a bit in his mouth". In most clauses, the nominal groups were appropriately used. The verbal groups were also transferred as appropriate tense forms, such as one core verbal group in past tense in a clause. A few problems, however, were found in terms of nominal groups, such as "accumulate" in clause 10 and "chief" in clause 15, which cannot exactly convey the meanings the writer wanted to express. Some verbal groups were misused such as "lived on the living in" in clause 3 and "house" as verb in clause 19, expressing the inappropriate meanings in the field.

The students whose pre-texts got medium score made great progress in their post-texts shown by long and complex sentences. In the pre-text (Text 6-4), though most meanings were accurately constructed, the story was very simple and unattractive for only several short sentences were used. In the post-text (Text 6-16), more complex sentences were used, construing rich experiential meanings to engage readers. Table 6-15 compares the clauses used in Texts 6-4 and 6-16.

From Table 6-15, we can see Text 6-4 only consisted of 4 clauses, while Text 6-16 included 24 clauses, some of which form complex sentences, such as clauses 1, 2 and 3, clauses 5 and 6, and clauses 7 and 8 and many others. Interference occurred at the clause rank in Text 6-4, such as clauses 1 and 4 (see Section 6.2.2). One point to note is that, in Text 6-16, one of the most common interferences is the lack of "be verb" in relational clauses, such as clause 4. The type of interference became less in the post-text, as it can be seen in clauses 21 and 22, in which the appropriate forms of "be verb" were used.

Except for a few grammatical errors, most sentences were appropriately developed with accurate grammatical structure in the post-texts. For the students of low-scored pre-texts, the significant progress in their post-texts was shown by the expansion of language resources and more appropriate use of verb groups in terms of tense change. For those medium scored students in the pre-texts, progress also involved the use of complex sentences. Since the language resources were expanded, plots in the post-texts became richer. Cross-linguistic influence occurred less and were only found at a lower language level. In addition, the appropriate and inappropriate English expressions caused by cross-linguistic influence also indicated the progressing way of taking control of English knowledge.

Table 6-15 Clause comparisons between Texts 6-4 and 6-16

Text 6-4 Clauses	Text 6-16 Clauses
1. yesterday was very an unforgettable day. 2. I've been studying all afternoon. 3. I finally learned how to ride a bike. 4. I very happy.	1. In the beginning of years, when the world was brand new, 2. There was a Horse, 3. and he lived on the edge of the grass. 4. he did not want to work. 5. He liked came to the river to take a bath, 6. and like to ate grass, most excruciatingly idle. 7. One day, the Horse did not want to work, 8. and he went to the grass land 9. and trotted. 10. And a Man played Horse tail, 11. That made Horse the very angry, 12. play the Man. 13. The Horse mater came to the grass land, 14. see the scene. 15. Presently the Horse came to the river to take a bath. 16. The Horse mater heard the Horse's cry 17. and came to the river. 18. And he saw a man 19. pulling the tail of a horse. 20. The horse was angry. 21. The Horse mater said to the Man, 22. the tail was the Key. 23. He found the Horse tail was key to him. 24. And said sorry. 25. And from that day to this, the Horse began to work for Man.

4. Graphic features

The development of the graphic features was also evident whether in spelling, punctuation or paragraphing.

As discussed in Section 6.2.3, most pre-texts, whether low or medium scored, were badly presented with poor punctuation and no paragraphing. In the post-texts, this has been greatly improved. Figure 6-1 below presents the comparison of graphic features between a low-scored pre-text (Text 6-19) and the post-text (Text 6-20) by the same writer, Student 13 from Class 2.

Pre-text

One day. We are family's go to the climb mountain, we went mountain climb tired and happy

Post-text

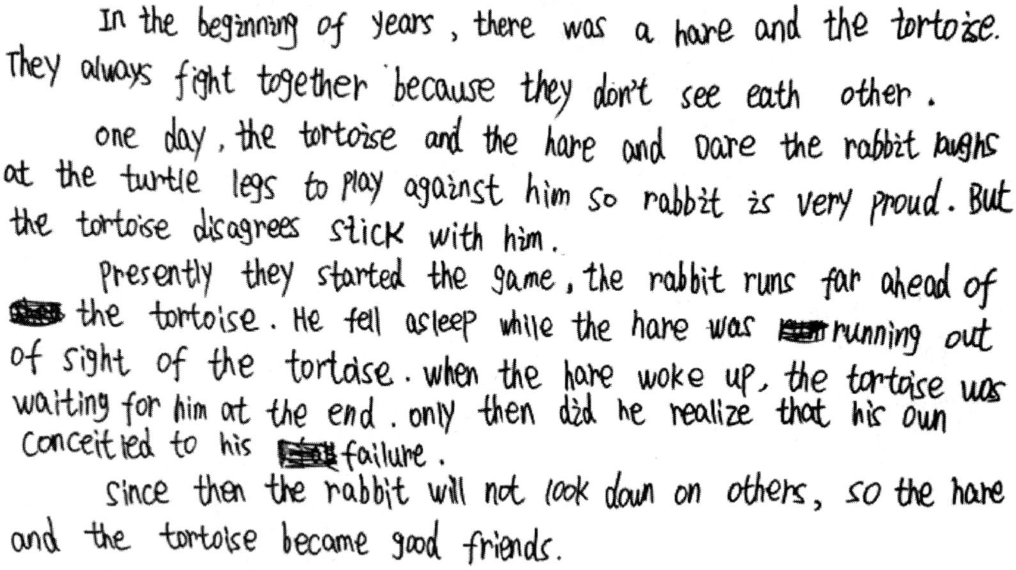

In the beginning of years, there was a hare and the tortoise. They always fight together because they don't see each other.

One day, the tortoise and the hare and Dare the rabbit laughs at the turtle legs to play against him so rabbit is very proud. But the tortoise disagrees stick with him.

Presently they started the game, the rabbit runs far ahead of the tortoise. He fell asleep while the hare was running out of sight of the tortoise. When the hare woke up, the tortoise was waiting for him at the end. Only then did he realize that his own conceitted to his failure.

Since then the rabbit will not look down on others, so the hare and the tortoise became good friends.

Figure 6-1　Comparison of the graphic features between the pre-text and post-text

Figure 6-1 shows great progress in terms of graphic features from the pre-text to the post-text. As we can see, the use of punctuation in Text 6-19 was not accurate and there was no paragraphing even not a clear sentence, while Text 6-20 demonstrated great development in control of punctuation and paragraphing. Commas and periods were accurately used, and paragraph were appropriately divided to organize the text, with one paragraph focusing on one stage or phase. This development was quite common in the post-texts from the students of low-scored pre-texts.

The spelling in the post-texts has also been greatly improved. Text 6-20, for example, had the right big letter for the first word to start a sentence. In many cases of the pre-texts, even very simple words were misspelt, such as "feind" (friend) in Text 6-2. This error become less in the post-texts. In addition, the handwritings in the post texts were more clear and clean. All in all, the improvement of graphic features composed a very important part in controlling the ways of English languaging.

6.5 Summary

The chapter set out to answer the main part of the second research question: "To what extent was the translanguaging genre-based pedagogy multilingual program effective in enhancing students' learning of English?" The answer to the question is that the designed pedagogy is greatly effective in enhancing students' learning of English, as demonstrated by various comparisons between the pre- and post-intervention texts.

The main goal of the intervention program was to enable the students to write stories in L3. The major challenge, as the results of the pre-text analysis indicate, was to move from commonsense discourse and cross-influenced inappropriate expressions into the literacy discourse. The pre-texts indicated pool English literacy level, as most multilingual beginners' writings. They were short and simple and cannot build a complete field, mainly using spoken words in everyday talk, even so a number of misspelling and inappropriate wordings and inaccurate grammatical structure were found. Most pre-texts also had problems in punctuation, particularly in the use of commas and periods.

The post-intervention texts presented great progress in not only L3 literature writing, but language skills and knowledge as well. With regard to L3 writing, the post-texts demonstrated a move from everyday experience to literary meanings. The post-texts narrated various attractive folk stories in a way that is expected in construing ethnic literature. This in turn promoted other language skills and knowledge. As abundant readings were prepared for it, talked around it and re-instantiated to interpret it, skills like reading, speaking, listening and translating were better developed. In these processes, KAEL at all levels has been negotiated, and thus better controlled. In addition, the post-texts realized the purpose of literary narrative by appropriate staging and phasing, achieved by proper lexis, grammar and graphic features.

Therefore, the L3 writing development indicated that the promise of advancing foreign language literacy by the TL-GBP. L3 literary writing has been demonstrated to be a feasible goal for multilingual classrooms in the Dong area. The high staking post-texts from the multilingual beginners showed that the strength of the intervention program as far as effective pedagogy is concerned.

CHAPTER SEVEN
OTHER IMPACT OF THE INTERVENTION PROGRAM

As set out above, the goals of the intervention program were not only to scaffold the students to take control over the way of English languaging, but also to ultimately develop their multilingual competence, and at the same time to promote their metalinguistic awareness and multilingual identity, which have been accomplished by a designed TL-GBP. It is to provide explicit KAL in systemic lesson steps and stages drawing from R2L program on the one hand, and to use the students' whole linguistic repertoire and cultural resources in English teaching drawing from translanguaging theory on the other hand. In this intervention program, the emphasis was on Dong students' language and culture. The chapter will examine other lesson activities involving Dong students' use of translanguaging strategies and their linguistic and cultural resources outside the TL-R2L cycle, and relevant impact on students' multilingual competence, metalinguistic awareness and multilingual identity.

The chapter is organized into five sections. Section 7.1 examines the students' strategic use of translanguaging in modelling their writing, based on the analysis of the interview data. Section 7.2 describes the translanguaging strategies outside TL-R2L cycle designed specifically for Class 2 to record the additional effectiveness of involving Dong language and culture as resources in L3 teaching and learning. Section 7.3 reports on the emerging patterns of learning in the multilingual context in terms of L3 talk development and L1 literacy development. Section 7.4 distinguishes different purposes of students' use of translanguaging in different writing periods, and the impact on their metalinguistic awareness. Finally, the impact on students' multilingual identity is investigated in Section 7.5.

7.1 Students' Use of Translanguaging Strategies

Translanguaging pedagogic strategies entail translation, code-switching and beyond

(García, 2009). In the investigation of the role of translanguaging in the learning process, the students reported that they used all languages throughout all learning stages and the process of their writings. The following categories of translanguaging strategies were identified: code-switching, translation, combination of translation and code-switching, and use of prior knowledge, which emerged from the analysis of the interview data. Each instance will be analyzed qualitatively to understand how the students used translanguaging techniques to achieve their learning goal in the following subsections.

7.1.1 Translation

Translation was the most frequently used translanguaging strategy in the students' writings. Translation refers to "the process or result of turning the expressions of one language into the expressions of another, so that the meanings correspond" (Crystal, 1992). The majority of students used translation at all stages of writing, especially in their pre-texts. As we can see, most students presented their English texts and Chinese translations in their pre-texts. However, if we scrutinized further, we would find that their English texts were indeed literally translated from the Chinese versions. Text 7-1 shows an example of translation—Student 1 stated that she was translating what she was thinking into written English.

Text 7-1　Example 1 of translation

S1：我写作文的时候通常会先用汉语思考，因为我会的英语不多，所以用英语我不能够想到很多东西，也不能深入。

S1：I thought in Chinese first when I wrote an English essay, because I know little about English and cannot think deeply about so many details in English.

In this case, Student 1 completed her writing by using her dominant L2—Chinese, to organize her thoughts, then translating her ideas into English. Forethought in Chinese, she had a clear idea that provided the foundation for the fluency of the writing process. As we will see in other examples, the use of two or three languages also mostly happened in all writing phases.

Another example showed that Student 2 also translated what she had written in Chinese into English in the writing process, outlined in Text 7-2.

Text 7-2　Example 2 of translation

T:写作的时候,你通常用什么语言思考?

S2:汉语。

T:你是怎样做的呢? 你的写作过程是怎样的呢?

S2:我会先把我想的用汉语写个大纲,打个草稿,然后再翻译成英语。

T：In which language did you think during writing?

S2：In Chinese.

T：How did you write your text? What's the process of your writing?

S2：First I wrote an outline in Chinese according to what I thought, and made a short draft, finally translated them into English.

In this instance, Student 2 managed the planning and drafting in Chinese by writing down her ideas and outlines in Chinese so that she could prepare for the next step in the writing process.

In other cases, the students would think in both Chinese and Dong, and then translate them in English. Text 7-3 shows an example.

Text 7-3　Example 3 of translation

T:写作的时候,你通常用什么语言思考?

S3:大部分情况下用汉语,有时候也会用到侗语。

T:什么情况用汉语思考?

S3:大多数情况,因为我们在学校上课都是用汉语,所以现在已经习惯用汉语思考,比如要怎样写,写什么,用哪些词什么的。

T:那什么情况用侗语思考?

S3:老师让我们写民族故事,有时候脑海里面就会想到以前老人跟我们用侗语讲的故事。

T:都是用这些熟悉的语言想好了,然后把它们翻译成英语的吗?

S3:大多数情况是吧,我的英语不行,感觉以前学得很混乱。所以就是把我想的直接翻译成英语。

T：In which language did you think during writing?

S3：In most cases in Chinese, sometimes in Dong.

T：In what cases did you think in Chinese?

S3：In most cases, as we mainly use Chinese at schools, we are used to thinking in Chinese, such as how to write, what to write and what words to use, and almost all things.

T: In what cases did you think in Dong?

S3: When teacher asked us to write folk stories, I had some Dong stories that the old people told us in my mind.

T: So did you often plan well in Chinese or Dong before you wrote English text?

S3: Yes, in most cases. My English was very poor. I felt what I have learned was in a mess, so I can't tell it out. I usually translated my thoughts into English.

Texts 7-1, 7-2 and 7-3 revealed that the students actively thought in their dominant language, Chinese, which supported them to write in English. These examples also demonstrated that the act of translanguaging was not a one-way process. This was especially apparent in Student 3's report. She was shuttling between Chinese and Dong to expand her ideas in the process of writing.

7.1.2 Code-switching

Code-switching in the literature often indicates language shifting that happens in oral communication. In this case, however, code-switching refers to more broad shuttling between codes during the writing, including the alternative use of languages in reading and thinking as writing emerges. In the students' interviews, most of them commented that they shifted codes for various purposes in their writing processes. The following examples present some typical patterns of such occurrences. In the students' views, code-switching occurred to them at a specific point during the writing activities in which they were engaged. Sometimes, the students would switch to English at the point that their English resources were relevant to their thoughts.

In the following example (Text 7-4), Student 4 showed her code-switching technique of organizing and writing her texts.

Text 7-4　Example 1 of code-switching

T:你在写作文的时候通常用什么语言思考?

S4:一般用汉语思考,但有时候用一点英语,相互结合学习的。

T:你的意思是你结合两种语言来写作的? 那你是怎样用两种语言思考的呢?

S4:如果我会写英文的话,我就可以直接用英语来写。如果不会的话,就直接写中文,然后用英文来翻译。

T: In which languages did you think during writing?

S4: I usually thought in Chinese and sometimes in English, and I combined them to learn.

T: You meant you combined both languages to write? How did you think in both languages?

S4: If I knew how to write in English, I would directly compose English wordings. If I didn't know, I would write my ideas in Chinese first and then translated in English.

In the intervention program, the students were scaffolded to take control of English language resources and to use these resources to construct a new text. Therefore, in the process of their individual writing, they reported they often switched languages to draw on all their semiotic resources. In Text 7-5, Student 4 further explained various patterns of code-switching at her different learning stages, showing the improving consciousness and ability to make full use of language resources negotiated in the class and from her own linguistic repertoire in individual construction.

Text 7-5　Example 2 of code-switching

T：在写作中间这篇文章时,用的什么语言思考?

S4：一般都是汉语和英语。

T：写这篇文章的构思过程和写第一篇文章一样吗?

S4：不一样。就是第一次写的文章很别扭,完全是汉语翻译过来的,不会用词,比如:time, thing, process, quality, place 这些几乎都没有用到。然后第二篇文章,就差不多都用到时间,事物,动作,过程,性质,地点这些写法。

T：很好! 就是写的时候更加注重英语的结构了,包括记叙文结构,句子结构,是吗?

S4：对对对,就是这样。

T：那这次还是大部分用中文思考吗?

S4：没有。如果我懂得怎样写的话,我就可以直接用英语写,或者可以仿造一些例子来写作,都可以。

T: In which language did you think when you wrote your middle-text?

S4: Mainly in Chinese and English.

T: So was the thinking process the same with the pre-text?

S4: No. The pre-text was somewhat awkward, because I just translated my Chinese thoughts into English, and I didn't know how to use English words, such as, time, thing, process, quality and place. In the second writing, I can use almost all these elements.

T: Good! It meant that you paid more attention to English structure, including narrative text and sentence structure, right?

S4: Yes, that's exactly right.

T: Did you think mostly in Chinese this time?

S4: No. If I knew how to write, I would directly write in English, or I can write following the samples, in both ways.

We can see from Text 7-5, after a learning iteration, Student 4 performed more frequent code-switching behaviors in the writing process. She explained that after learning the English reading text and jointly writing by using the language resources, she tried to think in English and use English language resources. As a result, she shifted the codes from Chinese to English more frequently to write a proper English text, which demonstrates that her metalinguistic awareness has been developed as she began to pay attention to the specific English language structures. In this interview, Student 4 practiced code-switching unconsciously, which indicated translanguaging was just a very common way in multilingual learners' daily communication and can be naturally used in their learning.

Code-switching practices commonly occurred in the processes of the students' writings, especially writings after the learning iterations. The students learned to employ the language resources they have accessed in their own writings. Text 7-6 shows how Student 2, mentioned in Text 7-2, was shifting the codes to gain the necessary linguistic resources for her independent writing.

Text 7-6 Example 3 of code-switching

T:在后面的写作中你是不是也是用汉语思考?
S2:不全是的,有时候想到一些英语句型和结构。
T:哪些句型和结构?
S2:就是上课学到那些,在英语阅读语篇和共同写作中教的一些内容。
T:你是如何找到你想要的英语表达的呢?
S2:在阅读中,把英语翻译成汉语,我就会印象非常深刻。因此在写作中,我就用中文去思考,但是会去想相应的英语表达,然后再看看英语语篇。有时候会想到一个英语句型,然后把汉语的想法套进去。
T:就是说有时候用汉语思考内容,然后再用英语思考句型,有时候是先想到英语句型再用汉语思考内容,对吗?

S2:是的。

T: Did you think mostly in Chinese when writing the last text?

S2: Not all, sometimes I thought of some English sentence patterns and structures.

T: Which ones?

S2: Those we learned in the class, taught in the reading text and joint construction.

T: How did you find the exact English expressions that you needed?

S2: When reading, I translated English into Chinese, then I would have deep comprehension. So when writing, I thought in Chinese and found equivalent English expressions, and then went back looking for the English text. Sometimes, I may think of an English sentence pattern first and then used it to express a Chinese idea.

T: So when you had ideas in Chinese first, you would switch to English for language patterns, and when you had English patterns, you would switch to Chinese for ideas, right?

S2: Yes.

After the reading and joint construction activities, Student 2 raised the consciousness of drawing on the previously learned English language resources when writing. She used her dominant language to help understand and memorize the main points of the reading text, and shifted to English knowledge gained from the text to write the sentences. In addition, she may think of English language patterns first, and then shift to Chinese to conceive of ideas. More precisely, Student 2 actually used two languages in the input phase. She depended on her Chinese to comprehend KAEL and developed her thoughts in Chinese. When writing, she had to go back to read the English text again. In other words, she depended on her Chinese language for knowledge input, and switched to English for language input. As such, unlike the William's pedagogic model—in which the learner used one language for input and switched to another language for output—Student 2 used two languages autonomously in one single segment of the process. Moreover, it did not only happen at the input stage, as some students reported that they seldom taught exclusively in the output language. On the contrary, they drew on all their linguistic repertoire to complete the task. Text 7-7 shows such an example that Student 5 explicitly stated that she used more than one language to think in the writing process.

Text 7-7　Example 4 of code-switching

T：在写作中你会一直用英文思考吗？

S5：我努力尽量不要用中文思考，要直接用英语写，但是我懂的英语不是很多，所以有时候用中文思考，再去用英语翻译。

T：有没有用侗语思考的时候？

S5：很少，有时候侗语和英语有类似的地方会联想到侗语。

T：那对你写作有什么帮助呢？

S5：能帮助我想起一些类似的英文表达。

T5：Did you always think in English during writing?

S5：I tried to think and write in English as much as I can. But I knew a little about English, sometimes I had to think in Chinese and translate my thoughts into English.

T：Did you think in Dong sometimes?

S5：Seldom, sometimes when there were some connections or similarities between Dong and English, I would think in Dong.

T：Was there any help for your writing?

S5：Yes, it can help me think of some similar English expressions.

It may be reasonable to conclude that, from S5's description of using English, Chinese and sometimes Dong to think while writing, that she had to switch among three languages whenever it was necessary, or where she could not manage in English; otherwise, the flow of her thinking would have been interrupted.

7.1.3　Code-switching and translation

From the above examples, we can see most students not only translated or switched codes separately, but usually combined them or mixed them as well. For example, as mentioned above, they switched languages to develop their writings. In most cases, they used L1 and L2 to organize their thoughts and then translate them into English in writing. This phenomenon also occurred in some students' final writing. For example, in the last sentence of Text 6-7 (repeated below), a student's individual construction text, the writer translated the English verb "play" into Chinese verb "踢", probably with the purpose of more explicitly conveying her meaning, as the idea may be firstly conceived in Chinese and then translated into English. To avoid misunderstanding, she added her Chinese idea besides her English text, which shows that she frequently shifted and translated languages to convey her thoughts best.

Text 6-7　Representative of individual construction text from Class 1

Long long ago, when the world was brand new, there was a Horse, and he live on the edge of the grass land, because he did not want to work. He liked to take a bath, and liked to eat grass, most excruciating idle.

One day, the Horse did not want to work, and he went to the grass land and trot. And a man play Horse tail, That made the Horse very angry, play（踢）the man.

The man came to the grass land, and said the man, sorry, I'm sorry for you. And from that day to this, the Horse began to work for man.

During the interviews, several students reported on instances where they mixed codes and ways of code-switching and translation. Text 7-8 serves as a typical example.

Text 7-8　Example 1 of code-switching and translation

T：你写作过程是怎样思考的,通常用什么语言?

S6：有时候会出现各种联想。

T：各种联想是什么意思?

S6：有时候在大脑里同时用几种语言想象同一个主题,有时候直接用英语想象按英文句型结构去写作,有时候先想到中文,然后翻译成英文。

T：How did you organize your ideas while writing, in which language did you usually think?

S6：Sometimes I thought connectedly in all languages.

T：What did you mean by connectedly?

S6：Sometimes I thought a topic or idea in several languages, sometimes I thought in English and wrote following the English sentence patterns, and sometimes I thought in Chinese and translated my thoughts into English.

To successfully complete the writing task, Student 6 connected all her language resources as a holistic repertoire. She went across languages and broke the linguistic boundaries by using the translanguaging strategy that combined code-switching and translation.

7.1.4 Application of prior knowledge

Finally, another translanguaging pattern, application of prior knowledge across languages is demonstrated. Multilingual students usually developed and used a variety of sophisticated translanguaging techniques in the process of multilingual practices for different communication purposes. These techniques were also used in their writing in this intervention program, and became more sophisticated with the development of the learning activities. Therefore, it was observed that the students used their prior knowledge more frequently and sophisticatedly mainly when writing their post-texts. In Text 7-9, Student 7 applied the knowledge about her native language to organize her ideas for a new field, and the knowledge about English she has just gained to construct her ideas into a new text.

Text 7-9 Example 1 of application of prior knowledge

T:你是怎么构思你的新故事的?
S7:我想写一个与阅读语篇类似的故事,牛在我们侗族也是很厉害的动物,就像英文文章中的骆驼一样,所以我就想到牛是怎么开始为人类做事受人管制的故事。
T:那构思过程主要用什么语言?
S7:先用侗语,我先尽量想一些侗族故事,有时候会用汉语。新故事是用不同的语言混合想出来的。
T:那写的过程呢,主要用什么语言?
S7:侗语、汉语、英语都能用到,比较混合。有时会学着用英文文章中的句型去写。
T: How did you conceive of your new story?
S7: I thought of writing a similar story with the English stories we learned. The Ox is a competent animal, like the Camel, so I thought of writing the story—how the Ox began to work for and obey the Man.
T: In which languages did you think of your ideas?
S7: I thought in Dong first. I tried to think some Dong stories, but sometimes I may use Chinese. I conceived of a new story by mixing various languages.
T: In which language did you think when writing?
S7: Dong, Chinese and English would be all used, in a mixed way. I learned to write English sentence patterns we have learned.

The above excerpt suggests that Student 7 actively translanguaged to use all his cultural and linguistic resources at every stage of the writing process to accomplish her writing task.

7.2　Additional Translanguaging Strategies for Class 2

Apart from the learning activities in TL-R2L cycle, additional translanguaging activities were designed for Class 2, the Dong Class, to help promote the students' motivation, establish identity, and ultimately improve their multilingual competence.

7.2.1　Learning multilingual idioms

The first translanguaging strategy was learning multilingual proverbs and idioms, with the main purpose of motivating the students' learning interest. As described above, the literacy scores of the students in the 2 classes were relatively lower, especially their English score when enrolled. After entering into the college, they had less academic pressure in learning English so they had hardly any interest or motivations in learning English. Therefore, the activity of learning interesting proverbs or idioms was inserted in the process of TL-R2L learning cycles.

The activity was usually conducted at the beginning of the lesson, lasting 5～10 minutes. In each lesson, one student presented two English proverbs or idioms, prepared before the lesson, and translated them into Chinese so that other students can easily get the meaning of the idioms without semiotic load for the next task. After the teacher guided the students to read and practice the proverbs or idioms, the students translated the English idioms into Dong language. Moreover, they could also bring Dong idioms and translate them into English. They need not necessarily translate the idioms literally, but they can find parallel expressions for them. The typical examples of multilingual idioms are presented as follows in Text 7-10.

Text 7-10　Some multilingual idioms

1. A bird is known by its note, a man by his talk.
   闻其歌知其鸟,听其言知其人。
   Qing soh wox mogc banl, qingk sungp wox longc nyenc.
2. Practice makes perfect.
   熟能生巧。
   Bens weex eis tags xus, bens qamt eis lamc luh (kuenp).
3. No pains, no gains.
   没有付出就没有收获。

Bai jenc eis jaems laic, laos yanc gai mangc (jedl) daos.

The students showed great interest in this activity. They found English idioms before class and clamored to write the idioms for the class. Most students actively engaged in the idiom translations and brought their ethnic idioms to the class. It is one of the most arduous task to understand proverbs and idioms in a new language in language learning. During this process, they learned languaging through proverbs and idiomatic expressions and thus their multilingual competence was also promoted. Some students even used these idioms in their independent writings later.

In the interviews, the students commented that the idiom comparisons and translations between English and Dong assisted the acquisition of idioms in English because they could relate some expressions in English to their own languages. In addition, some students expressed that they could also learn Dong language from this activity. They could not only learn the written scripts, which were new for them, but also recall some ethnic idioms, which were seldom said and almost forgotten now.

Text 7-11 Interviews in the activity of multilingual idiom learning

S1：和我们侗族谚语相似的，很容易理解也容易记住。就像"A bird is known by its note, a man by his talk"和侗族谚语几乎一样，通过这个谚语记单词也很容易，里面 bird 就是鸟，侗语中的 mogs。

S1：Some English idioms are similar to our Dong idioms, so that they are easy to be understood and remembered, like "A bird is known by its note, a man by his talk." It is almost the same with the Dong idiom. I knew "bird" is "鸟" in Chinese, and "mogs" in Dong.

S2：有的侗族谚语很有趣地解释英语谚语，如"no pains, no gains"，侗族中"Bai jenc eis jaems laic, laos yanc gai mangc (jedl) daos"，意思为进山不弯腰，进屋没柴烧。与我们侗族生活相关，很有趣。

S2：Some Dong idioms interpret English idioms interestingly, like "no pains, no gains", the parallel expression in Dong is "Bai jenc eis jaems laic, laos yanc gai mangc (jedl) daos." It means that if you don't bend down on the mountain to pick up firewood, you will not have firewood to burn in the house, which is closely related to our Dong lives, interesting!

7.2.2 Composing English idioms in Dong songs

Another activity was composing an English idiom song with a Dong song melody.

Dong song is one of the most important parts in the Dong area. It is a significant way of meaning making and making sense of the world for the Dong people. The students in Class 2, a special class for inheriting Dong culture, have deep love for Dong songs. Most of them sang Dong songs when they were little children. Now they have a Dong song course as a fundamental compulsory class. In addition, they often took part in concerts and competitions to perform Dong songs inside and outside school. It was often the case that some students practiced Dong songs during the break time of English class because, they said, they had to prepare for the next rehearse or performance.

For these reasons, the activity was to use their familiar Dong song melody to compile a song with English idioms as lyrics. At first, the teacher presented all English idioms that have been negotiated on the board, and then the class discussed the lyrics, namely, to select the idioms that fit in the melody. After the lyrics were composed, the whole class practiced the new song. The original Dong song and the newly created song with English idioms as lyrics and the Dong song as melody are presented below in Texts 7-12 and 7-13.

Text 7-12　The Original Dong song 小山羊（节选）

Text 7-13　Newly composed English idiom song with the Dong song melody

No pains, no gains ei. Knowledge is power. While there is life, there is hope. Believing in yourself, believing in, believing in yourself. A bird is known by its note, a man by his talk.

The song was sung at the beginning of the class or a learning stage to manage the class. The students showed that they were greatly impressed with this activity. By the way of singing English idiom song in their familiar melody, they had deep expressions about these English idioms.

Text 7-14　Interview: Impact of song composition activity

S3：印象深刻。下课的时候都会不自觉地去唱。

S3：Impressing! We would sing the song after class unconsciously.

S4：因为旋律很熟悉，所以经常唱，因此这几个英语谚语记得特别牢。

S4：As we were quite familiar with the melody, we often sing it. By this way, we remembered these idioms very well.

7.2.3　Reflections on the translanguaging strategies

From the above, the extra translanguaging practices greatly promoted the students' interest in learning English. Moreover, these activities improved their multilingual competence and established their agency as multilingual learners. Apart from learning English, the students also had a deeper understanding in the ways of meaning making in both Chinese and Dong. In the process of translating English idioms into Dong, the students would recall some Dong expressions, some of which even have been forgotten due to language attrition. These activities, it was argued, facilitated the students to trace their language repertoire. Moreover, the written scripts of the Dong idioms presented in the activities helped the students access a new form of Dong language in a meaningful multilingual context.

Another point to note is that the translanguaging activities reinforced the students' agency as multilingual learners and created a positive experience throughout the activities. These translanguaging experiences provided a space to authenticate the students' sense of plural selves of being and making sense of the world through multiple ways of meaning making. The languaging practices that included the students' language and songs in learning sustained their ethnic identity and established their multilingual identity. The translanguaging practices also reflected the ways of their life and revealed how multilingual students experience the world.

7.3 Tracing the Development of Students' Multilingual Competence

Throughout the intervention program, it was observed that the students actively participated in the lesson activities, involving a large amount of translanguaging behaviors. Translanguaging practices that indicate one of the main features of multilingual communities may provide insights into the development of multilingual competence. In this case, L2, as the major medium of instruction in most subjects, had already been the students' most proficient language, so it was not the concern of this investigation. The key points here were to trace the students' L1 and L3 development in the TL-R2L activities.

7.3.1 L3 talk development

Pronunciation in L3 is an important part in the program for it is an essential language skill of new languaging to be acquired. For example, the pronunciation acquisition of the grammatical terms ensured the understanding. Modelling pronunciation of new terms or words was commonly carried out in the Elaborate phase. The teacher first modeled the pronunciation, and then the students rehearsed it. During the exchange, translanguaging was used to ensure the success of the task. The typical example is shown in Table 7-1.

Table 7-1 Modelling pronunciation

Spk	Exchange	Gloss	Sourcing	Sources	Roles
T	请跟我读"Orientation"。	*Please repeat "Orientation".*	present	knowledge	dK1
Ss	[Pronouncing] Orientation.		recall	knowledge	K2
T	Good! Orientation.				K1'

As discussed above, although a dK1 move was realized by commanding an action, it was still a knowledge exchange, in which the teacher presented English knowledge at the level of phonology. The students recalled and repeated the knowledge as K2 role, then the teacher evaluated it (K1'). Here, L2 and L3 were used for different functions. L2 was to focus the students' attention on the task, and L3 was to present new knowledge. This translanguaging way was similar to the way the students usually practice at home and with their peers, so that the students can easily engage and actively participate in the learning task.

Rehearsing as knowledge exchange was often the case in various learning cycles, even when the teacher did not direct a pronouncing activity. In Table 7-2, the teacher concluded the grammar knowledge that has just been elaborated. Some students rehearsed the grammatical term together with the teacher each time without demanding. There was one thing to note that even though the teacher elaborated the English grammar in Chinese, the students still rehearsed the English expression but not the Chinese one, for they have been quite familiar with the translanguaging practices, like the ways they often act in their daily lives.

Table 7-2 Rehearsing pronunciation

Spk	Exchange	Gloss	Phases	Matter	Roles
T	我们来总结一下，句子成分通常有六个。第一个：thing。	*Let's conclude, there are usually six components in a sentence. The first one is thing.*	Elaborate	grammar	K1
Ss	Thing.		Rehearse	pronunciation	K2
T	第二个：process。	*The second is process.*	Elaborate	grammar	K1
Ss	Process.		Rehearse	pronunciation	K2
	…				

The students also asked the teacher for teaching pronunciations. One example is presented in Table 7-3. In this exchange, after an identification move, a student found that she cannot read the new long word, so she demanded the teacher to model its pronunciation. After the teacher pronounced it, some students repeated without being required.

Table 7-3 Querying pronunciation

Spk	Exchange	Gloss	Phases	Matter	Roles
S17	这个怎么读？	*How is it pronounced?*	Query	pronunciation	K2
T	Excruciatingly.		Extend	pronunciation	K1
Ss	[Pronouncing] excruciatingly		Rehearse	pronunciation	voc

Rehearsing the pronunciation is probably the most common part of multilingual culture. The multilingual speakers need to say the words correctly to express precisely in verbal communication. For example, the pronunciations of some Chinese words are difficult for the people, so they have to rehearse the pronunciation repeatedly in case the incorrect pronunciation would result in misunderstanding. When they learn a Dong song, they also have to first rehearse the Dong lyric many times following the standard pronunciation in order to express its exact flavor. It may be the students' learning habit to rehearse and they rehearsed whether intended as a practice or not in the program, which illustrated that they were more conscious about language differences and willing to internalize new languaging through rehearsing. In the context of multilingual education, the intervention program has scaffolded the students from what to "hear" to how to "say" in new L3 languaging.

7.3.2　L1 literacy development

In the intervention program, the students' L1 has also been improved through the lesson activities. As the minority language involved in this program was Dong, here the investigation of L1 literacy development was mainly concerned with Dong students in Class 2. Dong language is the students' mother tongue for most students in Class 2, but it has been attrited or even lost for them, because they had to learn and speak Chinese in a Chinese-speaking school context when they entered into school. In the lesson activities, they recalled their Dong expressions that they have almost forgotten.

Table 7-4 shows an example in detailed reading. After negotiating the word "world", the teacher asked the students to re-instantiate the word into Dong through eliciting their prior knowledge. However, they have forgotten this languaging in Dong because now they communicate mostly in Chinese rather than in Dong in their daily lives. A student proposed the Chinese word which was also used as the Dong expression now. The teacher implicitly rejected the response by reminding the student of the original Dong expression. The student finally recalled it.

Table 7-4　Re-instantiation in Dong: students' language source

Spk	Exchange	Gloss	Phases	Matter	Sourcing	Sources
T	World(世界)用侗语怎么样说？	How to say "world" in Dong?	Focus	wording	enquire	student knowledge
S18	也是"世界"。	"Shijie", too.	Propose	wording	recall	knowledge
T	是吗？侗语好像有 <u>manl kwangl</u> 说法吧。	Really? It seems that "world" is "manl kwangl" in Dong.	Reject	wording	remind	knowledge
S18	<u>Manl kwangl</u>? 哦！对,是有这个说法,但现在我们年轻人都习惯说汉语的"世界"了。	"Manl kwangl?" O, that's right! But now we are used to say "shijie", the Chinese word.	Propose	wording	recall	knowledge

From the above, we can see that some Dong expressions have been converted into Chinese as influenced by the dominant Chinese. In addition, Dong languaging has also taken in some newly appeared Chinese words as its part. As a result, translanguaging between Dong and Chinese is a common practice among their community members. When we translated English or Chinese expressions into Dong, there still existed code-mixing. Sometimes, the students would redress Dong expressions with the original ones.

In Table 7-5, the teacher prepared the students to translate English proverb "practice makes perfect" into Dong by first providing its Chinese meaning then reminding them of the equivalent Dong saying with Chinese explanation. After the students proposed the Dong saying, the teacher affirmed and repeated the responses. Here one student pointed out "luh" was borrowed from Chinese word, and the original one should be "kuenp". The teacher then affirmed his propose and redressed the saying.

Table 7-5 Redressing the original Dong expressions

Spk	Exchange	Gloss	Phases	Matter	Roles
T	Practice makes perfect. 这句话中文为熟能生巧,侗语有类似的表达吗?	The Chinese is "熟能生巧". Is there any similar expression in Dong?	Prepare/ Focus	L1, L3 idioms	dK1
T	咱们侗语有"常走不迷路,常做不生疏"这一说法,和这句英语谚语意思差不多。侗语是怎么说的呢?	There is an expression in Dong "you would not lose your way if you often walk, and not be unfamiliar with your work if you often do it?" How to say it in Dong?	Prepare	L1 idiom	dK1
Ss	Bens weex eis tags xus, bens qamt eis lamc luh (kuenp).	You would not lose your way if you often walk, and not be unfamiliar with your work if you often do it.	Propose	L1 idiom	K2
T	Great! Bens weex eis tags xus, bens qamt eis lamc luh.	You would not lose your way if you often walk, and not be unfamiliar with your work if you often do it.	Affirm	praise/ repeat	K1
S19	老师,luh 是汉语"路",应该是 kuenp。	Miss, "luh" is Chinese expression "Lu", it should be "kuenp".	Propose	wording	ch
T	Ok! 所以也可以说Bens weex eis tags xus, bens qamt eis lamc kuenp.	So it could be "Bens weex eis tags xus, bens qamt eis lamc kuenp".	Affirm	praise/ repeat	K1

Sometimes, the students proposed the wordings of other Dong dialects. In Table 7-6, after identifying the Dong word "xic unv" in L1 reading text, one student proposed another dialect expression. The teacher affirmed her Propose and elaborated the Dong dialects and the standard form. The teacher then checked whether the students from other Dong dialect areas can understand the standard form. The students clarified the understanding because there are only slight differences among different dialects. By querying the linguistic differences among the Dong dialects, the students had a full understanding of their L1. As more dialects they contact, they can access more knowledge about the L1 and communicated better with their peers from other dialect areas. The rich languaging experiences would indubitably promote their metalanguage awareness and facilitate them to learn new ways of languaging.

Table 7-6 Proposing other dialects of the Dong wordings

Spk	Exchange	Gloss	Phases	Matter	Roles
T	Xic nup 侗语语篇。	"When" in the Dong text.	Focus	L1 wording	K1
S20	Xic unv.	Long time ago.	Identify	L1 wording	K2
T	OK, great!		Affirm	praise	K1'
S21	我们那儿说的是qic kunv。	We say "qic kunv" in our town.	Propose	L1 wording	ch
T	Yes. 我们侗语有不同的方言，阅读语篇中的侗语为标准音，这是榕江章鲁方言。	We have different dialects in Dong, and take the one we are reading as standard. It is Rongjiang Zhanglu Dialect.	Elaborate	L1 wording	K1
T	能够听得懂吗？	Can you understand it?			tr
Ss	差不多，差别不大。	Almost. Most dialects only have a few differences.			rtr
T	Great!				K1'

In the context where Dong people live a mixed life with Han Majority and other ethnic groups, it is a common phenomenon that Dong language has borrowed an increasing number of words from the dominant Chinese in the modern age. Consequently, now young Dong students are more likely to shift their old Dong expressions to Chinese. Furthermore, even though they, as students of an ethnic inheritance class, learned some Dong culture like music and dance, they don't have a Dong language course. As a result, they could hardly get a comprehensive knowledge about Dong, and also language inheritance. In this intervention program, the translanguaging activities provided chances and resources for the students to recall and get full access to their Dong language. Specifically, they could have access to their written scripts, which is particularly necessary for them as to be ethnic inheritors. By comparing their written scripts with Chinese pinyin in the activities of reading multilingual texts, the students can easily grasp the written scripts. The results showed that the multilingual learning experiences and translanguaging practices can improve multilingual learners' metalinguistic awareness, which in turn promoted the learning of a new way of languaging.

7.4 Development of Students' Metalinguistic Awareness

The development of the students' metalinguistic awareness was shown by their ability of regulating their learning by the flexible use of their linguistic repertoire and skills. As the above interviews revealed, all students had frequent translanguaging practices in order to make sense of the reading text, and to construe experiences in their writings. Moreover, the sequence of translanguaging was not unidirectional. The students shifted between languages whenever they found it was expedient or necessary to successfully do their learning tasks. By using these translanguaging strategies in their learning process, the students demonstrated and developed metalinguistic and metacognitive awareness (Herdina & Jessner, 2002), abilities which can assist self-regulation in learning. They used translanguaging strategies for various purposes to self-regulate their learning during all learning stages. With the deepening of learning, the students who were emergent multilinguals have gradually developed into more experienced multilinguals who had more advanced metalinguistic awareness.

7.4.1 Translanguaging for support

As the above examples have shown, the students frequently used translanguaging as strategies throughout the writing process. They shuttled between codes whenever they found this action necessary to accomplish the learning tasks.

As analyzed above, the students used various translanguaging strategies at different learning stages. The driving force behind the translanguaging use exercised by the emergent trilingual students was the challenge posed in the process of their learning at different stages. During the activities of learning cycle, translanguaging strategies were used to deconstruct new reading text and understand new vocabulary in detailed reading and to re-instantiate the Dong text in joint construction. In addition, the reason for the students to switch to the dominant language was to develop ideas in their individual construction. In other learning phases, the students also used translanguaging strategies for different reasons and purposes.

In the pre-intervention texts, the students usually practiced pattern of translanguaging with heavy dependence on his or her dominant languages for support. Texts 7-1, 7-2, and 7-3 present how the students depended on their dominant language to develop their thoughts. In these examples, the students' translanguaging strategies indicated a proactive process that relied on their forethought and a clear idea of what they wanted to achieve. This self-support thought pattern showed much about their self-regulating process of learning. Before they created English written text, they set a goal in terms of the field and quality they wanted to achieve, and translanguaging supported them to pursue and reach these self-imposed standards. For emergent multilinguals, translanguaging can function as a self-regulatory mechanism that expedited the process of language learning, especially when the multilingual learners had difficulties in thinking in English.

7.4.2 Translanguaging for enhancement

After the learning iterations, students have read bilingual texts, acquired some English language resources and practiced joint-constructing new texts. All these greatly benefited the students. They no longer depended mainly on their dominant languages, but relied more on semiotic resources in their writings. They exercised translanguaging not only for support, but also for expanding meanings and enhancing their language skills.

Texts 7-7 and 7-8 show that students exercised translanguaging to use all their linguistic resources to expand meanings and to save cognitive space and time. For example, Student 6 in Text 7-8 used Chinese and Dong to organize her ideas, meanwhile she also used English language resources to expand and express her ideas. The learning of English resources in the learning cycles has expanded her ability to make meaning.

Texts 7-5 and 7-6 show that Student 4 and Student 2's translanguaging practices after the learning iterations were slightly different from those in the pre-texts. In Text 7-5, Student 4 presented her ways of thinking in English. She indicated that although in some cases, she needed to depend on Chinese to develop ideas, thinking in English permitted her to expand the meaning in English. In the translanguaging space of this special class, Student 4 has been moving away from one-way translanguaging to two-way translanguaging (Kano, 2013), that is from translanguaging with heavy dependence on her dominant languages to shuttling between languages. In this vein, she began to move towards what García, et al. (2007) termed "pluriliteracies", which refers to a recognition that written language modes of meanings are intricately linked with all kinds of modalities, including visual, audio and spatial semiotic systems. "Pluriliteracies" give the learner agency to engage in the literacy act that uses different literacy practices to expand the meaning of the text being received or produced. Student 4 has found the place where she translanguaged not for support, not even for expansion, but for enhancement.

In Text 7-6, Student 2 also stated how she made best use of her multilingual abilities, using all her linguistic repertoire to complete her writing tasks. Compared with the dependent translanguaging pattern in pre-intervention phase, she flexibly used all languages at her disposal. In the process of her translanguaging practices, she has been moving back and forth between languages and from the reading texts to her individual writing. By this way, she took every chance to use her entire linguistic repertoire, so that her multilingual competence has been enhanced.

One advantage of translanguaging pedagogy was that, by drawing on the students' full linguistic repertoire, it enabled them to self-regulate their enhancement of every language, even in English class. It turned out that, although the translanguaging pedagogy used in this class was special for the teaching and learning of English writing, the students also benefited from the sustenance and development of their L1 literacy, which has been demonstrated above (Sections 5.2.1 and 7.3.2).

In addition, they also used translanguaging strategy to learn and develop multilingual literacy. In Text 7-6, Student 2 stated that after the iterations, she was aware of using translation to reinforce her English knowledge and she usually went back to find proper English resources to make meanings in her independent writing.

After the teaching and learning activities, the students have been developing into more experienced multilinguals from the original emergent multilinguals. They were able to use their full linguistic repertoire for enhancement. They actively and flexibly translanguaged to enrich their languaging and academic experiences. Consequently, their metalinguistic awareness has been developed in a more sophisticated way.

7.5 Translanguaging for Multilingual Identity

Experienced multilingual students use their entire linguistic repertoire in a holistic way. They translanguage not only for strategic expediency, but also for developing multilingual identity.

In the intervention program, all the experienced multilinguals fluidly and flexibly used their linguistic resources in order to participate in class discussion, mostly in Chinese, to read the multilingual texts, and to write in English. Text 7-15 shows an example. Student 4, a balanced bilingual, when asked in which languages she used to discuss with her classmates, she acknowledged that she usually used Chinese. The exercises of translanguaging also occurred for expediency, and for constructing multilingual identity.

Text 7-15　Translanguaging for multilingual identity

T：课堂讨论的时候你通常用什么语言呢？

S4：汉语。

T：有用到侗语吗？

S4：问别人问题的时候说的是侗话，但是还是会讨论中文怎么翻译英语。

T：上课的时候和同学讨论你觉得用侗语方便还是汉语？

S4：汉语。因为上课都用汉语，我们已经习惯汉语课堂用语，也习惯了汉语思维。

T：上课讨论的时候会不会有时用侗语有时用汉语？

S4：有。有的时候还会说侗语突然冒出一句汉语，或者是英语。

T：什么情况下会这样呢？

S4：就是有的时候，用汉语和同学聊天，突然想到一个东西，但是又忘了用汉语怎么说，然后就用侗语说出来了。

T：Which language did you speak when discussing in the class?

S4：Chinese.

T：Did you use Dong?

S4：Sometimes when asking others questions I would speak Dong, but we also discussed how to translate Chinese into English.

T：Which language did you think was expedient for your discussion in the class?

S4：Chinese. As we mainly used Chinese in class, we were used to using Chinese as medium of instruction and Chinese mode of thinking.

T：In the class discussion, were there some cases that you used both Chinese and Dong?

S4：Yes. Sometimes when we talked in Dong, I would occasionally speak Chinese or English.

T：In what situation would this happen?

S4: Sometimes I talked to my classmates in Chinese, and I thought of a thing, but I forgot how to put it in Chinese, so I said it in Dong.

From the above example, Student 4 demonstrated how she flexibly used her linguistic repertoire in order to communicate appropriately and expediently. In the social space of the classroom, Chinese as the official language occupied the dominant status. In all subjects, including English, Chinese is the major medium of instruction in schools of the Dong area, and the modes of communication in the class are associated with academic success and social mobility. The students have to learn and practice Chinese. English, as the international language, is the target language of teaching and learning, and thus occupies the core place in the classroom. As majority of the students are emergent multilinguals, they can hardly communicate in English, so they tend to discuss in Chinese and translanguage, and produce their writings in English.

However, learning a way of languaging, as García and Li (2014, p. 70) stated, is not easy for learners as it also involves learning "a new way of being in the world". They (2014, p. 70) further pointed out that "new language practices can only occur in interrelationship with old ones, without competing or threatening an already established sense of being that languaging constitutes". Norton (2000) termed it "investment" in learning or practicing a new language. On the one hand, students must cognitively engage in and act on the learning. On the other hand, they also need a secure sense of self that allows them to appropriate new language practices as they engage in a continuous becoming.

Therefore, in the classroom, multilingual students translanguaged frequently and flexibly not only for support, not even for enhancement, but for claiming for their agency, a sense of being. Such translanguaging act has also been termed inclusion, an important function of translanguaging. The students used Chinese in order to be included in Chinese academic community, and English for investment in mobile future successful community, and Dong language for inclusion in their own community. By this way, they have sustained their ethnic identity and at the same time established their multilingual identity.

By allowing the voices of minority students in L3 teaching and learning, as García and Leiva (2014) argued, translanguaging is transformative and it could serve as a mechanism for social justice. In the intervention program, all students' language practices were allowed to use as resources [what Bakhtin (1981) called "raznojazycie"]. In so doing, such practices also encompassed a commitment to multi-discursivity [what

Bakhtin (1981) called "raznorecie"] that includes students' discourses, culture, concerns, and topics of interest. Translanguaging as pedagogy here took what Busch (2011) referred to a "critical gesture" of language practices, aiming to develop a high degree of linguistic and social awareness.

7.6 Summary

This chapter attempted to answer the question: "To what extent is the TL-GBP program effective in improving the students' multilingual competence, promoting their metalinguistic awareness, and developing their multilingual identity?"

Translanguaging strategies which took into account minority students' entire linguistic repertoire produced better English written texts. As the students flexibly used L1, L2 and L3 at all the teaching and learning stages, their multilingual competence (e.g. L3 talk, L1 literacy, L2 metalanguage knowledge) has been reinforced and developed.

Evidence was also provided through the interviews that the students developed greater awareness of the similarities and differences of the three languages by translanguaging between languages. Translanguaging strategies, which enabled the students to shift back and forth between their languages, actually not only helped students to overcome the difficulties brought by language differences, but also added discourse and idea inventory in writing. These L3 learning activities also had repercussions for their understanding of L1 speech and written scripts. Moreover, as they translanguaged for different purposes (e.g. for support, for enhancement, for multilingual identity), their metalinguistic awareness was enhanced as they have become more efficient language learners.

In addition, translanguaging practices enabled the students to invest in any language communities, thus their multilingual identity has also been established—to learn L3 as target language for academic success, to employ L2 as medium and resources to enter into mainstream society and for social mobility, and to develop and sustain Dong culture and language. In the process of reading and re-instantiating Dong ethnic folk stories, their ethnic identity was build and Dong ethnic classics have been translated and inherited.

CHAPTER EIGHT
CONCLUSIONS

This study reports a research that investigated English teaching as a third language (L3) in the context of multilingual education of the Dong area in Guizhou. The research aims to make a significant contribution to pedagogic practices for the third language teaching in the Dong area and other ethnic minority areas in China. Moreover, it seeks to provide effective ways of sustaining and developing Dong language and culture. English teaching in the Dong area is typically characterized by multilingualism, so the research seeks to show how the students' multilingual repertoire is used to facilitate the teaching and learning of a new way of languaging (L3), and to develop students' multiliteracy and multilingual identity at the same time. Therefore, the approach, unlike some common practices, is inclusive by actively involving the students' knowledge and everyday multilingual practices in English teaching over time to develop their confidence in L3 practice. It is thus argued to make a contribution to educational equity and thus social justice.

This chapter presents the major findings, strengths and implications of the research, and then points out the prospects for future research.

8.1 Summary of the Findings

8.1.1 TL-GBP

This research is an intervention program of teaching English in multilingual classrooms of the Dong area. TL-GBP (translanguaging genre-based pedagogy) was designed and implemented by incorporating translanguaging approach and genre-based pedagogy from systemic functional linguistics (SFL). Translanguaging was taken as the holistic approach that takes students' linguistic and cultural resources into account in English teaching and learning, which served as pedagogic strategies to facilitate them to access the new ways of languaging. Reading to Learn (R2L) model, which is itself based on genre-based pedagogy, was taken as a pedagogy. It was employed to design the specific curriculum that makes a planned and deliberate use of translanguaging approach while introducing English in a systemic way.

Translanguaging approach, formulated as teaching strategies, was planned in every step of the R2L curriculum. With regard to the design of the knowledge genres, narrative from story genre family was selected. The translanguaging strategies were the use of multilingual reading texts and multilingual and multicultural resources as teaching materials. The design of the curriculum genres involved the three-layered circle of R2L, including different stages and steps. Translanguaging strategies were alternating use of L1, L2 and L3 at each lesson stage for different purposes. L1 and L2 were used as a scaffold by carefully shifting the discourse towards L3. Moreover, the alternative use of L1, L2 and L3 provided the ways of developing multilingual competence and multilingual identity.

8.1.2 The pedagogic practices of the intervention program

The program was implemented in two ethnic classes (Miao Class and Dong Class) in Kaili University in Guizhou Dong area. The students were selected because most of them are bilinguals or multilinguals, who speak their mother languages, Mandarin Chinese and the dialects and/or other ethnic minority languages. Moreover, they were both educated with the same objective of becoming the special local ethnic minority heritors.

The program involved two iterations in both classes. The teaching steps in Iteration 1 included "preparing for reading—detailed reading—sentence making—joint construction—individual construction". L1 and L2 were mostly used in class talk in Iteration 1 to scaffold students to access to L3 reading text. In Iteration 2, L1 and L2 reading texts were used, and there was a need of re-instantiating L1 and L2 into L3. Therefore, the teaching steps in Iteration 2 involved "preparing for reading—detailed reading—translating—joint construction—individual construction". L1 and L2 were also used in class interactions, meanwhile L3 talk was increasingly used. L3 text was jointly constructed as a result of the re-instantiation of L1 and L2 reading texts. Throughout the learning iterations, the students gradually developed L3 practice in classroom interactions.

In terms of the students' ethnic minority language, the emphasis was on Dong in Class 2 in this program. On the one hand, Dong was used in both classroom interactions and written materials. On the other hand, some additional translanguaging activities (i. e. learning multilingual idioms, composing English idioms in a Dong song) were conducted. In so doing, Dong students' L1 literacy and ethnic identity and further multilingual identity were developed. Furthermore, this practice also provided implications of translating and publicizing Dong ethnic classics, as well as training the ethnic inheritors.

8.1.3 The impact of the pedagogy

In the teaching of English writing, the focus was on handing over control of story genre and register, particularly with regard to field, literary elements, grammar (e. g. identifying clauses and verbal groups), and presentation (e. g. paragraphing, spelling, and graphic features).

Over the iterations, the students can write whole and longer texts with well-organized stages and phases, achieving the purpose of writing narratives about folk stories in L3. Their stories demonstrated considerable progress in the use of literary elements, such as thing, people, time, place, quality. The accurate use of L3 grammatical patterns showed diminishing cross-linguistic influence. For example, their sentences presented growing control of some difficult or specific knowledge about English grammar, such as the proper use of identifying clause (e. g. "be" verb and "there be" sentence pattern), the tense change of verbal groups (e. g. he went to the grass land). The students also showed enhanced competence of spelling in L3, to do with literary elements, and control of punctuation and paragraphing.

The intervention program also had great impact on the students' multilingual competence, metalinguistic awareness and multilingual identity. Throughout the intervention program, L1 and L2 KAL were reinforced and L3 metalanguage talk were also developed. In addition, the use of the Dong reading text provided access to Dong written scripts for the students.

During the teaching and reading process, they developed greater metalinguistic awareness, shown as their awareness of language differences and self-regulation in writing. They became more aware of the differences in the construction of Chinese and English written texts, thus attempted to diminish the interference from their L1 and L2 (e. g. tense change of verbal groups). They used translanguaging strategies to self-regulate their learning, such as translanguaging for support, translanguaging for enhancement, among other things. Furthermore, the students translanguaged for identification as multilingual learners. In this process, the students not only developed

L3 literacy, but also maintained a high standard of their L1 and ethnic identity.

8.2 Strengths and Implications of the Research

8.2.1 Strengths

The research evaluated a design-based TL-GBP program. The methodology underpinning the pedagogy was drawn from genre-based pedagogy and translanguaging approach, and both notions aim at addressing socio-linguistically based inequality. The research drew on the undoubted strengths of genre-based pedagogy while adopting translanguaging approach to explore the teaching of L3 in the context of multilingual education in the Dong area. Several strengths were obtained from the development and implementation of the program.

Translanguaging approach provided a precise way of approximately utilizing multilingual students' advantages to teach/learn L3. Translanguaging that involved students' learning through a process of deep cognitive bilingual engagement promoted a deeper understanding of knowledge. Translanguaging also established bridges between L3 teaching at school and multilingualism in real-life communication. Therefore, not only students' L1/L2 language resources, but also their metalinguistic awareness, communicative competence, language knowledge and even their learning experience can be actively used to learn L3 in a more efficient way.

Translanguaging that encouraged multilingual communication also provided the ways in which students combined different linguistic and other modal resources to negotiate socio-cultural identities. By adopting translanguaging approach, the research changed the traditional approach of trilingual education in which the focus only on English in ethnic minority areas. Translanguaging enabled students to make meanings by engaging their whole linguistic repertoire and expanding it, i.e. to promote additive trilingualism by alternatively using L1, L2 and L3. Therefore, the pedagogy developed in this research was arguably different from some language education types, such as immersion and two-way dual language bilingual programs, which argued for controlling carefully the language use within the different spaces they construct. In this way, the two languages keep in what Cummins (2008) called "bilingual solitudes." However, as García and Li (2015, p. 228) pointed out, "in this more dynamic world of interaction, it is practice in translanguaging that students need."

With respect to pedagogy, the R2L established a clear goal for the curriculum. Its pedagogical focus was on the text, while looking at the context for its use. Therefore, it provided a principled basis for manipulating the curriculum design, planning the specific lesson activities and implementing pedagogy. The approach adopted a "top down method": it began with the genre, proceeded to the register, and moved to discourse, grammar, graphology and presentation. By this way, the pedagogy covered all language levels in teaching a genre across a series of lessons, so the connections between all language levels were maintained. As the pedagogy outlined clear stages and steps of lesson activities, it was simply operable to be extended by incorporating translanguaging strategies in each specific step.

The pedagogy was validated in this research for it provided the researcher a way of introducing the metalanguage about the text type and aspects of its grammar, and scaffolding towards the metalanguage by using students' all linguistic repertoire as resources in teaching and learning. The metalanguage used in all students' languages could be used to assist them in switching between their familiar languages to L3 with confidence and deeper comprehension as they have gradually taken control of it.

The R2L methodology also provided a set of criteria for assessing students' writing development, which effectively assisted the researcher in obtaining a general view of the overall accomplishment of language criteria in writing. This helped inform the researcher to evaluate the teaching and learning and then immediately conduct an appropriate action.

As for learning experience, the approach created engaging ways for all students to learn and to collaborate with their peers. The students became more collaborative as they had to do the tasks together with the other students. The relations among the peers became closer. In addition, as students engaged in the pedagogical activities by actively using any languages at their disposal, their confidence in accomplishing the tasks individually was promoted and their multilingual identity was maintained as well.

A further strength of the research was that it was situated in a real classroom context to address the needs of ethnic minority college students. The teaching units in the program, though innovative by using new teaching materials and pedagogy, were based on the curriculum objectives of tertiary education in minority areas, i. e. mastering three languages: English, Chinese, and the minority language. The program aimed not only at L3 literacy, as most other research has focused, but also involved abundant use of their L1 and L2 to develop multilingual competence.

8.2.2 Pedagogic implications

The Sydney School genre-based pedagogy has been implemented in various contexts in Australia and many other parts of the world, including multilingual contexts, but the main focus of attention has been on one language only (normally the national language or target language). In this research, however, genre-based pedagogy was implemented in teaching/learning L3 with the emphasis on trilingualism, contributing significantly to the development on the application of genre-based pedagogy.

One important implication is that multilingual education should take a real holistic approach that considers students' whole linguistic repertoire for a more effective learning. The use of students' mother tongues in the teaching of the target language has always been subject to debate. In theories of bilingual and multilingual education, there is a strong idea that only the target language is expected to be used, while other languages are often suppressed. The use of students' mother languages and code-switching have thus often been conceived as only interference in developing students' target language competence. Code-switching, however, is inevitable for its pragmatic use to assist students in foreign language learning. In recent years, the term "translanguaging", interrelated discursive practices involving students' L1, L2 and L3, is offered as a more feasible approach to differentiate it from random switch or shuttle between languages. The research has provided evidence about the values of actively utilizing students' language and cultural resources in L3 teaching/learning, for the use of students' L1 and L2 could improve performance in L3 as well as L1 and L2.

It is timely to reapproach multilingual education by planning and promoting pedagogy which values students' ways of learning and being as multilinguals. This research reported here developed a TL-GBP pedagogy by taking the students' whole linguistic repertoire and their multilingual practices into account, attempting to challenge those who theorize the exclusive use of target language. The program deliberately used L1 and L2 as part of L3 teaching and learning and legitimated translanguaging practices whether in teacher's instruction or in students' learning, which enabled students to access high-staking literacy and gain considerable control of the target language (L3). By comparing grammar, re-instantiating lexical items and metalanguage, students' L1 and L2 were also enhanced. The research showed that L3 learning had repercussions for their L1 and L2 understanding, which indicates that students' home languages and cultures are not necessarily depreciative or assimilated in learning L3, but instead they were maintained and indeed enhanced.

Students' mother language should be actively used in trilingual teaching practice to develop their confidence in using L3 and enthusiasm in talking L1. The systematic use of the students' mother tongue to introduce L3 enabled them to proceed in their L3. It is indubitably necessary for students to speak in L3, but to envelope students directly in L3 without adequate scaffolding by using their linguistic repertoire may be counterproductive. In addition, the interrelated discursive practices across the three languages offer their increasing opportunities and interest of multilingual practices. This sheds light on the long-standing concern associated with L3 motivation and multilingual identity. When a pedagogic practice prepares the students to be successful multilingual learners, as modeled in the intervention program, the student will be greatly motivated in investing the target language, meanwhile maintaining their ethnic identity. By this way, diverse linguistic and cultural repertoire are expanded to their fullest extent.

The use of text-in-context model in assessing L3 writing allowed a more comprehensive examination of students' L3 writing development than those only on specific language strata. As articulated above, it examined all language levels in a given context, from genre and register, to discourse, grammar, and presentation, which were first taught and then assessed. Another impact of the text-in-context model on assessment was that cross-linguistic influence and the awkward lexical re-instantiations were viewed as transitional parts of students' progress towards L3 proficiency. The views of considering language interference and lexical re-instantiation in assessing students' L3 development provided a new perspective.

The further step is to familiarize teachers into the new pedagogic practice designed specifically for multilingual education. Teachers should be trained to grasp the theoretical and linguistic knowledge based on SFL. They should familiarize new ways of designing and teaching lessons, such as when and how to use metalanguage, how to introduce KAL, and how to plan the use of students' language resources, among other things.

8.3 Limitations and Prospects for Future Research

It was desirable to consider how successful the study was as an exercise in a design-based action research project. There were, however, some limitations of the research, and accordingly, several considerations were proposed to give directions for future research.

Firstly, as it was the first time to build a theoretically based teaching model by combining translanguaging and genre-based pedagogy, elements of the two theories cannot be all considered in this research. In terms of translanguaging, the design of the teaching model should take all students' linguistic and cultural resources into account. In the intervention program, only Dong language and culture were involved in the lesson activities, while other ethnic minority students' language resources, such as Miao, were not taken into consideration. As reported above, although all students have gained from the program, Dong students from Class 2 benefited more in terms of their L1. Hence, in the future research, all languages, not only one ethnic minority language, in the multilingual classroom should be taken into account to explore the authentic multilingual approach, and to realize true educational equity.

In terms of genre, this curriculum dealt with narrative about folk stories in literary art. Other genres like reports, expositions and explanations, in which embedded literacy might be involved in science subjects, could be planned by incorporating translanguaging approach in the teaching of academic English in minority tertiary education. Accordingly, not only KAL, but also knowledge about disciplinary content should be taken into consideration. One point to note is that, if the language and knowledge of science in these genres are involved, but some terms and concepts are not expressed in local minority languages for they have never needed to do so, will the same method of teaching be applicable to those minority students? Will teaching English involve three languages, or only two languages? If only two languages are needed, what is the role of minority language in teaching genres in science? Therefore, how to maximize the value of students' full linguistic repertoire in disciplinary language teaching when incorporating translanguaging into genre-based pedagogy should be further explored.

One apparent limitation of the research concerns the relatively short period time of the program. The total time in which the study was undertaken was only over two months because this time arrangement reflected the amount of time to learn one genre knowledge for junior college students and this was what the school would permit as the students have to learn the school English curriculum. Ideally, such an intervention program should be conducted longer, so that more time could be permitted to deal with more stories or other genres and to use other linguistic and cultural resources (such as Miao), as well as to provide more evidence for the overall development trajectory to testify the established pedagogical model.

Another unfortunate limitation of the research was related to the small scale of the data sample. The program was designed and implemented to teach English as a third language in two ethnic classes of the local ethnic college, involving mainly Dong, Chinese and English. When it comes to teach English to speakers from other ethnic minority groups in China, for whom their L1 is dominant, will the pedagogy be suitable? Or could the use and roles of three languages be adjusted to suit for students from other ethnic minority groups in other regions? Will this approach also be applicable for multilingual education in similar contexts around the world, in which students are from disadvantaged background or speak indigenous languages? How to adapt or fine tune the model to teach multilingual learners, whose mother tongue might belong to the same language family with the target language? In addition, the pedagogy was designed for college students, will it be feasible for the schoolchildren whose L1 or L2 has not been well developed?

Therefore, the small scale action research can be considered as a pilot study towards more ambitious studies that could be developed in other regions of China and the world in the future. A larger scale project could be conducted in a larger period of time, which could include more diverse ethnic participants in terms of language and socioeconomic background and involve different levels of schooling different subject areas and genres.

References

[1] ACEVEDO C. Will the implementation of Reading to Learn in Stockholm schools accelerate literacy learning for disadvantaged students and close the achievement gap? [M]. Stockholm: Multilingual Research Institute, 2010.

[2] ADAMSON B, FENG A W. A comparison of trilingual education policies for ethnic minorities in China [J]. Compare, 2009, 39(3): 321-333.

[3] ADAMSON B, FENG A W. Models for trilingual education in the People's Republic of China [C]// GORTER D, ZENOTZ V. Minority languages and multilingual education: Bridging the local and the global. Dordrecht: Springer, 2014: 29-44.

[4] ARTEAGOITIA I, HOWARD L. The role of the native language in the literacy development of Latino students in the U. S. [C]// CENOZ J, GORTER D. Multilingual education: Between language learning and translanguaging. Cambridge: Cambridge University Press, 2015: 61-83.

[5] ATKINSON D. Alternative approaches to second language acquisition [M]. New York: Routledge, 2011.

[6] AUER P. Language and space: An international handbook of linguistic variation. Theories and methods (Vol. 1) [M]. New York: Walter de Gruyter, 2010.

[7] BAILEY B. Heteroglossia [C]// MARTIN-JONES M, BLACKLEDGE A, CREESE A. The Routledge handbook of multilingualism. London: Routledge, 2012: 499-507.

[8] BAKER C. Foundations of bilingual education and bilingualism (vol. 79) [M]. Bristol: Multilingual matters, 2011.

[9] BAKHTIN M. Dialogic imagination: Four essays [M]. Austin: University of Texas Press, 1981.

[10] BERNSTEIN B. Vertical and horizontal discourse: An essay [J]. British journal of sociology of education, 1999, 20 (2): 157-173.

[11] BERNSTEIN B. Pedagogy, symbolic, control, and identity: Theory, research, critique [M]. Rev. ed. Lanham: Rowman & Littlefield Publishers, Inc. , 2000.

[12] BLACHFORD D Y R, JONES M. Trilingual education policy ideals and realities for the Naxi in Yunnan [C]// FENG A W. English language across Greater China. Clevedon: Multilingual Matters, 2011: 228-259.

[13] BLACKLEDGE A, CREESE A. Multilingualism [M]. London: Continuum, 2010.

[14] BOSTES. Board of studies [S/OL]. NSW: Board of Studies Teaching & Educational Standards NSW, 2001 [2014-08-15]. http://www. boardofstudies. nsw. edu. au/7-10-literacy-numeracy/.

[15] BUSCH B. Building on heteroglossia and heterogeneity: The experience of a multilingual classroom [C]. The 3rd International Conference on Language, Education and Diversity (LED), November 22-25, 2011. New Zealand: University of Auckland, 2011.

[16] BRISK M E. Engaging students in academic literacies: Genre-based pedagogy for K-5 Classrooms [M]. New York: Routledge, 2014.

[17] CANAGARAJAH S. Lingua franca English, multilingual communities and language acquisition [J]. The modern language journal, 2007(91): 923-939.

[18] CANAGARAJAH S. Codemeshing in academic writing: Identifying teachable strategies of translanguaging [J]. The modern language journal, 2011, 95(iii): 401-417.

[19] CANAGARAJAH S. Literacy as translingual practice [C]. London: Routledge, 2013.

[20] CENOZ J. The additive effect of bilingualism on third language acquisition: A review [J]. International journal of bilingualism, 2003, 7(1): 71-87.

[21] CENOZ J. Towards multilingual education: Basque educational research from an international perspective [M]. Clevedon: Multilingual Matters, 2009.

[22] CENOZ J. The influence of bilingualism on third language acquisition: Focus on multilingualism [J]. Language teaching, 2013, 46(1): 71-86.

[23] CENOZ J, GORTER D. Focus on multilingualism: A study of trilingual writing [J]. The modern language journal, 2011, 95(iii): 356-369.

[24] CENOZ J, GORTER D. Focus on multilingualism as an approach in educational contexts [C]// CREESE A, BLACKLEDGE A. Heteroglossia as practice and pedagogy. Berlin: Springer, 2014: 239-254.

[25] CENOZ J, GORTER D. Multilingual education: Between language learning and

translanguaging [M]. Cambridge: Cambridge University Press, 2015.

[26] CENOZ J, GORTER D. Translanguaging as a pedagogic tool in multilingual education [C]// CENOZ J, GORTER D, MAY S. Language awareness and multilingualism. Switzerland: Springer, 2017: 309-321.

[27] CENOZ J, GORTER D, MAY S. Language awareness and multilingualism [C]. Switzerland: Springer, 2017.

[28] CENOZ J, HUFEISEN B, JESSNER U. Cross-linguistic influence in third language acquisition: Psycholinguistic perspectives [M]. Clevedon: Multilingual Matters, 2001.

[29] CENOZ J, TODEVA E. The well and the bucket: The emic and etic perspectives combined [C]// TODEVA E, CENOZ J. The multiple realities of multilingualism: Personal narrative and researcher's perspectives. Berlin: Moutou de Gruyter, 2009: 265-292.

[30] CHRISTIE F. Curriculum genres: Planning of effective teaching [C]// COPE B, KALANTZIS M. The power of literacy: A genre approach to teaching writing. Pittsburgh: University of Pittsburgh Press, 1993: 154-178.

[31] CHRISTIE F. Classroom discourse analysis [M]. London: Continuum, 2002.

[32] CHRISTIE F. Language education throughout the school years: A functional perspective [M]. Hoboken: Wiley-Blackwell, 2012.

[33] COOK V. Evidence for multicompetence [J]. Language learning, 1992, 42(4): 557-591.

[34] CREESE A, BLACKLEDGE A. Translanguaging in the bilingual classroom: A pedagogy for learning and teaching? [J]. The modern language journal, 2010, 94(ⅰ): 103-115.

[35] CRYSTAL D. An encyclopedic dictionary of language and languages [Z]. Oxford: Blackwell, 1992.

[36] CUMMINS J. Teaching for transfer: challenging the two solitudes assumptions in bilingual education [C]// HORNBERGER N H. Encyclopedia of language and education. New York: Springer, 2008: 1528-1538.

[37] DE ANGELIS G, DEWAELE M. New trends in cross-linguistic influence and multilingualism research [M]. Bristol: Multilingual Matters, 2011.

[38] DE SILVA JOYCE H, FEEZ S. Text-based language & literacy education: Programming and methodology [M]. Outney: Phoenix Education, 2012.

[39] EDWARDS J. Foundations of bilingualism [C]// BHATIA T, RITCHIE W. The handbook of bilingualism. Oxford: Blackwell, 2004: 7-31.

[40] EMILIA E, CHRISTIE F. Factual genres in English: Learning to write, read and talk about factual information [M]. Bandung: Rizqi Press, 2013.

[41] FENG A W, ADAMSON B. Trilingualism in education in China: Models and challenges [C]. Dordrecht: Springer, 2015.

[42] FINIFROCK J E, SCHILKEN D. Emerging trilingualism among the Dong minority in Guizhou Province [C]// FENG A W, ADAMSON B. Trilingualism in education in China: Models and challenges. Dordrecht: Springer, 2015: 199-221.

[43] FLYNN S, FOLEY C, VINNITSKAYA I. The cumulative-enhancement model for language acquisition: Comparing adults' and children's patterns of development [J]. International journal of multilingualism, 2004(1): 3-17.

[44] FU D L. An island of English: Teaching ESL in Chinatown [M]. Portsmouth: Heinemann, 2003.

[45] GARCÍA O. Bilingual education in the 21st century: A global perspective [M]. Oxford: Wiley-Blackwell, 2009.

[46] GARCÍA O. Educating New York's bilingual children: Constructing a future from the past [J]. International journal of bilingual education and bilingualism, 2011, 14(2): 133-153.

[47] GARCÍA O, BARTLETT L, KLEIFGEN J. From biliteracy to pluriliteracies [C]// LI W, AUER P. Handbook of applied linguistics on multilingual communication. Berlin: Mouton de Gruyter, 2007: 207-228.

[48] GARCÍA O, KANO N. Translanguaging as process and pedagogy: Developing the English writing of Japanese students in the US [C]// CONTEH J, MEIER G. The multilingual turn in languages education: Benefits for individuals and societies. Bristol: Multilingual Matters, 2014: 258-277.

[49] GARCÍA O, KLEIFGEN J. Educating emergent bilinguals: Policies, programs and practices for English language learners [M]. New York: Teachers College Press, 2010.

[50] GARCÍA O, LEIVA C. Theorizing and enacting translanguaging for social justice [C]// CREESE A. BLAKLEDGE A. Heteroglossia as practice and pedagogy. New York: Springer, 2014: 199-216.

[51] GARCÍA O, LI W. Translanguaging: Language, bilingualism and education [M]. London: Palgrave Mc Millan, 2014.

[52] GARCÍA O, LI W. Translanguaging, bilingualism, and bilingual education [C]// WRIGHT W E, BOUN S, GARCÍA O. The handbook of bilingual and multilingual education. Chichester: Wiley Blackwell, 2015: 223-230.

[53] GARCÍA O, SYLVAN C. Pedagogies and practices in multilingual classrooms: Singularities in pluralities [J]. The modern language journal, 2011, 95(iii): 385-400.

[54] GORT M. Strategic codeswitching, interliteracy, and other phenomena of emergent bilingual writing: Lessons from first-grade dual language classrooms [J]. Journal of early childhood literacy, 2006, 6(3): 323-354.

[55] GORTER D. Multilingual interaction and minority languages: Proficiency and language practices in education and society [J]. Language teaching, 2015, 48(1): 82-98.

[56] GORTER D, ZENOTZ V, CENOZ J. Minority languages and multilingual education [C]. Dordrecht: Springer, 2014.

[57] HALLIDAY M A K. Learning how to mean: Explorations in the development of language [M]. London: Edward Arnold, 1975.

[58] HÉLOT C. Linguistic diversity and education [C]// MARTIN-JONES M, BLACKLEDGE A, CREESE A. The Routledge handbook of multilingualism. London: Routledge, 2012: 214-231.

[59] HERDINA P, JESSNER U. A dynamic model of multilingualism: Perspectives of change in psycholinguistics [M]. Clevedon: Multilingual Matters, 2002.

[60] HEUGH K. Epistemologies in multilingual education: Translanguaging and genre—companions in conversation with policy and practice [J]. Language and education, 2015, 29(3): 280-285.

[61] HORNBERGER N H. Continua of biliteracy [J]. Review of educational research, 1989, 59(3): 271-296.

[62] HORNBERGER N H, LINK H. Translanguaging and transnational literacies in multilingual classrooms: A bilingual lens [J]. International journal of bilingual education and bilingualism, 2012, 15(3): 261-278.

[63] HUMPHREY S, MACNAUGHT L. Revisiting joint construction in the tertiary context [J]. Australian journal of language and literacy, 2011, 34(1): 98-115.

[64] JOHNSON E, MA F, ADAMSON B. Developing trilingual education in western China [C]// LEE J C K, YU Z Y, HUANG X H, et al. Educational development in Western China. The Netherlands: Sense Publishers, 2016: 177-189.

[65] JØRGENSEN J N. Polylingual languaging around and among children and adolescents [J]. International journal of multilingualism, 2008, 5(3): 161-176.

[66] KABUTO B. Becoming biliterate: Identity, ideology and learning to read and write in two languages [M]. New York: Routledge, 2011.

[67] KANO N. Translanguaging as a process and a pedagogic tool for Japanese students in an English writing course in New York [D]. New York: Columbia University, 2013.

[68] KARTIKA-NINGSIH H. Multilingual re-instantiation: Genre pedagogy in Indonesian Classrooms [D]. Sydney: University of Technology, 2016.

[69] KENNER C. Becoming biliterate: Young children learning different writing systems [M]. Stoke on Trent: Trentham, 2004.

[70] KIBLER A. Writing through two languages: First language expertise in a language minority classroom [J]. Journal of second language writing, 2010(19): 121-142.

[71] KLEIN E C. Second versus third language acquisition: Is there a difference? [J]. Language learning, 1995,45(3): 419-465.

[72] LEVINE G S. Code choice in the language classrooms [M]. Bristol: Multilingual Matters, 2011.

[73] LEWIS G, JONES B, BAKER C. Translanguaging: Origins and development from school to street and beyond [J]. Educational research and evaluation: An international journal on theory and practice, 2012, 18 (7): 641-654.

[74] LEWIS G, JONES B, BAKER C. 100 bilingual lessons: Distributing two languages in classrooms [C]// ABELLO-CONTESSE C, CHACON BELTRAN R. Bilingualism in a school setting. Bristol: Multilingual Matters, 2013: 107-135.

[75] LIN A M Y. Toward paradigmatic change in TESOL methodologies: Building plurilingual pedagogies from the ground up [J]. TESOL Quarterly, 2013, 47(3): 521-543.

[76] LIN A M Y. Conceptualising the potential role of L1 in CLIL [J]. Language, culture and curriculum, 2015, 28 (1): 74-89.

[77] LIN A M Y, LO Y Y. Translanguaging and the triadic dialogue in content and language integrated learning (CLIL) classrooms [J]. Language and education, 2017,31(1):26-45.

[78] LIU Y. Commitment resources as scaffolding strategies in the reading to learn program [D]. Sydney: University of Sydney, Guang zhou: Sun Yat Sen University, 2010.

[79] LYSTER R, COLLINS L, BALLINGER S. Linking languages through a bilingual read-aloud project [J]. Language awareness, 2009, 18 (3-4): 366-383.

[80] LYSTER R, QUIROGA J, BALLINGER S. The effects of biliteracy instruction on morphological awareness [J]. Journal of immersion and content-based language

education, 2013, 1(2): 169-197.

[81] MAKALELA L. Moving out of linguistic boxes: The effects of translanguaging strategies for multilingual classrooms [J]. Language and education, 2015, 29(3): 200-217.

[82] MARTIN J R. English text: System and structure [M]. Philadelphia: John Benjamins Publishing Company, 1992.

[83] MARTIN J R. Life as a noun [C]// HALLIDAY M A K, MARTIN J R. Writing science: Literacy and discursive power. London: Falmer, 1993: 221-267.

[84] MARTIN J R. Embedded literacy: Knowledge as meaning[J]. Linguistics and education, 2013, 24 (1): 23-37.

[85] MARTIN J R, ROSE D. Working with discourse: Meaning beyond the clause [M]. London: Continuum, 2007.

[86] MARTIN J R, ROSE D. Genre relations: Mapping culture [M]. London: Equinox, 2008.

[87] MATON K. Knowledge and knowers: Towards a realist sociology of education [M]. London: Routledge, 2014.

[88] MAZAK C M, HERBAS-DONOSO C. Translanguaging practices at a bilingual university: A case study of a science classroom [J]. International journal of bilingual education and bilingualism, 2015, 18(6):698-714.

[89] MICHAEL-LUNA S, CANAGARAJAH S. Multilingual academic literacies [J]. Journal of applied linguistics, 2007, 4(1): 55-77.

[90] MIN-ZHAN L, HORNER B. Translingual literacy and matters of agency [C]// CANAGARAJAH A. Literacy as translingual practice. London: Routledge, 2013: 26-38.

[91] NORTON B. Identity and language learning: Gender, ethnicity, and educational change [M]. Harlow: Longman, 2000.

[92] OTHEGUY R, GARCÍA O, REID W. Clarifying translanguaging and deconstructing named languages: A perspective from linguistics [J]. Applied linguistics review, 2015, 6(3): 281-307.

[93] OTSUJI E, PENNYCOOK A. Metrolingualism: Fixity, fluidity and language in flux [J]. International journal of multilingualism, 2010, 7 (3): 240-254.

[94] PAINTER C. Into the mother tongue: A case study of early language development [M]. London: Pinter, 1984.

[95] PENNYCOOK A. Language as a local practice [M]. London: Routledge, 2010.

[96] PROBYN M. Pedagogic translanguaging: Bridging discourses in South African

science classrooms [J]. Language and education, 2015, 29(3): 218-234.

[97] ROSE D. Beyond literacy: Building an integrated pedagogic genre [J]. Australian journal of language and literacy, 2011, 34(1): 81-97.

[98] ROSE D. Analysing pedagogic discourse: An approach from genre and register [J]. Functional linguistics, 2014(1): 1-32.

[99] ROSE D. New developments in genre-based literacy pedagogy [C]// Mac Arthur C G. Handbook of writing research. 2nd ed. New York: Guilford, 2015a: 227-242.

[100] ROSE D. Building a pedagogic metalanguage I: Curriculum genres [C]// MARTIN J R. Appliable linguistics and academic discourse. Shanghai: Shanghai Jiao Tong University, 2015b: 1-28.

[101] ROSE D. Building a pedagogic metalanguage II: Knowledge genres [C]// MARTIN J R. Appliable linguistics and academic discourse. Shanghai: Shanghai Jiao Tong University, 2015c: 29-59.

[102] RORE D, MARTIN J. Learning to write, reading to learn: Genre, knowledge and pedagogy in the Sydney School [M]. Bristol: Equinox Publishing, 2012.

[103] ROSE D, MARTIN J. Intervening in contexts of schooling [C]// FlOWERDEW J, LI W. Discourse in context: Contemporary applied linguistics (Vol. 3). London: Bloomsbury Academic, 2014: 273-300.

[104] SAFONT-JORDA M P. Third language learners: Pragmatic production and awareness [M]. Clevedon: Multilingual Matters, 2005.

[105] SAFONT-JORDA M P. Third language acquisition in multilingual contexts [C]// CENOZ J, GORTER D. Language awareness and multilingualism. Switzerland: Springer, 2017: 137-148.

[106] SKUTNABB-KANGAS T, HEUGH K. Multilingual education and sustainable diversity work: From periphery to center [M]. New York: Routledge, 2012.

[107] SOLTERO-GONZALEZ L, ESCAMILLA K, HOPEWELL S. Changing teachers' perceptions about the writing abilities of emerging bilingual students: Towards a holistic bilingual perspective on writing assessment [J]. International journal of bilingual education and bilingualism, 2012,15(17): 71-94.

[108] SWAIN M, LAPKIN S. A Vygotskian sociocultural perspective on immersion education: The L1/L2 debate [J]. Journal of immersion and content-based language education, 2013, 1(1):101-129.

[109] TAYLOR S K. From "monolingual" multilingual classrooms to "multilingual" multilingual classrooms: Managing cultural and linguistic diversity in the Nepali

educational system [C]// LITTLE D, LEUNG C, AVERMEAT P V. Managing diversity in education: Languages, policies, pedagogies. Clevedon: Multilingual Matters, 2014: 257-272.

[110] TSUNG L. Minority languages, education and communities in China [M]. Basingstoke: Palgrave Macmillan, 2009.

[111] UNESCO. Mother tongue matters: Local language as a key to effective learning [M]. France: UNESCO, 2008.

[112] UNESCO. MTB MLE RESOURCE KIT including the excluded: Promoting multilingual education [M]. Bangkok: UNESCO, 2016.

[113] VELASCO P, GARCÍA O. Translanguaging and the writing of bilingual learners [J]. Bilingual research journal, 2014, 37(1): 6-23.

[114] WANG G. Pains and gains of ethnic multilingual learners in China: An ethnographic study [M]. Singapore: Springer, 2016.

[115] WRIGHT W E, BOUN S, GARCÍA O. The handbook of bilingual and multilingual education [C]. Chichester: Wiley Blackwell, 2015.

[116] WHITE P R, MAMMONE G, CALDWELL D. Linguistically-based inequality, multilingual education and a genre-based literacy development pedagogy: Insights from the Australian experience [J]. Language and education, 2015, 29 (3): 256-271.

[117] WOOD, BRUNNER J, ROSS G. The role of tutoring in problem solving [J]. Journal of child psychology and psychiatry, 1976(17): 89-100.

[118] ZHANG Y, GUO Y. Exceeding boundaries: Chinese children's playful use of languages in their literacy practices in a Mandarin-English bilingual program [J]. International journal of bilingual education and bilingualism, 2017, 20 (1): 52-68.

[119] ZHANG Z A, LI G H, WEN L T. Trilingual education in China's Korean communities [C]// FENG A W, ADAMSON B. Trilingualism in education in China: Models and challenges. Dordrecht: Springer, 2015: 47-64.

[120] ZOU W C, ZHANG S L. Family background and English learning at compulsory stage in Shanghai [C]// FENG A W. English language across Greater China. Clevedon: Multilingual Matters, 2011: 189-211.

[121] 阿斯罕.布迪厄实践理论视角下的语言认同:四位蒙古族三语人案例研究[D].北京:北京外国语大学,2015.

[122] 蔡凤珍,杨忠.L2(汉语)对新疆少数民族学生L3(英语)习得的影响研究[J].外语与外语教学,2010(2):10-13.

[123] 曹艳春,徐世昌.三语习得中的元音迁移研究——以[a]、[i]、[u]为例[J].语言与翻译,2014(4):79-84.

[124] 陈丽云.三语教育视阈下的少数民族语言与英语语言习得对比研究[J].民族教育研究,2012(6):66-69.

[125] 陈亚杰,花拉.语境视角下蒙古族大学生英语作文语篇错误分析及对策研究[J].内蒙古师范大学学报(教育科学版),2017(1):123-127.

[126] 崔占玲,张积家.藏-汉-英三语者语言联系模型探讨[J].心理学报,2009(3):208-219.

[127] 冯祖贻.侗族文化研究[M].贵阳:贵州人民出版社,1999.

[128] 盖兴之,高慧宜.浅论三语教育[J].民族教育研究,2003(5):65-69.

[129] 顾有识,罗树杰.中国民族志[M].黑龙江:黑龙江人民出版社,2003.

[130] 古丽夏·阿克巴尔.科学编写适合新疆少数民族学生语言学习特点的英语教材之思考[J].新疆教育学院学报,2011(2):97-99.

[131] 胡德映.云南少数民族三语教育[M].昆明:云南大学出版社,2007.

[132] 黄习中.文化典籍英译与苏州大学翻译方向研究生教学[J].上海翻译,2007(1):56-58.

[133] 姜秋霞,刘全国,李志强.西北民族地区外语基础教育现状调查——以甘肃省为例[J].外语教学与研究,2006(2):129-136.

[134] 教育部.教育部关于积极推进小学开设英语课程的指导意见[S/OL].北京:中华人民共和国教育部,2001:1 [2022-01-23]. http://www.moe.gov.cn/s78/A26/jces_left/moe_714/tnull_665.html.

[135] 教育部高等学校大学外语教学指导委员会教育部.大学英语教学指南(2020版)[M].北京:高等教育出版社,2020.

[136] 李嵬.新中式英语和后多语主义[J].语言学研究,2016(1):16-26.

[137] 李玉霞.英语影视剧迷在中国社交媒体中的超语嬉戏[J].语言学研究,2016(1):39-52.

[138] 刘承宇,单菲菲.贵州侗族地区三语教育现状调查研究[J].民族教育研究,2016(1):61-69.

[139] 刘承宇,谢翠平.《第三语言习得中跨语言影响的心理语言学研究》述评[J].当代语言学,2006(4):372—377.

[140] 刘承宇,谢翠平.外语专业学生第二外语学习中的跨语言影响研究[J].外语教学,2008(1):43-47.

[141] 刘惠萍,张绍杰.请求策略语用对比研究——以新疆维吾尔族大学生为例[J].外语与外语教学,2012(3):24-28.

[142] 刘全国.三语环境下外语教师课堂语码转换研究[D].兰州:西北师范大学,2007.

[143] 刘全国,李倩. 我国民族地区英语课堂三语教学模型探索[J]. 青海民族研究,2011(1):75-78.

[144] 刘懋琼. 三语习得中的跨语言影响分析[J]. 人民论坛,2010(10):206-207.

[145] 马玉蕾. 马丁基于语类理论的写作教学框架[J]. 当代外语研究,2010(10):50-54.

[146] 马玉蕾. 阅读、写作和学习三者之间的对接——《为写而学,为学而读——悉尼学派的语类、知识和教学法》评介[J]. 当代外语研究,2014(11):69-72.

[147] 马玉蕾. 语类教学法本土化与外语教师发展[J]. 北京科技大学学报(社会科学版),2017(1):9-17.

[148] 欧亚丽,刘承宇. 语言距离对英语作为第三语言学习的蒙古族学生语音迁移的影响[J]. 西安外国语大学学报,2009(4):93-97.

[149] 热比古丽,白克力,闻素霞,雷志明. 维一汉一英三语者三种语言语义通达模型的实验研究[J]. 心理科学,2012(2):287-293.

[150] 史民英,邢爱青. 西藏地区三语教学存在的问题与对策[J]. 西藏大学学报(社会科学版),2011(2):137-141.

[151] 谭爱华. 语言可加工性理论下的三语迁移现象及其对少数民族外语教学的启示[J]. 西南民族大学学报(人文社会科学版),2012(3):218-220.

[152] 王慧,孔令翠. 藏区英语教学媒介语问题与基于藏族学生母语的藏授英语教师培养[J]. 外语学刊,2013(5):109-113.

[153] 吴白音那. 从蒙授英语专业教育实习分析蒙古族学生三语教学[J]. 内蒙古师范大学学报(教育科学版),2010(3):113-115.

[154] 吴白音那,文秋芳. 三语教师课堂语码转换结构类型与功能分布特征研究[J]. 外语学刊,2015(5):106-111.

[155] 吴启禄. 贵州省民族语言综述[J]. 贵州民族学院学报(社会科学版),1999(4):11-16.

[156] 熊向阳. 在侗族地区英语教学中构建"三语教育"模型的思考[J]. 柳州师专学报,2007(4):75-76.

[157] 杨信彰. 英语专业学生的语类意识与外语能力[J]. 外语与外语教学,2015(3):25-28.

[158] 杨学宝. 第三语言学习倦怠与元语言意识关系实证研究——以云南沧源佤族中学生为例[J]. 外语与翻译,2016(1):82-87.

[159] 杨筑慧. 走近中国少数民族·侗族[M]. 沈阳:辽宁民族出版社,2015.

[160] 袁妮娅,周恩. 超语言技能:概念、理论机制与研究进展[J]. 外语界,2015(2):7-15.

[161] 原一川,胡德映,冯智文,等. 云南跨境民族学生三语教育态度实证研究[J]. 民族教育研究,2013(6):80-87.

[162] 曾丽. 苗族学生在三语习得中元语言意识的发展[D]. 重庆:西南大学,2010.

［163］曾丽. 儿童三语习得中元语言意识的发展对我国少数民族外语教育政策制定的启示［J］. 外语教学与研究, 2011(5): 748-755.

［164］张春梅. 三语习得及其对蒙古族中学生英语教学的启示［J］. 语文学刊(外语教育教学), 2011(11): 135-138.

［165］张先刚. 语类读写教学法对学术论文摘要写作的启示［J］. 外语教学, 2012(1): 56-60.

［166］张先刚. 悉尼学派的语类教学法理论［J］. 外语界, 2013(2): 24-32.

［167］张贞爱. 朝汉双语人与英语教育［J］. 延边大学学报(社会科学版), 1998(1): 152-155.

［168］张贞爱, 俞春喜. 北方少数民族师生三语教育认同研究——以维吾尔、蒙古、朝鲜、哈萨克族师生为例［J］. 民族教育研究, 2012(1): 16-23.

［169］照格申, 张布和, 吉日木图. 构建蒙语授课学生"三语"教育体系的思考［J］. 中国民族教育, 2008(9): 29-31.

［170］周祥. 悉尼学派语类教学法对大学英语写作教学之启示——"以读促学"与王初明"以写促学"的结合［J］. 西安外国语大学学报, 2017(1): 72-77.

Appendix Ⅰ
Questionnaire

学生基本信息调查问卷

1. 姓名：_____ 出生年月：_____ 出生地：_____ 性别：_____
2. 民族：_____
    (1)汉族 　　　　　　(2)侗族 　　　　　　(3)其他民族
3. 有人用侗语跟你说话时，你_____
    (1)全部能听懂 　　　(2)大部分能听懂 　　(3)能听懂一半
    (4)少部分能听懂 　　(5)一点都听不懂
4. 你认为你的侗语水平_____
    (1)流利 　　　　　　(2)还行 　　　　　　(3)知道很少
    (4)不会
5. 你用_____跟本族人交谈？
    (1)全部都是侗语 　　(2)大部分是侗语 　　(3)一半侗语
    (4)很少侗语 　　　　(5)不用侗语
6. 你在家使用_____跟你的父母和兄弟姐妹说话。
    (1)侗语 　　　　　　(2)汉语 　　　　　　(3)侗语和汉语
7. 在学校，你使用_____和你的同学们说话。
    (1)全部都是侗语 　　(2)大部分是侗语 　　(3)一半侗语
    (4)很少侗语 　　　　(5)不用侗语
8. 你认识侗语的文字形式吗？_____
    (1)认识 　　　　　　(2)认识一部分 　　　(3)认识很少
    (4)不认识
9. 你认为侗族的孩子应该学会说本民族的语言吗？
    (1)完全应该 　　　　(2)基本应该 　　　　(3)说不准
    (4)不太应该 　　　　(5)完全不应该
10. 侗语对你的英语学习有什么影响？_____

(1)正面影响　　　　　(2)负面影响　　　　　(3)没有影响

11. 你认为侗语对以后有用吗？_____
    (1)用处很大　　　　(2)用处比较多　　　　(3)一般
    (4)用处比较少　　　(5)没有用

12. 你了解侗族的历史和传说吗？_____
    (1)非常了解　　　　(2)了解比较多　　　　(3)一般
    (4)了解比较少　　　(5)不了解

13. 你了解侗族的风俗习惯吗？
    (1)非常了解　　　　(2)了解比较多　　　　(3)一般
    (4)了解比较少　　　(5)不了解

14. 你参加侗族的节日和活动吗？_____
    (1)经常　　　　　　(2)有时　　　　　　　(3)无所谓
    (4)偶尔　　　　　　(5)从不

15. 你会因为自己是一个地道侗族自豪吗？_____
    (1)经常　　　　　　(2)有时　　　　　　　(3)偶尔
    (4)从不

16. 你愿意住侗族传统的房屋，并穿戴侗族传统服饰吗？_____
    (1)很愿意　　　　　(2)比较愿意　　　　　(3)无所谓
    (4)不太愿意　　　　(5)不愿意

17. 你认为有必要积极地保护和宣传侗族文化吗？_____
    (1)很有必要　　　　(2)有必要　　　　　　(3)无所谓
    (4)不很必要　　　　(5)不必要

18. 你愿意向别人介绍侗族传统文化吗？_____
    (1)很愿意　　　　　(2)比较愿意　　　　　(3)无所谓
    (4)不太愿意　　　　(5)不愿意

Appendix Ⅱ
Interview questions

◎**Teachers**

Part 1　Experience in teaching English in class

1. 你从事英语教学有几年了？你在课堂教学中主要使用什么教学方法？
2. 你是少数民族吗？你会说少数民族语言（侗语）吗？
3. 你在课堂中通常使用什么语言（侗语、汉语、英语）教学英语，为什么？
4. 你在英语教学中会使用或涉及侗族文化材料吗？
5. 你怎样看待在英语教学中使用学生的母语和文化资源的？

Part 2　Experience in attending the program

1. 你怎样描述你作为英语教师参加本次项目的感受？
2. 你能描述一下在本次项目英语教学中语言的使用，教学材料和方法与你平时英语教学的差别吗？你的印象和感受是什么？
3. 你对学生在本次项目中的表现有何评价？对教学活动、师生互动、学生学习态度积极性等各方面有什么感受？
4. 本次项目中学生的任务能够促进学生学习吗？如果是，怎样促进的？
5. 本次项目对学生的英语学习有什么影响？对学生后续的学习有影响吗？

◎**Students**

Part 1　Experience in studying English in class

1. 你学习英语多久了？怎么评价你的学习经历和成效？
2. 你在学校学习英语的经历是怎样的？
3. 你认为你的本民族语言和汉语对英语学习有影响吗？如果有，是怎样影响的？
4. 你有过使用民族语和汉语学习英语的经历吗？你怎样看待英语教学中本民族语言和文化的使用？
5. 你对学校英语课的看法是什么？期待在学校英语课上学到什么？

Part 2　Experience in studying English under the program

1. 你在本项目中学习英语的体验是什么？
2. 本项目的英语教学与你平时的英语学习有什么差别？

3. 你怎样看待项目中分配给你的任务？

4. 本项目对你英语学习有什么影响？

5. 你对本民族语言和文化是否有了更进一步的理解和意识？

Part 3　Translanguaging practices

1. 你的整个写作过程是怎样的？

2. 写作的时候你通常用什么语言思考？

3. 什么情况下用汉语/侗语/英语思考？

4. 你有没有用两种或两种以上语言思考和写作的情况？如果有，你是怎样做的？

5. 你在前、中、后三篇作文的写作中的语言使用和构思过程是否一样？如果否差别在哪里？

6. 你在写作中是怎样使用语言资源的（包括汉语、侗语、原来掌握的及新学的英语知识）？

7. 你课堂讨论的时候通常用什么语言？

8. 你有使用两种或两种以上语言讨论的情况吗？如果有为什么？每种语言的角色和作用是什么？

Appendix Ⅲ
Teaching materials

1. Reading text 1 (the extract of the story)

How the Camel Got His Hump?

In the beginning of years, when the world was so new and all, and the Animals were just beginning to work for Man, there was a Camel, and he lived in the middle of a Howling Desert because he did not want to work; and besides, he was a Howler himself. So he ate sticks and thorns and tamarisks and milkweed and prickles, most excruciatingly idle; and when anybody spoke to him he said "Humph!", Just "Humph!", and no more.

Presently the Horse came to him on Monday morning, with a saddle on his back and a bit in his mouth, and said, "Camel, O, Camel, come out and trot like the rest of us."

"Humph!" said the Camel; and the Horse went away and told Man.

Presently the Dog came to him, with a stick in his mouth, and said, "Camel, O Camel, come and fetch and carry like the rest of us."

"Humph!" said the Camel; and the Dog went away and told the Man.

Presently the Ox came to him, with the yoke on his neck and said, "Camel, O Camel, come and plough like the rest of us."

"Humph!" said the Camel; and the Ox went away and told the Man.

At the end of the day, the Man called the Horse and the Dog and the Ox together, and said, "Three, O, Three, I'm very sorry for you (with the world so new-and-all); but that Humph-thing in the Desert can't work, or he would have been here by now, so I am going to leave him alone, and you must work double-time to make up for it."

That made the Three very angry (with the world so new-and-all), and they held a meeting (palaver, and an indaba, and a panchayat), and a pow-wow on the edge of the

Desert; and the Camel came chewing on milkweed, most excruciatingly idle, and laughed at them. Then he said "Humph!" and went away again.

"I shouldn't say that again if I were you," said the Djinn; "you might say it once too often. Bubbles, I want you to work."

And the Camel said "Humph!" again; but no sooner had he said it than he saw his back, that he was so proud of, puffing up and puffing up into a great big lolloping humph.

And from that day to this the Camel always wears a humph (we call it "hump" now, not to hurt his feelings); but he has never yet caught up with the three days that he missed at the beginning of the world, and he has never yet learned how to behave.

2. Bilingual reading text in Iteration 2
◎**Dong reading text**

NYONC GUEEC DANGH JIH

Xic unv, jih xenp xangh eis biees, ul laic kop kongk, dingl buh beeuv nyaoh dees longc, qamt saengc eis qamt weengc.

Xic jav gueec buh eis qingk sungp, nyenc daol aol maoh aemv keip bail yav weex ongl, maoh hangt keip suh keip, eis haengt suh bail nuic, nyenc daol deic maoh nyaengc eis lis banl fac.

Lis il maenl, jih nyaoh aox guis daenl jil, gueec soic weex ongl laengh map aox guis abs, piat xenp bail, piat xenp map, eis xingl ngic il dingl xait daml dav laic jih, jih banl menl banl deih, gas gueec yenl dinl, jih aov laoh douh xait biees yangx, ul laic naengl douv jiagc jangs dinl laox, dinl jih buh douh xait miedl bail yac mangv. Dah xic jav qit, jih suh biinv wenp yangh naih, qamt bail nas eis lis, gobs lis qamt weengc.

Jih douh gueec xait biees, nuv gueec gav laox lail soh, eis ams xunp il bags, wanp wanp nyenh nyaoh aox longc.

Maenl lenc, gueec yuh touk aox guis map abs, jih jaemc nyaoh aox ngamc bial jah, eip yac guv suit, gas gueec deic gaos nyabp laos aox naemx xic jah, maoh suh songk legc deic jagc nangl gueec jah nyaeml, gueec qingk ids banl menl banl dih.

Xus yanc qingk gueec banl menl banl dih, ganx bieeuv map naengc, lis nuv duc jih idx naengl gueec, nyaengc qingk lail gol gungc.

Gueec nuv xus yanc touk map, ganx jit xais xus yanc juv maoh. Xus yanc xenh naih xih wox naengl gueec jangs jemc yaol haip, suh laengc deic jiuc lanh ul xenp suic doiv jih idx tongh jah xonp laos aox naengl gueec bail, lenc sip seik seik deic jih kat luih map, xonv songk laos aox guis bail.

Dah xic jav qit, gueec douh nyenc daol deic lamh xonp naengl, yidx maoh bail dongl, maoh buh eis ams bail siip, kip yav weex ongl, xais maoh bail nas, maoh buh eis ams xonv lenc yangx.

◎**Chinese translation**

牛和螃蟹的故事

很久很久以前,螃蟹的身子并不扁,背上是光滑的,脚也长在肚皮下,行走时是向前爬,而不是横着爬行。

那时候的牛一点都不服人们的使唤,人们叫它耕田种地,它高兴就耕,不高兴就睡,人们拿它没办法。

有一天,螃蟹正在溪中觅食,牛懒得干活,逃到小溪中来洗澡,翻来覆去地洗,好不自在! 一不小心一脚踩在螃蟹的背上,痛得螃蟹喊天叫地。等牛把脚抬开,螃蟹早已被踩扁了,背上还留下一个深深的牛脚印,螃蟹的脚也被踩得挤散到身子的两旁。从那时起,螃蟹变成现在这个样子,不能向前爬行,只能横着走了。

螃蟹被牛踩扁,眼看牛个子那么大,力气那么大,连一句话都不敢吭,只好忍气吞声,恨在心头。

第二天,牛照例又来到小溪中洗澡。螃蟹躲在岩缝里,张开两只锋利的大爪,等牛把头余入水下时,它就狠狠地把牛鼻子夹住,痛得老牛喊爹叫娘。

主人听到牛的哭叫声,赶忙跑到溪边来看,见到螃蟹咬住牛的鼻子,忍不住笑出了眼泪。

牛见主人到来,急忙跪下求救。主人这才发现牛鼻子是牛的要害之处! 就把随身带来的绳子往螃蟹咬通的地方穿了过去,然后再慢慢地把螃蟹取下来送到溪中。

从此,牛被人们拴上了鼻绳,牵它往东,它不敢往西;耕田耕地时,叫它往前走,它就不敢后退了。

Appendix IV
Scores of pre- and post-texts

Class1's scores	S1	S2	S3	S4	S5	S6	S7	S8	S9	S10	S11	S12	S13	S14	S15	S16	S17	S18	S19	S20	S21	S22	S23	Average score
pre-text	8	7	8	6	5	8	10	8	6	5	12	6	5	5	15	5	6	8	6	8	10	9	20	8
post-text	32	34	20	24	15	18	28	25	30	19	30	28		10	33	14	16	26	31	22	34	28	27	25

Class1's scores	S1	S2	S3	S4	S5	S6	S7	S8	S9	S10	S11	S12	S13	S14	S15	S16	S17	S18	S19	S20	S21	S22	S23	S24	S25	S26	Average score
pre-text	4	8	12	5	3	15	3	5	14	3	5	14	6	5	6	3	6	6	14	5	5	10	3	8	12		7
post-text		23	24	29		28		15	32	20	15	18	24	16	14	14	31	18	21	12	20	27	34	24	31	30	23

Appendix Ⅴ
Samples of pre- and post-text assessment

1. Sample of pre-text assessment

Criteria	Score	Comments	Pre-text (Text 6-1)
Purpose	0	No clear genre	
Staging	1	No clear stages	Today, I'm and feind eat Practice jump dance
Phases	0	No phases	
Field	1	No clear field	Today, I'm and feind eat Practice jump dance
Tenor	1	Simple personal evaluations	Tired, pleasure
Mode	0	Too spoken for junior college students	
Lexis	1	Very simple	
Appraisal	0	Simple judgements (underlined)	
Conjunction	0	No conjunction	
Reference	0	No reference	
Grammar	0	Inaccurate	
Spelling	1	Some errors	
Punctuation	0	Wrong punctuation	
Presentation	0	No paragraph, less legible	
Total	5/42	Extremely below the grade standard	

Appendix Ⅴ   Samples of pre- and post-text assessment

2. Sample of post-text assessment

Criteria	Score	Comments	Post-text (Text 6-13)
Purpose	2	Well-achieved purpose	Narrative about a folk story
Staging	3	Clear and appropriate stages	Orientation, Complication, Resolution
Phases	3	Well organized phases in most stages	Setting, problem, solution, reaction
Field	2	Settings, plot and characters are built	Rich plots
Tenor	2	Simple personal evaluations	Happy, angry
Mode	2	Some written language is used	In the beginning of the years
Lexis	2	Use new language resources well to construct the field	See Table 6.13
Appraisal	1	Simple judgements	Happy, angry
Conjunction	2	Appropriate conjunction	And, so
Reference	2	Clear reference	The Dog, the Man
Grammar	2	Appropriate sentence structure but some errors	Accurate use of verbal tense
Spelling	2	Good spelling but a few errors	
Punctuation	2	Appropriate punctuation	
Presentation	2	Good paragraphing but less cleanly presented	
Total	29/42	Above the standard	